THE ELEMENTS

OF

NETWORKING STYLE

THE ELEMENTS

OF

NETWORKING STYLE

And Other Essays and Animadversions

on the Art

of Intercomputer Networking

M. A. PADLIPSKY

PRENTICE-HALL, INC., Englewood Cliffs, New Jersey 07632

Library of Congress Cataloging in Publication Data

Padlipsky, M. A. (Michael A.)
  The elements of networking style and other essays and
animadversions on the art of intercomputer networking.

  1. Computer networks. I. Title.
TK5105.5.P34   1985   001.64'404   84–22247
ISBN 0-13-268129-3
ISBN 0-13-268111-0 (pbk.)

Editorial/production supervision and
  interior design: *Lynn Frankel*
Cover design: *Photo Plus Art*
Manufacturing buyer: *Gordon Osbourne*

Printed in the United States of America

10 9 8 7 6 5 4 3 2 1

ISBN 0-13-268111-0 01   {PAPER}

ISBN 0-13-268129-3 01   {CASE}

Prentice-Hall International, Inc., *London*
Prentice-Hall of Australia Pty. Limited, *Sydney*
Editora Prentice-Hall do Brasil, Ltda., *Rio de Janeiro*
Prentice-Hall of Canada Inc., *Toronto*
Prentice-Hall of India Private Limited, *New Delhi*
Prentice-Hall of Japan, Inc., *Tokyo*
Prentice-Hall of Southeast Asia Pte. Ltd., *Singapore*
Whitehall Books Limited, *Wellington, New Zealand*

In empathic memory of the Emperor Julian
—and, of course, Voltaire

Contents

CHAPTER 3

The Elements of Networking Style

58

CHAPTER 4

A Perspective on Intercomputer Networking

69

CHAPTER 5

A Perspective on the ARPANET Reference Model

89

CHAPTER 6

The Host-Front End Protocol Approach

116

CHAPTER 7

Slaying the "TCP-on-a-LAN" Woozle

132

CHAPTER 8

The Illusion of Vendor Support

144

CHAPTER 9

Low Standards: A Critique of X.25

153

CHAPTER 10

Gateways, Architectures, and Heffalumps

167

CHAPTER 11

An Architecture for Secure Packet-Switched Networks

177

APPENDIX 1

Two Introductions That Were Too Good to Go to Waste

190

APPENDIX 2

The Arouet Papers

196

APPENDIX 3

The Self-Framed Slogans Suitable for Mounting

204

Foreword

Brace yourselves. We're about to try something that borders on the unique: an actually rather serious technical book which is not only (gasp) vehemently *anti*-Solemn but also (shudder) takes sides. I tend to think of it as "Constructive Snottiness."

If you find that sort of thing inconceivable, all I can say is that I hope this is a library's copy you're reading. If, on the other hand, you're tired of Dull when it comes to "professional reading," I trust you'll wind up getting your own copy even if this is a library one—you'll want the Self-Framed Slogans Suitable for Mounting for your walls, if nothing else. (No "off the wall" jokes, please.)

One other prefatory sort of thing you should be aware of is that I've taken great pains and exercised incredible self-restraint to avoid even the faintest suggestion of Libel here (even though Truth is supposed to be a fine defense to that sort of thing) by not actually naming any of the villains. After all, they know who they are, and after you've read the book you'll be able to recognize their like for yourself. There is, however, a reference to not being "scandalous" in the Usual Papers, and on that score all I can say is that the Publisher joins me in hoping the only sort of scandalous you'll find it is scandalously witty. (Well, the Publisher actually said "funny," but I prefer "witty." Think about it.)

Happy reading.

M. A. PADLIPSKY

Preface

I know almost nobody reads Prefaces, and I hadn't even planned to have one originally, but I've discovered I've got to say the following somewhere, and this *is* the Right Place for it:

Many of the forthcoming chapters were circulated in what might be called the "semi-open literature" previously, and a couple of them started life as conference papers. Based upon the responses to those relatively limited modes of dissemination, I feel compelled to issue a *caveat lector.* I *know* many readers will consider many of my positions (or, more accurately, many of what they assume to be my positions, because as a devoted proponent of Constructive Snottiness it's not even always clear to me when I'm being sarcastic) to be what's usually euphemized as "controversial"(or maybe "provocative"). I *know* that both of the widely publicized approaches to "networking" I've taken shots at here have more or less achieved the status of sacred cows in some circles. (I *also* know they're not one and the same, but see the Prefatory Afterthoughts to Chapter 9.) I *even* know that some readers will be offended by the Content and others by the Form and still others by the Form and Content. *However,* honest, it won't help to call me up, more in sorrow than in anger, and try to tell me "What 'OSI' really means" or "Why X.25's really needed."

If you feel you absolutely must try to correct my thinking, drop me a note in care of the Publisher, and if you include a stamped, self-addressed envelope I'll probably respond eventually—but I'm tired of having to sort out on the fly who's sincere and responsible from who's trying to play Thought Police games. So if you really are a serious and responsible True Believer and sincerely think I've blasphemed, try writing me off as Invincibly Ignorant if you possibly can (please don't, however, assume you can treat me the way they did I.I.'s in the Old Days), because even if I did believe that it's fair to my employer to waste time trying to be polite to non-work-related phone callers, and even if the phone callers were so thoughtless as to call me at home, the Publisher's simply not paying me enough for this book to make it worth my while spending a major fraction of the next year or two repeating again and again and again what I'm about to say as unambiguously as I can, right here, right now:

Although this book is by no means intended to be solely an exercise in bone picking and axe grinding, there certainly is an element of that sort of thing going on in it. The bone/axe I call "ISORMites." By ISORMite, I mean a self-proclaimed advocate/partisan of the International Standards Organization's "Open System Interconnection Reference Model" (which I choose to refer to as the "ISORM" for reasons dealt with subsequently) who is either (a) deliberately attempting to pass it off as a panacea/"finished product" (as of 1984)/"ideal solution for all your networking problems"/whatever, as his or her professional "bag" (or "ricebowl," in some circles), without admitting to any of its shortcomings (about which more later), and usually ignoring or belittling without good evidence the *current* state of the Intercomputer Networking art, which I take to be those protocols in use on what is usually called "the ARPANET" (and based on the ARPANET Reference Model, or ARM, about which much more later); or (b) not really experienced in Intercomputer Networking and insistently accepting and parroting the ISO party line because he or she is naive enough to think that's all there is or that it makes such good sense on paper that no "reality testing" is required. [I *think* that turns out to be the longest sentence in the book, but I wouldn't want to make any promises.] That is, I'm mainly against con artists and truly sloppy scholars, of whom I've met aplenty.

(For future reference, let's define "ISORMist" as an advocate of the ISORM who isn't an ISORMite—that is, one who is serious and responsible, albeit, in my view, wrong.)

It ought to go without saying that category (a) is a lot more offensive to me than category (b), but I am after all trying to be unambiguous here. And I really should mention that *if*, as I rather suspect, there turns out to be a category (c), consisting of those who do it as a consciously cheap way of coming off like "experts" when they're not, I do have a special infernal circle reserved for them.

That's *not* to say that I believe everybody who has anything good to say about what I call the ISORM is *ipso facto* a scoundrel/villain/con/huckster. One of my close personal friends, whom I consider to be an Old Network Boy, is a prominent figure in "OSI" circles. We happen to disagree professionally. Big deal. (Actually, the world is probably a safer place because of it: Back when we agreed professionally, we used to do marvelous numbers on hapless hucksters who got caught between us at Design Reviews . . . we called it "stereophonic snot.") And there are certainly some properties of the ISORM that make a fair amount of sense to me. (Don't worry, by the way, if you don't know what the

ISORM is yet. Chapter 2 will make an explicit try at describing it, and there are implicit tries here, there, and almost everywhere.) Just one example: They make a great virtue of "Layering." So do We. Indeed, so did We a number of years before They existed (see especially Chapter 5). Unfortunately, however, They don't seem to be willing to acknowledge that fact—and They also have, in my considered opinion, mechanized Layering in an inefficient, inhibiting fashion. So, as I said somewhere, it's not that we've got a Not Invented Here attitude, it's that we've got a Not Reinvented Right one. But unless you've actually heard and seen the kind of guff that *some* vendors try to palm off on the Government, or the kind of fuzzy thinking *some* people in the Government try to palm off on others, all in the name of the ISORM, you can't begin to appreciate the provocation I was subjected to which resulted in the following essays and animadversions. (Again, perhaps needless to say, but I've worked—indirectly, but at only one remove—for the Government for eight of the last nine years, so I've seen a *lot* of foolishness.) The story in Appendix 1 is true, by the way: I really did run into a turkey who asked, when I told him the ARM predated the ISORM, "But does the ARM conform to the ISORM?" Grrrrrrr.

Another reason why I decided to write a Preface, despite what I say about them in Chapter 1, is that I just (on the day of the 1983 Autumnal Equinox) got another phone call of the type that I described earlier and in the Prefatory Afterthoughts to Chapter 9. Though apparently one of the well-meaning variety, the caller made annoying reference to "the Ivory Tower Attitude," and I decided I wanted my response to go into The Book. So . . . since 1970 I've put two systems onto the ARPANET, personally implemented a few protocols, personally integrated them with a few others, designed—both as working group member and chairman—a few more protocols, had numerous rather searching conversations with my peers, and reviewed more paper "architectures" and protocols than I'm willing to count. *I'm* not in an Ivory Tower (even though I must confess I think the only thing wrong with Ivory Towers is the leaving of them). On the other hand, ISO, as a Voluntary Standards Organization, has to take *whomever* it gets sent and let them decide on the merits and demerits of various proposals—irrespective of the depth, breadth, or duration of their technical expertise and/or experience. That sounds more Ivory Tower, in the common-usage sense of being removed from Reality, to me than a position which holds that the notion of "Good Art" is fair game as an evaluation criterion even for application to a proposal that has the *apparent* cachet of coming from an international standards organization—or even a national one. It also seems to me that the best judges of Good Art, when it comes to technology anyway, though I don't advise having analytical/aesthetic discussions with dancers and painters, are . . . practitioners of the art in question. In other words, to my few friends and several acquaintances whom I do find serious and responsible, but who have elected to "play the game" (and who usually admit in private that they, too, deplore the ISORMites) who urge me not to ignore the "political realities," I say again, *I am* aware of the political realities. That's why I doubt I'd accept an invitation even if you could figure out how to get one for me from what you keep reminding me is, after all, a *voluntary* standards organization.

I imagine that to some, that will still sound rather Ivory Towerish. Well, here's my last, best offer by way of prefatory disclaimer: I'm sure I've misinterpreted a few points of Their theology here; I've probably even misrepresented a few points of Our theology. *But,* in the first place, look at the title: This ain't meant to be mathematics. Indeed, I submit it's not only licit to be openly qualitative about a technological art—it's a damn sight more intellectually honest than pretending to be able to quantify the qualitative. *And,* in the second place, I'll say it right out: Unlike what I call the panacea pedlars, *I don't claim to be writing on the backs of the tablets the Ten Commandments came down on* (though I do get annoyed when those who clearly know a lot less about the field than I do try to convey just that impression). In other words, if you do so it's at your own risk, because

I never asked to be taken for granite.

NP

Acknowledgments

Much of the work contained in this book was performed under the sponsorship of the Electronic Systems Division of the United States Air Force Systems Command. The views expressed herein represent the author's opinion and are not necessarily those of the United States Air Force.

I'd also like to acknowledge my gratitude to the following people and organizations (roughly in order of receipt of written permission):

Dr. Robert M. Metcalfe, for permission to quote the definition of "process" from his doctoral dissertation.

The Macmillan Publishing Company, Inc., and the Council of Trinity College, Cambridge, for permission to quote from *The Golden Bough,* One-Volume Abridged Edition, 1938, by Sir James G. Frazer. (Copyright 1922 by Macmillan Publishing Company, Inc., renewed 1950 by Barclays Bank Ltd.)

The Institute of Electrical and Electronics Engineers, Inc., for permission to reprint those of my conference papers that appear as Chapters 5 and 11, and my Session Chairman's Introduction that appears as Section 2 of Appendix 1. (Copyright notices on the respective first pages.)

IFIP and North-Holland Publishing Company, for permission to quote from the article by Danny Cohen and Jon Postel, "The ISO Reference Model and Other Protocol Architectures," in "Information Processing '83," R. Mason (ed.), Amsterdam, North-Holland 1983.

My old friend John Bean, for the Cover Cartoons for Chapters 3–5, and 7–10.

My friend David Omar White, for the Cover Cartoons for Chapters 1, 2, 11, and the Appendices.

E. P. Dutton & Co., Inc., for permission to paraphrase Benjamin Hoff's *The Tao of Pooh* and quote from A. A. Milne's *Winnie-the-Pooh,* © 1926 by E. P. Dutton Inc; renewed 1954 by A. A. Milne and reprinted by permission of the publisher.

Methuen Children's Books for permission to quote from A. A. Milne's *Winnie-the-Pooh.*

Finally, though only because the copyright holder required a particular phrasing that didn't fit into the list, the quotations in the Prefatory Afterthoughts to Chapter 1 are:

Reprinted by permission of Linda G. Sprague and Christopher R. Sprague, "Management *Science*?", *Interfaces,* Volume 7, Number 1, November, 1976, Copyright 1976, The Institute of Management Sciences.

In addition, even if it costs me a dreaded Author Alteration, I must add my deep thanks to Karl Karlstrom of Prentice-Hall, for deciding to do a "fun book," and to Lynn Frankel of Prentice-Hall, for diligently shepherding this neophyte author through the treacherous fields of Production to the (relative) haven of First Book.

The author writes, "There being, as far as I know, precious few Protocols groupies out there to appeal to, I feel that the above picture is far more worthy of display than one of me menacing a windmill (though you could have one of those, too, if you wanted it). The symbolism of this particular piece of *art trouvé* is too important to pass by: Although innocently plunked down a block or so from Trafalgar Square ostensibly to promote a local newspaper, it suggests to the discerning that those who join the Stampede to Standardize will wind up in fetters, after paying a high price (1P > $.0125, after all), and will get something basically jury-rigged. The pushiness of it all is also Meaningful. Further, at a deeper level we must consider that a former psychologist (turned "System Engineer") friend of mine assures me that Standards-yearning is related to Fromm's views on the Urge to Trust, and another friend assures me that Trust is also the wellspring of B & D, so we can see that the picture also suggests the psychopathology of what you'll get if you trust the Standardsmongers. All in all, then, a much more important picture than one of dear, sweet, kindly, Constructively Snotty, old Uncle Mike."

CHAPTER 1

On Style
and Style

PREFATORY AFTERTHOUGHTS

Both because several of the chapters to come were written during the course of my employment and hence had to be "cleared for public release," which makes revision a nuisance, and because I rather like the idea anyway, each chapter will have a few prefatory afterthoughts—even those which, as is the case here, were written from scratch for this book.

The point I'd like to try to make about "On Style and Style" is that, after I had completed the first draft, I realized that I could capture the spirit of what I was up to quite nicely by appealing to a marvelous paper written by two very old, very good friends of mine for an entirely different discipline. The friends are (Professors) Linda G. Sprague and Christopher R. Sprague. The paper is entitled "Management *Science?*" (*Interfaces*, November 1976, The Institute of Management Sciences, pp. 57–62, Vol. 7, No. 1). The different discipline had better be obvious.

Apparently, an earlier letter in another journal in the field had excited some comment by complaining of a lack of "journal readability." The Spragues took the essence of that argument a step or three further and, to oversimplify their own rather elegant argument, observed that, in essence, by trying to sound Science-y, management science journals were all too often letting "Bad Science" drive out "Good Engineering." "The bulk of our science never finds application and the bulk of our engineering is never brought to our professional associations."

As you'll see, I think the same problem applies with a vengeance in Computer Science in general and with a fierce (perhaps Sophoclean?) vengeance in Intercomputer Networking in particular. The Spragues' suggested alternative, which I commend to you along with their paper as a whole, is, if I may flatter myself a bit, what I "really" had in mind for Chapter 1. We should, instead of trying to make noises like learned scientists, "preach what we practice."

LITERARY STYLE

My friend F. M. Arouet is fond of saying—for reasons known only to him, me, and a passing Emily—that nobody ever reads Forewords and/or Prefaces. As usual, he's right. Also as usual, he prevailed upon me, in this case to do what would ordinarily be a Preface and/or Foreword as Chapter 1. (He additionally prevailed upon me to include a few of his milder pieces at the back of *my* book—mainly because he's a silvery-tongued devil, but also because he does include the Ultimate Answer in one of them.) This way, a few people might actually pass their eyes over it. *Don't* skip to the next chapter, though, now that the cat's out of the whatever, unless you're willing to infer for yourself what the book is about—and *do* go back and read what is here as a Preface: It's got a very fair warning in it, and a great pun.

For the benefit of those whose attention has been inveigled, I'd like to take advantage of the moment by telling you a couple of Great Truths about Technologists (by which I mean to include scientists, engineers, programmers, and their usually-parasitic-but-sometimes-symbiotic entrepreneurs). The first G. T. is that we are almost always heard casually referring to "the State of the Art," but we almost all think—if we even bother to think about it at all—that Art is a metaphor. Well, it isn't.

Sure, what we do for a living isn't a Fine Art; but each and every technological discipline *is* an Art, at some fairly real level.

I'll save the detailed argument for a future book (working title "Prolegomena to Technicoaesthetic Theory," © M. A. Padlipsky). What matters in the present context is that no technologist *should* be surprised to see the sorts of analyses and arguments usually found in, say, literary criticism cropping up in a work about a particular technology/art, but altogether too many technologists *are* surprised by it.

An example: My employer circulates the titles and abstracts of internal documents which have entered the publication mill to interested employees. When the title of my actually quite serious critique of the overly well-known communications protocol X.25 appeared on one of the pubs sheets as "Low Standards: A Critique of X.25," a few old-line engineers (a.k.a. Old Poops) objected so strongly that I decided, in the interests of getting the thing cleared for public release so that eventually you could get to see it, to drop the lovely pun before the colon (and, being moderately scrupulous, the colon as well).

There are two points to this little anecdote: One is that the original title was perfectly appropriate. Being at least *a* mechanization of the bottom three layers of the "reference model" the standardsmongers are currently monging, X.25 does, literally, comprise low standards. But the reactionaries reacted to the word play and somehow didn't think it was Right and Proper to poke fun at a Standard, or, perhaps, that a quasi-learned/"technical" paper was the Right Place to do so. Which leads to the second point: Art is not only allowed to be amusing as well as edifying, some even expect it to be both. So if you don't want to run the risk of being amused while you're being edified, you almost certainly don't want to read most of the rest of this book—and you surely didn't read the Foreword. Of course, I'd like to think that if you don't read the rest of the book you'll forego your chance to become properly edified on the *real* state of the Intercomputer Networking Art, but that remains to be seen.

A digression on solemnity.   I didn't want to waste this one on the Foreword, so even though it breaks the flow, I'd like to tell you the first of a number of true stories I've snuck in here and there. Around a dozen years ago, I was at a party in Cambridge (Massachusetts). Spotting a young woman whose cigarette was unlit, I was inspired to say, "Unless you're terribly militant," as I offered her a light. Unfortunately, she thought she was, and began to remonstrate. "Hmmm," I said, "you don't seem to know the difference between capital W–capital L and lower-case w–lower-case l." ("Women's Lib" was almost as big a buzzword in Cambridge in those days as "Structured Programming" was a few years ago.)

Well, she still didn't get the joke. Indeed, she called a couple of friends over to help remonstrate. When they paused for breath, I observed—being rather amused at the overreaction to an actually quite harmless jest—that "It's a pity True Believers almost never have senses of humor," and they were off again. Finally, I got bored. "I've gotten bored," I said, "I will now reveal my impeccable credentials: It just so happens that I'm the only known member of the Class of '60 at M.I.T. who took a classmate to the Freshman Dance. [In the Bad Old Days, the mandatory response to 'I didn't know there were coeds at M.I.T.' was 'Oh, yes: 80 coeds . . . and 20 girls'. As this *was* a Cambridge party, I didn't have to explain that part at the time.] I invented 'sexual egalitarianism' independently before you lot had even heard of puberty—but I don't feel any compulsion to be so damn Solemn about it."

That worked. (It's also true, which just might have helped.) They calmed down, and at that moment the host came by and asked if I wanted to play tennis the next day; this prompted the original young woman to say, "Oh, you play tennis. Would you care to play with me some time?" I of course replied, "Fine. But I wouldn't think of asking you to be untrue to your principles: I'm in the book, call me." (Do you really need to be told that she never did?)

There are a couple of morals to this Digression. One is that a large number of people do feel impelled to be awfully Solemn about Serious Matters; I hope you're not one of them. The other is that you shouldn't get the impression that I'm a totally fanatic fun-poker: The Y. W. in question was actually rather unattractive (spiritually and physically); had she not been, I'm quite confident I could have resisted taking the call-me shot.

(One of the simple joys of authorship, by the way, is contemplating how much the Old Poops are going to *hate* Arouet's stuff. After all, I just said I'm not a fanatic about it, but I never said I believe fun isn't for poking.)

OK. If you're still with me I can make the next part quick: The other Great Truth about technologists is that they are almost all allergic to Literary Style. Most of us seem to think that to be "scientific" we have to write as dully as possible; that the first person singular pronoun is Unclean; that "technical writing" must consist of short, simple sentences; that having recourse to a dictionary because an author has used a word common to the working vocabularies of graduates of good Liberal Arts colleges but not to "straightforward engineers" is grounds for censuring the author, not the technomacho subliteracy myth; that even though block diagrams are almost as good as equations, cartoons are *infra dig;* and, worst of all, that polemics—if we know the word at all—can only deal with theology.

It ain't necessarily so.

I could try to cop a plea on the literary style issue by offering to grant mass absolution to any and all readers of this book as a one-time teacher of Freshman Comp (I didn't mention what I majored in at the 'Tute, did I? how remiss) who's still empowered to Make Exceptions, but that wouldn't satisfy me even if it worked for some—or most—of you. Perhaps I've overdone the fair warnings bit, but what *I* think it all boils down to is whether you're willing to have a go at something off the beaten track because it just might turn out to be good for you . . . either as amusement, as edification, or, if I'm right, as edification *and* amusement.

Besides, you can at least be grateful that most of the chapters have been "handkerchiefed": Some of the early drafts even raised my friend Arouet's eyebrows now and then.

A digression on vocabulary.   At the risk of gilding the ragweed, I can't resist closing out the literary style portion with another true story. I worked on the first draft of this chapter on an airplane from Boston to L.A. I had planned to finish it on the return trip, but my business in L.A., coupled with the heat wave they were having, left me in a state fit only for reading on the way back. In what I was reading, I found a delightful sentence that in one breath expected the reader to recognize Dr. Pangloss and know what "Kirkegaardian" implied. To quote the dozen or so words in question for you would have cost me $75, which I consider indecent, and required an Acknowledgment of the "Courtesy of" the magazine in question, which I consider obscene, so you'll have to settle for what I've just told you. (If you're an aspiring author, by the way, be warned: Don't quote anything in/under copyright if you value your time, wallet, sanity, and gorge. Even quoting yourself can lead to nuisance.) The cream of the jest, though, is that I was reading a "sports magazine" at the time. What a glorious moral, eh? Jocks can be asked to recognize allusions to Voltaire and to existential *Angst*—or at least to accept such things at some level—but technojocks get terribly fussed over little things like "animadversions." Well, cheer up gang, at least I didn't call them "floccinauncinihilipilifications."

[Well, OK, I guess that does border on the vicious. I'll give you a break: It's the longest word in the latest edition of the *Oxford English Dictionary* (according to a probably reliable newspaper story I read a few years back anyway).]

[Sigh. After months of internal debate, I suppose it *would* be gratuitously snotty rather than constructively so to make you find an OED. It means the art of estimating as valueless.]

We'd better forge ahead rapidly. If we don't, I'm liable to succumb to the not altogether unworthy temptation of also taking some shots at the hardcore types who keep grousing about "fancy writing" beyond the mere level of disliking mildly recondite vocabularies. (You know, the ones who find a "literary" literary style to be somehow threatening and want to score sentences by word count—and as if the game were golf rather than basketball. I'd call them perverse See Spot Run lovers, but they'd probably think I was talking dirty.) Let's just note in passing that, on the word choice front, it is particularly ironic that those who complain the loudest about occasionally having to look in a dictionary are the likeliest to be scandalized by the thought of using 22/7 for π in a calculation. Perhaps precision in arithmetic expressions is more important than precision of verbal expression after all, but I don't see why you can't have it both ways.

A digressive conjecture on pyschopathology.   Do you suppose the reason so many technologists eschew "the literary" is that they're fundamentally analytical types and simply built up a heavy resentment of the preachments of spinster schoolmarms (of whatever sex and marital persuasion) that they *had to* admire the Classics . . . without ever explaining why? I do know that my own fondness was only triggered by exposure to an incredibly sharp M.I.T. E.E.-turned-literary-critic whose style was extremely analytical/explicatory, and that I've always loathed the "You *must* like it because it's Great Art" circularity myself; whether or not it generalizes, I can't really say.   If, however, the stereotyped technologist's distaste for things artsy isn't merely a manifestation of technomacho and does indeed have something to do with High School English Trauma, then I would at least like to point out that there actually do exist objective criteria for judging whether something is "Good Art"—even though any detailed examination of them clearly doesn't belong in this book—so if you're a victim of the Trauma yourself, you might want to reconsider . . . and maybe even urge the Publisher to try to get me to follow up on the threat to do the Technicoaesthetics book.

At any rate, since all I'm trying to do at this juncture is suggest that even if you can't relax and enjoy my admittedly (maybe even insistently) rather idiosyncratic prose you really shouldn't use your reaction to the Form as a basis for rejecting the Content, not trying to "prove" that Words Can Be Beautiful, I'll just offer a true confession as the final—I semi-promise—thought on literary style and let it go at that: Even though I know it's likely to alienate some readers, I feel obligated to admit that I personally am prouder of having committed the "taken for granite" line in the Preface than I would be if I'd managed to break the world Fast Fourier Transform record by fifty or even a hundred microseconds.

TECHNICOAESTHETIC STYLE

So much for the first kind of style I wanted to deal with in this sneaky Foreword.   The Old Poops (of whatever chronological age) will probably have ignored the book based on the title—or anyway the cover—and the Young Turks are probably wondering why I even bother to raise the point because they think it's perfectly fair to be snotty in a good cause, but perhaps those between the extremes will feel a little better about the fact that the sexton does encourage laughing in his particular church.

[**Digression on psychodynamics.**   Perhaps what's really going on is a recapitulation of the old Medicine Must Taste Bad To Do Good ethic. If so, perhaps you should think of me as asking you to take the Sweet with the Bitter. . . .]

Let's get on with the other kind of style.

Actually, there are two other kinds of style we're concerned with. The first, however, has been dealt with in the eponymous chapter. (Take that, Old Poops.) It has to do with whether it's appropriate to "do networking" by emulating devices already known to each of the various operating systems being "networked." (It's not.) As you can come to grips with that one when the appropriate chapter rolls along, though, we won't bother with it here. After all, having conned you into reading what amounts to an extended Foreword and/or Preface I don't want to let this "chapter" go on *too* long.

Before digging in to the real point of the present exercise, however, I can't resist a small Digression on Forewords: My new friend Karl Karlstrom of Prentice-Hall told me, when he heard that my Chapter 1 was actually going to be a sort of trick, that he'd recently published a book called *STATLIB*, and had received an earnest letter asking where one could get licensing information on the software described therein. If you can't work out the answer to where it was all the long, you might not get much out of the rest of this.

So much for the preliminary pleasantries. In one sense, this whole book may be viewed as a treatise on what at least one Old Network Boy thinks is good style—the Right Way to do Intercomputer Networking. (The "Intercomputer" part is significant: I'm not concerned with mere communications between terminals and central systems any more than I'm concerned with "networking" as a euphemism for singles clubs.) Said Right Way, however, turns out to be at variance with certain widely touted beliefs. That is, I'm not here to praise "Open System Interconnection" and/or the "Reference Model" still being evolved for it under the aegis of the International Standards Organization. I "don't like their style."

I know, I know. That's *shocking*, isn't it? Why, nobody's ever heard of anybody doing a non-OSI book in recent memory, have they? Well, in the first place, see Appendix 1 for a couple of true stories about the PR Wars; and in the second place, be aware that the Fuller Context is "He who is more Right than his neighbors constitutes a Majority of One" if you're thinking what I think you're thinking. A central position to be taken here is that OSI (as they call "Open System Interconnection" familiarly) is not a panacea. More importantly, there isn't anything *magical* about having a "reference model" to aid in attempting to achieve OSI, no matter what you may have heard. Though even I am not sufficiently quixotic to tilt at the sacred RM bovine at the level of whether you actually need such a thing at all, making a cult out of your reference model *is* a great deal like being thrilled to discover in middle age that you've been talking prose all your life. As we'll see, it's the protocols that are supposed to realize/mechanize the RM that *really* matter ... and besides, there are demonstrable flaws in the most-touted RM anyway. Indeed, for reasons my friend F. M. Arouet will expand upon at the very end of the book, I refer to that particular world view as the "ISORM"—pronounced "Eyesore-mmm"—rather than the "OSIRM," and, as you'll see if you persevere, think I have a number of good and sufficient reasons for doubting the verity of the propaganda that's been issued in its behalf in recent years. One thing I don't like about their style, then, is that it's too pushy.

That's not to say I think the ISORM is utterly without value, by the way, as those of you who took the hint and read the "real" Preface will already know. But as (Doctors) Jon Postel and Danny Cohen—another couple of Old Network Boys—observe in a recent paper (given at IFIP '83), too many ISORM camp followers make noises too much like "In 1978, ISO invented the ISORM and Communications became much easier," and that in turn is too reminiscent of "In 1778, Lavoisier invented oxygen and breathing became much easier." Jon and Danny also observe in a footnote that it turns out Priestly had discovered oxygen several years earlier. As you'll see, that turns out to be a strong candidate for World's Most Significant Footnote. (The paper also casts some valuable light on the ISORM's preoccupation with Seven—which ISORMites hold to be the Right Number of layers or levels . . . even though by my count they've actually got eight or nine in their RM by now.)

So despite the apparent fact that "everybody knows" the ISORM is the wave of the future, my position is firmly rooted in the reference model that was evolved by those of us who worked on the ARPANET, which I call the ARM, and I will, of course, have more to say about both reference models later. In particular, I've been asked to furnish a "sort-of-tutorial" to accompany the separately written, somewhat independent, admittedly rather specialized essays which comprise the bulk of the book. It's the next chapter, actually, and for the benefit of those who haven't been trained always to read the Table of Contents first, it's called "What the Windmill Looks Like Up Close."

By the way, no matter what you might have heard, the rumor is *not* true that I refer to the ISORM as "the Dark Side of Networking" in private. That's actually the coinage of still another friend, whom I'd like to credit but can't get in touch with to clear it with. He said something about being incommunicado for a while on Tatooine. . . .

All of which finally brings us to the other kind of style, because once you realize that what I'm up to here is an attempt to inculcate you with the right way of thinking about Intercomputer Networking it's no distance at all to realizing that if there are two contenders for the crown of King Reference Model, each probably has its own technicoaesthetic style, and that's what I want to say a few things about in broad terms now. (Details, of course, show up in subsequent chapters.)

Here's where things get a bit dicey in terms of literary style, or at least literary methodology, by the way. The problem is that a lot of people (myself included, in some contexts) legitimately dislike being exposed to inductions based on non-enunciated data, but that's by and large what I'm about to do for purposes of this chapter—which you should realize is being written *after* Chapters 3–10 . . . and after some 14 years in the networking game, for that matter. That is, I'm going to characterize the ISORM and the ARM based on my reading of both of them (and, as a matter of fact, my writing of one of them; see Chapter 5), without going all Scholarly and doing much finger pointing at what it was that made me come to the conclusions I came to. There are several reasons for taking this tack, ranging from laziness (which, by the way, I suspect underlies all good technology), through distaste for poring over literature I dislike in general looking for specifically bad points ("I don't have to eat a whole egg to know it's rotten" is a particularly apt Old Saw on that score), all the way to the most compelling consideration of them all: that most technologists don't really give a damn for any kind of style, much less technicoaesthetic style, so why should I suffer trying to convince them of something that won't have much of an impact on them even if I succeed?

Therefore, I'll present only a few pieces of evidence for my inductions here (though more will appear in later chapters, of course) and then get on to the inductions themselves. The evidence: The ISORM insists that all "*n*-entities" (which are protocol interpreters at a given level in a hierarchy, according to two-thirds of the *soi-disant* ISORM experts I've asked—where "interpreter" means "program that obeys/implements the protocol" . . . and you'll have to wait a few pages to get even an attempt at a definition of "protocol"—but are protocols themselves, whatever that means, according to the other third) communicate with each other via "*n*-1 entities" and in terms of "data units" (which are headers, near as I can tell). As dealt with in somewhat more detail later on, if you visualize it as a high-rise apartment house, you have to climb up and down all the stairs to get anywhere, and you have to be wearing the right color coat for each floor.

The style, then, is extremely prescriptive.

That is, even making allowances for the vagaries of the literary style standards documents flounder in, with all those silly "shalls" and "wills" and "musts," the ISORM really is trying to tell you how you've *got to* do things. And, at one level, that's a commendable effort. Even I agree that standards should be as complete as possible, and as helpful as possible; indeed, in a couple of the essays that follow, I fault the "ISORMites" (see the "real" Preface) for not having *enough* to say—in particular about how protocol interpreters are to be integrated into/with the participating operating systems. (If you don't know what an "operating system" is, you're not alone; most Communications Engineers don't either. Try Chapter 2 before you decide the whole thing is outside of your sphere, though.) The problem is that even if the Voluntary Standards Organizations did attract experienced Intercomputer Networkers in large numbers (which I doubt they do, based on having looked at a lot of their documents and having met a few of their members), it's just too hard to be able to prescribe "in advance"—i.e., in your Reference Model—for *everything*. (Evidence for that assertion will be found throughout the book.) Indeed, it's sometimes too hard to do so even in your protocol specs, but what I'm fussing about here is that the prescriptive style of the Model per se makes it even harder to come up with good protocol specs than it needs to be, because the Model overconstrains the protocol designers.

Digression on definitions. Somewhere in my piling system I have several sheets of paper a former co-worker put together for a course he was teaching on operating systems. The sheets contain something like 28 "definitions" of the crucial Computer Science concept, "process." I think, though I may be misremembering, that they were culled from the writings of something like 26 reputable—or at any rate well-reputed—"computer scientists." (I'll have more to say about *that* interesting phrase in the future—but it may have to wait for another book.) At the risk of gilding the ragweed again, I'll go on: Although you'll have to trust me on my assertion that "process" is incredibly important in understanding operating systems if you're not into that sort of thing, it does seem clear that there's something wrong somewhere if fundamental concepts require multiple definitions for large values of multiple. (And I may well have remembered incorrectly—given the state of my piling system, there's not much chance I'll ever re-find the sheets of paper—there may only be umpteen definitions . . . but it's still a lot.) What's wrong, I submit, is the underlying assumption that Rigorous Definitions are achievable outside of the strictly mathematical disciplines (e.g., and probably i.e., math and physics—and I have some doubts about the latter). Yet the ISORM literature is rife with what look like rigorous definitions. Why? Well, at the risk of taking a potshot, my guess is that it's part and parcel of their prescriptive style: However hard (perhaps impossible) it is to come up with rigorous definitions, if you want to achieve a "scientific" style you have to attempt it. My own position, in contrast, is that an occasional Non-Rigorous Definition is clearly in order, but I'm not going to pretend I've codified the uncodifiable.

At any rate, the style of the ISORM comes off as what I call Prescriptive, and that in turn may well stem from a desire to look Science-y. The style of the ARM, on the other hand (oops, sorry 'bout that . . . but not sorry enough to excise it), is Descriptive. That is, we tried to set down what worked, at some suitable level of abstraction, rather than to give the impression that our precepts had been discovered on the backs of the tablets that the Ten Commandments came down on. You want to skip a layer or two? You know what you're doing? Feel free. *Our job is to furnish suitable primitive operations*, and suitable groupings or "packagings" of them, for each layer of protocol we feel is needed, not to pretend to be exhaustive. A good motto for this Descriptive style is "If you know what you're doing, three layers is enough; if you don't, even seventeen levels won't help." Indeed, our reference model is so far from being a strait jacket that it didn't even get written up explicitly until years and years after it was evolved—when I got annoyed at all the ISORMite braying over the ISORM, which I think *is* a strait jacket.

Before concluding this crypto-Foreword with another way of character-izing the contending networking styles, I really must digress a bit on Descriptive versus Prescriptive in the abstract, because a number of readers of what stands here as Chapter 5 ("A Perspective on the ARPANET Reference Model") have told me that they had trouble grasping the distinction. (By the way, if you hate all these digressions, cheer up: The chapters comprising previously published papers—3–11—are not in anywhere near so naturalistic a style as this one and the next. Of course, if you dig the digressions, don't despair; the style there, even though "handkerchiefed," never gets all that close to what you'd expect to find in a Learned Journal.) In any event, "Descriptive versus Prescriptive" is a handy dichotomy I picked up in freshman Philosophy of Science. The allusion is to the two kinds of Laws we encounter: natural/"scientific" being Descriptive, and societal/"legal" being Prescriptive. The first kind of "law," deals with what *is*, and the other with what *should be*. Examples: $f = ma$ (or $f = mdv/dt$, depending on where you took Freshman Physics) is a Descriptive Law; "Thou shalt not bear false witness" is, on the other hand, a perhaps rather pointed instance of a Prescriptive Law. (That's not, by the way, to say that I find the ISORM utterly useless. I often say something like "speaking of what should properly be called Layer Soandso *functionality*, as opposed to merely Layer Soandso"; in other words, the ISORM can indeed be used as a reasonable common tongue for Description. As a matter of fact, if you read their "Draft Proposal"—at least the version I have of it—you'll find that's pretty much what they profess they're up to. It's the ISORMites who do most of the Prescribing, although there are some inducements in the document that might well have encouraged them to.)

Another way of putting it is that whereas the Descriptive approach is suitable for technology, the Prescriptive approach is suitable for theology.

In a roundabout way this brings us to the other point I want to try to make about the ISORM style versus the ARM style. As you'll see (particularly in Chapter 5) there *are* a fair number of points of commonality between the ARM and the ISORM—which shouldn't be very surprising, given that the ARPANET was, after all, the proof-of-concept of geographically dispersed, resource-sharing, packet-switching oriented, heterogeneous intercomputer networking [an incredible mouthful, but fraught with meaning nonetheless], and even Voluntary Standards Organizations don't operate in a complete vacuum, no matter what my friend F. M. Arouet suggests. Despite the points of com-monality, though, there are still several differences, and there's still that annoying

Prescriptive style . . . annoying both because I don't think there ever can be a Book complete, clear, and cogent enough to Go By and because I do harbor severe reservations about the sort of people who volunteer for the Voluntary Standards Organizations. Not all of them, mind you; maybe not even most of them. But Great Babbage's Ghost, it really *is* the case that the ISO Standard designation for the film we knew as ASA 400 and/or DIN 27 is ISO 400/27 (or maybe 400/27°: the box I've got may turn out to be more accurate than the newspaper article I saw, and I trust you're aware that there's no way in the world you're going to get me to look that one up). That simple fact has got to cast considerable light on how ISO resolves political versus technical trade-offs/issues.

It's the theological connotation that really bothers me, though.

Let me sneak up on it. (After all, if you've gotten this far you've probably figured out that I do get there eventually.) I came across a marvelous book the other month, courtesy of a co-worker who said something like "Given your great fondness for A. A. Milne, have you ever seen *The Tao of Pooh?*" As it happened, I hadn't, so he lent me his copy. It turns out to be by Benjamin Hoff and was published by E. P. Dutton in 1982.

It also turns out to have given me what I've come to think of as the master metaphor for ISORM versus ARM style. You see, Brother Hoff starts out his rather more serious than not attempt to explicate the Oriental religion called Taoism (Tao = The Way) in terms of the "character" of Winnie-the-Pooh by describing a classic Chinese painting called "The Vinegar Tasters." To paraphrase, there are these three men standing around a vat of vinegar, tasting the contents. They represent the founder of Confucianism (another Oriental religion, for those still too lazy to look up words they don't know—and, significantly, a quite widespread one, we're told), the Buddha (I assume even Oldest Poops have heard of him), and the founder of Taoism. The first two are making variously displeased faces, but the latter, Lao-tse, is smiling.

The symbolic content of the picture, we're told, is profound. Confucianists are extremely concerned with Propriety; they're "into" Order; they're basically Establishment. "If the mat is crooked, the Master will not sit" is said to be a Confucianist maxim. (Indeed—and I am indebted to my friend Sheldon Orlov, a rising scholar of Chinese history, for the observation—the *rigidity* of the entrenched, Confucianist-dominated bureaucracy probably brought about the fall of the Ch'ing Dynasty.) Try chanting "All n-entities must communicate with other n-entities via n-1 entiteeheeheeees" in Plainsong (or even Gregorian Chant); if you get the flavor, you'll see where I'm heading. Omitting the Buddha (nothing personal, Gautama old thing, I just don't feel like taking on SNA right now) (an in-joke; I apologize), Lao-tse is smiling because Taoists are said to believe in accepting things as they are, in "going with the flow," and—in my reading of Hoff anyway, and for the purpose of my metaphor irrespective of whether it's accurate Taoism—are rather Anti-Establishment.

At the risk of gilding the ragweed still again, doesn't the ISORM, even as sketchily as it's been depicted here so far, feel awfully Confucianist to you? Doesn't the ARM feel pleasantly Taoist? I mean, not that I'm trying to take sides between real Confucianists and real Taoists, but if we've got to turn the whole business into some sort of Holy War (and several of Them sure sound like they have done just that), wouldn't you feel . . . cleaner somehow, as a professed technologist, to associate with the less Religious religion, at least in terms of the metaphor we've got going?

Just to suggest that I am capable of some seriousness (if not Solemnity) after all, I hasten to add that I don't take the style arguments to be decisive. Our stuff isn't necessarily better, and Their stuff isn't necessarily worse, just because Their style is presumptuous/theocratic. I do take the style points to be suggestive, though, and I hope you'll at least keep them in the back of your mind as you plow or zip through the rest of this stuff—which, by the way, you should feel perfectly free to view as just another perspective on Intercomputer Networking and not as some sort of Taoist tract. We didn't start the squabble by calling Their stuff no good, after all (when they even bothered to admit our stuff [pre-]existed), nor did We advertise how great our stuff was years before it even existed at all. . . .

[I sometimes think we should have advertised/proselytized more, though; that's why I let Arouet talk me into the Slogans campaign. (See Appendix 3.) If you don't like them, tear 'em out and throw 'em away; the argument of the book won't suffer. For that matter, if you do like them, tear 'em out (carefully) and put 'em up on your walls; the argument of the book still won't suffer—nor should it benefit—but perhaps some of the more hypocritical and pushy ISORMites will. Hmmm, if I survive this one, maybe the next book should be an anthology of Our papers, collected from the various, rather scattered conference proceedings they appeared in. Postel would be willing to co-edit, and we can have some good arguments over appreciating the significances. . . . Are you listening, Karl?]

What we've got going, then, is a couple of Form versus Content problems, which in some sense is what Style is all about. On the one hand, I'm asking you to accept my preferred non-Solemn (literary) form on the grounds that it's the way I find it feasible to convey some fairly Serious content. On the other hand, I'm asking you to consider the possibility that, despite the extremely Solemn form you'll have seen in "the literature," if you're reading this book as a serious student of Intercomputer Networking (not your only possible reason, of course: it could be for collateral reading in Computer Science; it could be for collateral reading in History of Technology; it could even be for fun—and I do hope the latter enters into your personal equation in any case), the content of the best known approach to Intercomputer Networking isn't actually as Serious as its proponents would have you think.

Resisting the temptation to digress on Form versus Content in the abstract, though it is a fascinating topic and I'd be so bold as to commend it to your attention as a subject for independent study, there are a couple of open questions lurking in the Us versus Them card I've blithely forced on you so far. Taking the easier one first, if you've read this far and don't care whether We or They are right, should you stop here? Well, I certainly don't think so, or I wouldn't have bothered with the whole proceeding. The point is that irrespective of the relative merits of the ARM and the ISORM it's not easy to learn how to think about Intercomputer Networking issues if you want to think for yourself about them, rather than just accept what Authority has to say. That is to say, this book is not *merely* a pro-ARM, anti-ISORM polemic. Indeed, as an example to some extent of what might be called Technological Criticism (by analogy to Literary Criticism, and emphatically *not* in the sense of Neo-Luddite polemics), it even has some claims to being not even merely a book about Intercomputer Networking, but I don't care to push too hard on that point.

I also don't care to push too hard on the Catholic/Protestant stereotype echoes triggered by the "think for yourself" versus "take what They tell you" point. There really is too much Religion kicking around in my particular Art . . . and besides, in case anybody cares I'm neither Catholic, Protestant, Confucianist, nor Taoist myself. (I'm also not what you probably think I am either.) In a funny kind of way, though, the Individualism versus Authoritarianism issue ought to be raised in red ink: The prose style here might well be too much like Luis Tiant's pitching style—incredibly long, herky-jerky windups followed by somewhat sneaky pitches—for everyone's taste, even though I'm not the only one who has fun with it. (Blame it on a surfeit of Nietzsche [in translation] in sophomore Western Civ if it makes you feel better.) There might even be so many parentheses floating around that you'll never believe I'm not a diehard LISP programmer. (In reality, I don't do LISP at all.) You might find yourself in intense agreement with a friend of mine who accuses me of speaking in clear text with encrypted headers, and I don't know what it would take to convince you that the vocabulary *isn't* dictated by former English major's malice. (The most I'll admit to is a somewhat imperfect touch of the poet.) *However*, the style I'd most like to see you adopt as a result of reading all this stuff isn't the ARM style over the ISORM (though it is preferable, in my view), or the litterateur's over the injuneer's (though I, for one, would have a lot less trouble putting up with "the literature" if more did): it's the *inquirer's style* over the accepter's. Granted, you need a lot of background to be in a position to make judgments you'd like to have become binding on others, but still **THE UNDERLYING MORAL OF ALL THIS IS "THINK ABOUT IT."** That is, although I am nowhere near snotty enough to presume to attempt to influence you one way or the other on issues of *real* Dogma (as a technical term in theology), on which your views are strictly your own business in my view, I *do* want to help you to realize that the pious-sounding pronunciamenti of the ISORMites *neither have nor deserve* the weight of positions declared by a duly constituted Sacred authority to be undebatable by communicants [pun intended] . . . even if the ISORMite style seems to encourage you to react as if they did. (It would also be nice if you read the Preface.)

Coming at last to the final lurking question, if, as I've more than hinted already, I'm going to take a fundamentally anti-ISORM (and extremely anti-X.25) stance, does that mean that I'm (gasp, shudder) anti-Standards?

Wellllll . . . not *really*.

We don't have to rehearse the economic reasons for having Standards. I'll stipulate. *However*, no matter how economically desirable it is to standardize, that's still no excuse for promulgating bad standards. (By the way, I'm addressing primarily "logical" standards—about which I expect I'll have more to say in Chapter 2—not physical ones. Clearly it's advantageous to be able to reclose bottles that contain carbonated beverages with reusable, interchangeable bottlecaps, as I've observed elsewhere. Physical standards are often Good Things. There is, ironically enough, a certain piquancy to the observation that when I was last in Europe—that ISORMite bastion, by all reports—the nifty "dual voltage" hairdryer which had arrived in the mail the very day I left turned out to be useless anyway because I couldn't plug it in to any of the wall sockets, which, as you probably know, require different sorts of prongs from country to country even though the voltage is supposed to be the same. [And don't bug me about adaptor plugs; it was much too heat-wavy out to go looking for such gizmos.])

Probably the classic example of the Stampede to Standardize Syndrome ("So manufacturers will know what to manufacture and the public won't get stuck with incompatible systems") is American television, which, according to my hardware-wise friends, settled on an inferior standard of 525 (or so) lines (of something per something) in the expressed interests of "getting something on the air fast," while the subsequently agreed-upon European standard of 800 (maybe) lines (of the same thing) is "better." (See the Afterthought on Scholarship for why the foregoing wasn't terribly specific.)

Now, I once met a man who was actually in the TV transmission field at the time, and he assured me that the situation was even worse than I'd heard, and was all "political" anyway, but I don't want to appeal to that. I don't even want to appeal to the private conversation I had last month with an Old Network Boy who's still a personal friend even though he's become a leading ISORM proponent, who assured me that ISO would never have gone for the ARM suite of protocols because the European governments didn't want their manufacturers to cede a head start to the American manufacturers. (I *do* wish he'd pass that on to the ISORMites who keep squalling that the ARM protocols are undesirable because they're not "vendor supported," though.) Instead, I want to try to convey what I think is really important about Standards by means of another true story:

On June 28th or 29th of 1971, I was in the throes of getting my home operating system (Multics, of which more later) "on the air" on the ARPANET, for "Telnet" (the archetypal Virtual Terminal Protocol, of which quite a bit more later). The reference standard (or "touchstone," a very nice word which you should look up if you don't know for sure what it means) for Telnet implementations was at the Network Measurement Center at UCLA, on their Sigma 7 (under the SEX operating system). So I took the Development System (among many other significant properties, Multics was one of the first systems to do dynamic reconfiguration), "brought up the network," and told my then-not-so-Old Network Boy friend Ari Ollikainen (who managed the SEX system, and was on the other end of a conventional telephone line) to have a go at logging in to us. He said, "It's saying 'Multics, Cambridge, Mass., System soandso, Load suchandsuch'!! What do I do now?" I told him the appropriate login ritual and then he said, "It's saying 'L is not a command'!" I thought furiously for a beat or two and then asked what kind of terminal he was at. "A Model 33," he replied. "Well, make it send lower-case letters. Multics doesn't think capital 'L' is the same as lower-case 'l'." "I can't," he replied. "But the protocol says you've got to be able to!" I howled. "Not yet," he replied. "*!\$!!**!\$!," I said, "I'm declaring it a success anyway."

The moral ought to be clear, but I'll say it anyhow:

What I want is good protocols, properly implemented, not bad Standards for the sake of having Standards.

That's not very rigorous. It also skips a lot of steps. But it's the best I can do by way of conveying the style I advocate for Intercomputer Networking. Call it Descriptive, call it Taoist, call it the programmer's approach as opposed to the computer scientist's—call it what you will . . . but do it right.

AN AFTERTHOUGHT ON SCHOLARSHIP

Having been exposed somewhere along the line to the Learned Tradition, I *do* feel some vestigial pangs of guilt for not feeling like looking up the TV "lines" business, and, in general, for not coming off like a good little Scholar in terms of content as well as form by crossing all the *i*'s and dotting all the *t*'s, even assuming that if you care about the Luddite allusion you'll look it up if you don't already know it. By way of apology, I'd like to tell one more true story: I once took a Sixteenth-Century English Literature course. One of the exam questions was, Where is the manuscript of Raleigh's poem, "The Weed and the Wag" kept? I got it right, because I *do* read Forewords (most of the time) and it was a funny-looking sort of name (the Bodleian, in case anybody cares; not having taken to reading Dorothy Sayers at the time, I didn't appreciate its significance, of course). I was also appalled that the question had been asked. The concern with Form it betrayed is preposterous. It became my master metaphor for giving up on the Humanities and letting my other head (the Numbers one—the first being the Words one) earn me a living thereafter. It's Confucianist to the *n*th degree. It's the sort of style that gives librarians a bad name (the stereotypical "soul of a librarian" not being at ease until and unless every volume is on the shelf in its proper DD or LoC place). It's the sort of thing I'd expect only from one of the ArchISORMites. It's *silly*.

Isn't that making too much of what is in fact just a form of pettifoggery? Not, I submit, if it grows up into a full-fledged hypocrisy, as it's quite capable of doing. What I consciously decline to offer you, then, is, to me, the false coin of Jive Scholarship, which looks Learned but lacks substance. So, unfashionable though it may be, I choose to furnish duly labeled informed opinion rather than feigned objectivity. An example of the sort of thing I dislike: "State machines" are all very nice in protocol specs, but where are the appendices on Wisdom (sometimes known as Notes to Implementors)? For that matter, consider "One-half approaches infinity for small values of two." It sure sounds Science-y, and would even be true if the premise could be—but the premise can't be true, and the result is ludicrous. Granted, not pretending to be touching all the proper bases does spare me some distasteful digging, but it also saves you from the risk of being conned—or, even worse, cowed. After all, we shouldn't ignore the (apparently true) story of the medieval Schoolmen who were wondering how many teeth horses had. The problem was that the answer wasn't in Aristotle. When one of their students suggested going out and looking in some horses' mouths, they expelled him for attempting to undermine Authority. A classic example of the Prescriptive dominating the Descriptive—as well, of course, as of the power of the wrong kind of scholarship. (Perhaps there should be a Padlipsky's Corollary to Gresham's Law: Bad intellectual currency does seem to have a tendency to drive good I.C. out of circulation, too.)

If, despite all that, you still demand the ultra-rigid, frequently phony Scholarly style, find another book; this one's meant to be evocative . . . and maybe even provocative.

CHAPTER 2

What the Windmill Looks Like Up Close: A Sort of Tutorial

PREFATORY AFTERTHOUGHTS

The main—and only—thing I have to say about "What the Windmill Looks Like Up Close" (other than to offer a friendly hint that if the title is obscure to you and *Don Quixote* doesn't ring a bell you might want to think about *Man of La Mancha* . . . even though I never do, myself) is that I do dearly wish I hadn't let myself get talked into it. It was a lot of effort, and I'm sure it won't satisfy those who need it most (i.e., total neophytes when it comes to Intercomputer Networking). I'm not even sure it particularly satisfies me. It certainly seems to be Snotty enough, but I worry about the Constructive part. The trouble is that however much I wanted to make it come out much more edifying than amusing, it seemed to insist on being amusing (if even that) instead of edifying. The old aesthetic sensibility kept getting in the way, and judgments kept supplanting, preceding, or at best coinciding with evidence: I really *don't* "do" tutorials, I'm afraid.

(I'd like to make a separate apology for having been unable to avoid using terms in advance of their semi-definitions even in a nominal tutorial, and in general for continuing to toss in comments, barbs, and "in jokes" that can only be appreciated by those who know more about the field than beginners should be expected to know. I *am* sorry, but I just can't break myself of the loathsome habit. Well, I never said I was *against* peer-peer communications, did I? [Drat! I did it again. Guess there's absolutely *no* hope . . . .])

Oh well, it did give me an excuse to tell a few more interesting true stories, and at least nobody can accuse me ever again of never showing pictures of headers—and the second and last sections *were* fun. Tell you what, if you ever happen to meet me, I won't blame you if you tell me you skipped most of the middle part and/or just looked at the pictures if you won't blame me for my unwillingness to deal with Tedium, which is what I feel winnowing out all sorts of corroborative detail on the vendors and the ISORM would have constituted.

INTRODUCTION: WHAT THIS CHAPTER ISN'T

When what stand here as Chapters 5 and 7 through 10 were published internally by my employer as what I referred to as Off-White Papers, I realized that they might well be worth broader circulation than they would be afforded as corporate documents (and, in one case, a conference paper). Perhaps, I thought, I'm not too lazy to do a book after all. So I took the five papers (originally known as the Teabag Papers because their early-form blanket cover sheet had some rather pointed "Taglines" from a particular tea company on it—but that can go unreproduced here, if only not to offend any few remaining EE types who weren't driven off by Chapter 1, and, as usual, to save me the trouble of having to request permission to quote them), added the other papers, which stand as Chapters 3, 4, 6, and 11, all of which had been cleared for public release already, and went off in search of a publisher.

I got lucky. As you can readily infer from the fact that you're reading this, Prentice-Hall liked the idea of doing an insistently non-stodgy technical book. Indeed, I was even encouraged to add my collection of unabashedly satirical pieces as Appendices and to come up with as many cartoons as I could, and my proposed cryto-Foreword was also welcomed.

Unfortunately, from my point of view, it was rightly observed that the field of Intercomputer Networking Protocols is, after all, rather highly specialized. So specialized, in fact, that most potential readers couldn't be expected to appreciate the technical points at issue without some sort of—oh, dear—"tutorial material." But if you've paid any attention at all to the pages preceding this one you'll have already figured out that I'm not the tutorial type, so you may well wonder how the impasse came to be resolved. Well, it just so happens that the Publisher had already paid some attention to Chapters 3–11 and wasn't so cruel (nor so unrealistic) as to insist on a "straight" tutorial from such as me. . . .

So what this chapter isn't is a Primer on Networking.

An Aside on Punctuation

Another thing it isn't is particularly Scholarly—in two senses, one of which will be dealt with later. At this juncture, though, it should be observed that I've also taken liberties with punctuation: To wit, I've invented a new use of "square brackets" here, as "strong parentheses." In other words, since my borrowed "word processor" isn't supposed to be very good at footnotes and I didn't want to run the risk of using end notes (the risk of their not being read, of course), at several points I've interjected paragraphs demarcated by "["and"]" which would otherwise have been footnotes, in the sense that they're even further from whatever flow there is here than what comes in normal parentheses. Just thought you'd like to know.

PSYCHOPATHOLOGY

Rather than tease you with the cover cartoon, I decided to start with what might otherwise have been the conclusion of this chapter. The chapter will, when we get around to it, deal with the History, Present State, and Future of what I've been calling Intercomputer Networking. (Be of good cheer: The non-rigorous definition is only a few pages away.) It's a somewhat strange story in that, as you'll see, once a reasonable working model had been built it was largely ignored by a number of hardware manufacturers, standards organizations, and even Government agencies I'm just barely tactful enough not to mention specifically— almost all of whom decided to invent their own "networks" rather than adopt, or even carefully adapt, the proof-of-concept one. It was only while I was planning this chapter that I had the insight as to exactly why the strangeness transpired, and I'd like to get it out of the way first so the reader won't be distracted by trying to account for the perverse phenomena as they go by, instead of, as intended, trying to acquire whatever knowledge and wisdom there may be to be found floating around in the chapter.

Thoughtful readers will probably already have figured it out for themselves long ago. Astute ones will almost certainly have worked it out from the cover cartoon. Just to make sure we're all on the same metaphorical wavelength, though, let me say it outright: A central factor in the psychopathology of the technologist is the It's *My* Ball Syndrome. That is, in case you haven't encountered the expression before, there's an awful lot of playing the old childhood trick of insisting on making the rules of the game by the owner of the ball, who will otherwise take the ball home, going on in the world in general, in technology in particular, and, based on my own experience, in Intercomputer Networking to a fare-thee-well.

(It also accounts for why just about every "Hollywood adaptation" you've ever seen of a good novel or play is a disappointment: Give a turkey a ball and he insists on trying to have one . . . by "improving" the rules of the game. Bah. But there *is* an awful lot of that going around.)

This isn't meant to be a personal vendetta, so I won't offer finger-pointing examples. I could, though, based just on my own recent existence as a Protocols Guru Without Portfolio, without even bothering to collect stories from other Old Network Boys. Even some people in a few organizations I've worked for/with have flat out said, "Mike, I don't care if you guys have already tried it that way and it doesn't work; this is *my* project and I want to learn from my own mistakes"—or words to that effect. Others haven't even been that honest with themselves. So, to explain the cover cartoon more than it probably needs, the It's *My* Ball Syndrome even crops up when dealing with an inventor of the game at hand. (I don't claim as distinguished a position in the pantheon of Intercomputer Networking as Dr. Naismith does in the pantheon of basketball, but I *was* there.)

That might seem rather harsh. Isn't there a more charitable explanation for the apparent refusals to attempt to benefit from deep understanding of the state of an art before attempting to advance it? Good scholarship is very difficult, after all. As you know, I don't claim to do it myself. (Of course, I can usually get away with the claim that I don't have to deal with secondary sources, being a primary source myself. Heh, heh.) Certainly, the well-known desire to sound Science-y mentioned in Chapter 1 has held more than some little sway in this field, too, so perhaps "the literature" was too hard to grasp? Maybe. But I doubt it. I'd better give you one example after all, so you can get the flavor:

The other month I went off, rather reluctantly, to learn about the position of a *major* manufacturer on Communications. Without being too specific—not out of kindness, but because I didn't tape record the proceedings and don't want to risk a libel action—the first shock was when I was told that their particular approach to networking would work just fine on Local Area Nets with only a change of "Level 1" (the ISORM "Physical" level, which we'll eventually have to discuss, I'm afraid). As "Level 3" is the ISORM "Network" level, and as a LAN is a network, I found the assertion rather off-putting, though I do realize, and will return to, the subtlety of end-to-endness in talking about the ISORM. The shock was that it was simply assumed to be the only possible interpretation.

Things got worse, though. They trotted out one of their heavyweights, who told us all about his view of the Right Way to do LANs. In the course of his actually rather plausible-sounding remarks, he gave me another shock: He said he didn't believe "Ethernet" would work on optical fibers. (Don't worry about what Ethernet is for a while . . . but I guess you're allowed to infer that I wasn't visiting Xerox Corp.) Since I was "there to learn"—and since, as usual last summer, it was too hot out for me to be in the mood for a gratuitous fight—I didn't bother to tell him that unless Dave Boggs is a liar I'd actually been permitted to touch a fiber Ethernet the last time I was in Palo Alto. (I don't like hardware, as you may already have figured out, but I do know just enough about it to have realized it would have been impolite to stare at the connector between the fiber and the computer; we agreed I was authorized to say "Ethernet does so work on fiber; I've touched it; it's orange" should the need arise, but, as I said, I wasn't in the mood to on the occasion I'm telling you about.)

So far, so relatively minor. I'd scarcely demand euthanasia for some marketeer for not understanding a somewhat subtle issue of reference model theology, after all, and the heavyweight seemed sincere about his inability to understand how you could do Ethernet on fiber, even if he was wrong. (I find it helps to consider hardware to be magic, myself; of course, that might make me more gullible than most about it . . . if I weren't convinced that I don't believe in magic.) I even forgave some earlier casual references to "interoperating via Gateways": After all, they hadn't had a chance to decline to read Chapter 10 yet. The real clinker dropped a couple of minutes later, when said heavyweight caused to be projected a nifty-looking picture which bore considerable resemblance to the Olympic Symbol (you know, all them interlocking circles) and said that he believed that with *his* pet LAN "technology" you could even interconnect LANs of different speeds. That was too much for me to take, even if I was there to learn. "Surely," I asked, "you're not attempting to imply that your way is the *only* way to do that?" "Gee," he replied, "I hadn't thought about that." "Aren't you familiar with the ARPA Internet?" I asked. "No," he replied. "Ah, well," I said, "I'm here to learn."

Now, it's still going to be several more pages before you get to see a schematic sort of picture of the ARPA Internet, and even a few more pages before I tell the few of you who haven't heard of it what "ARPA" is, but you can trust me that it's been interconnecting *dissimilar* communications subnetwork "technologies" for a number of years. The ARPA Internet, and the "AR-PANET" before it, are also readily accessible in "the literature." But this *major* manufacturer's heavyweight, who had apparently been instrumental in convincing them to go with his pet LAN, hadn't heard of it.

Pick your own expletive.

I forget whether I decided their corporate position on Communications was prone or supine, but I sure as hell realized it was *their* ball.

"HISTORY"

Whether or not you accept my analysis of the Psychopathology, you'd better brace yourself: After only one more digression, we get to the make-believe history lesson—as best I recall it, and with no particular claims to Accuracy. (Real Scholars wouldn't believe anybody who writes as snottily as I do anyway, and besides, I don't like library "research" any more than hardware.)

On the Futility of Technohistorical Endeavor

But first, a sort of disclaimer: Another thing I know from personal experience is that pinning down who invented what is damn near impossible. Let's go over a few quick examples, if only because I think they're fun.

Who invented the computer? Eckert and Mauchly (however you spell 'em)? The Professor from the Midwest, whose name escapes me? How about Turing's "Bombe" that we only got to hear about 30 or so years later because it was part of the "ULTRA Secret"? I dunno.

Who invented the video game? There was an article in a Boston newspaper the other week about one Ralph Baer of Sanders Corp. who seems to have a sound claim to precedence over the commonly accepted one (according to the article, anyway) of Nolan Bushnell of Atari. But what about Space War on the PDP-1 in Bldg. 26 at M.I.T? I saw that one myself in '65, and it wasn't brand new then as I recall.

Who, for that matter, invented "packet switching"? I thought for years it was Larry Roberts, when he was head of ARPA's (whatever that is . . . but you'll get to know soon) Information Processing Techniques Office; then I met Bruce Taylor and his wife at a party (he was Roberts' immediate predecessor at ARPA IPTO), and she told me *he* did it. Then there's the somewhat-known report Paul Baran did at RAND even earlier, which many *cognoscenti* give the credit to. But what about the Englishman I heard at an otherwise dreadful conference the other month who claims the credit should actually go to Donald Davies at NPL (the National Physical Laboratory—*their* Standards Bureau)? He sounded pretty convincing too. (To make matters worse, I've since come across an article by Roberts crediting J. C. R. Licklider, Taylor's predecessor, with the original inspiration. Gee, maybe I should ask Lick what *he* thinks. . . . Nah, it can't be worth it.)

Speaking of the English—or at any rate the British—for most of the years I worked on Multics I thought Virtual Memory was the brainchild of Glaser and Corbató . . . then somebody went and told me about some system across the sea called Atlas. Hmmm. Never thought to ask if they got the idea for *it* from the D-825. Oh well, never mind—the D-825 is too far afield even for me to pretend to explicate. (After I wrote this I happened to hear from Bob Daley, who was there before I was, that Ted and Corby *were* aware of Atlas. Sigh.)

Perhaps all of those could be determined by sufficiently expert Scholarship, though, so why do I claim it's futile? Well, I'll tellya. Around five years ago I ran into an Old Network Boy friend (Gary Grossman, actually) I hadn't seen for a while. We got to reminiscing about the good old days five or so years previously on the "New" Telnet (again, you'll hear about that one later too) working group and I said, "You know, I always liked your IAC trick." (I haven't decided yet whether I'll go deeply enough into Telnet to let you know what *that* means, but for present purposes it may be taken as a fairly important second-order mechanism of the ARPANET's second-pass Virtual Terminal Protocol.) "Wait a minute," he replied, "IAC was one of *yours*."

After considerable discussion, he semi-convinced me it was indeed one of mine. After considerable thought, and numerous conversations with Jon Postel, whom I refer to as the Senior Guru (of the ARPANET protocols—I'm only the Eldest Guru), wherein we couldn't even pin down exactly which few of the important first-order mechanisms weren't his, I'm totally convinced that you just can't "do" Technohistory. Therefore, what's to come should be viewed as just my own recollections and impressions, not Revealed Truth—nor, of course, even particularly assiduous Scholarship. Remember, I said pages ago that I think laziness is the wellspring of technology. But it's as close as I can bring myself to a tutorial/history on/of Intercomputer Networking, and I did promise the Publisher, so take it for whatever it's worth. . . .

The NWG's Role

We can't delay it any longer: "ARPA" is an acronym for the Advanced Research Projects Agency . . . of the U.S. Department of Defense. Indeed, at the first ARPANET Network Working Group meeting I attended, in May of 1971, Larry Roberts was introduced as being from the more formal-sounding—and probably more correct—"DARPA." This occasioned some anxious whispering in the back of the room. Then one of the best and brightest of the Old Network Boys—who's still a good friend, so whose identity I'll conceal in case he ever decides to drop back into the field—came up with the first Great Network One-Liner: "Cheer up, you guys, *our* money only has blood on one side."

There's a lot in that one. Yes, the funding for the ARPANET *did* come from the DoD. Yes, the latter-day concerns for Reliability and Security did stem in some measure from a desire to serve the sponsor's needs. But NO, NO, Several K times NO, the NWG (which I'll use from now on to indicate the Network Working Group, even though the non-rigorous definition won't come for a while yet) wasn't particularly concerned with—nor even particularly aware of—those facts. As a matter of fact, most of us looked—and in some ways were— sufficiently like our contemporaries that four of us really were shooed away from the booth of a semi-major Southwestern manufacturer by one of its superstraight salesmen when we wanted to find out how much its then-new portable terminal weighed. (This occurred at the SJCC which coincided with the NWG meeting just mentioned.) So if the rumors I've heard are true and the ISO troops in Europe distrust Old Network Boys because of our "tainted associations," They're even wronger than usual . . . but it's really probably just a rationalization for wanting to keep Dr. Naismith away from *their* gym.

To understand why I claim that the DoD involvement was not dominant, you have to understand the composition of the NWG. To understand that, it helps to consider a Creation Myth: Once upon a time (somewhere in the late 1960s), the Director of the Information Processing Techniques Office of the Advanced Research Projects Agency (of the Department of Defense) got the umpteenth call that month from a university requesting a PDP-10 (or maybe -6) of its very own. "Hmmm," he thought, "if only phone calls weren't so expensive I could just have 'em use the ones I'm already paying for at other universities, there must be plenty of cpu cycles to spare. Say, how about an ARPANET!" That is, as discussed somewhat less frivolously in Chapters 3–5, one of the underlying ideas of Intercomputer Networking is "Resource Sharing" in its simplest sense, of just making it economically feasible to "get at" computing power elsewhere. Remote Access, in other words. But for present purposes what matters is that the Creation Myth implies who became the NWG: the system programmers and Computer Science students from a number of universities with ARPA-sponsored systems, mainly. (In fairness, a few nonacademic organizations were also involved . . . and even one or two for-profits.)

If you want the "official" story, get in touch with Bolt, Beranek, and Newman, Inc. in Cambridge, Mass., and ask for a copy of the ARPANET History document they put out a while back for the Tenth Anniversary (of "being on the air with Telnet," I think). I actually blundered across my copy of it recently and would love to give you the document number but now I can't find the slip of paper I wrote it down on. Of course, if you do get a copy it'll read as if BBN did almost all of the work, but don't let that fool you. They certainly were major contributors, but what really happened is that they got the contract to build the communications subnetwork processors: the IMPs (for Interface Message Processors), which either were or weren't the first packet switches but certainly got a lot of attention in any event. (Generically, I call such gadgets CSNPs, for Comm Subnet Processors.) They also had supplied what turned out to be the most numerous Host type, "TENEX" (for [PDP-] 10, EXtended [or maybe EXpanded]) to a number of the participating institutions. They didn't, however, run the NWG.

By "Host," by the way, I mean a resource-bearing computer system/operating system attached to a communications subnetwork for purposes of participating in what I've been calling Intercomputer Networking with other Hosts, which don't have to bear the same operating system or even be of the same manufacture. The fancy word for the latter property is "heterogeneous," of course. (Note, by the way, that the heterogeneity made it natural to posit *separate* CSNPs; as we'll see, not everybody makes that distinction.) By Intercomputer Networking, while I'm at it, I mean something very much like Resource Sharing in the sense of Chapters 3–5. Indeed, I keep using the awkward locution "communications subnetwork" in an attempt to distinguish between what too many people think "the network" "is"—the IMPs of their equivalents— and what I think the network is: the Hosts and their subsidiary (though unarguably necessary, and even interesting) communications gadgets. Well, I warned you I'm not big on Rigorous Definitions, didn't I?

The object of the NWG's game, then, was to "network" *all* of their home systems, not just TENEXes. Among the early players were SEX on the Sigma 7 at UCLA and Multics on the GE (or maybe by then Honeywell) 645 at M.I.T., as mentioned earlier; OS/TSO on the 360/91 at UCLA; ITS (the "Incompatible Time-sharing System") on (originally) the PDP-6 at M.I.T.'s AI Lab (which was actually on the same floor of the same room of the same building as Multics, but was institutionally . . . different, Multics being under the aegis of what was then called Project MAC); NLS on a PDP-6 or -10 at SRI; TSS on the 360/67 at NASA–Ames; OLS on the 360/75 at UCSB; I-forget-which-operating-system at RAND (probably TSO, but with different enough "Access Methods" to make it an essentially different system than UCLA's); and what was then called CP/CMS on, I think, a 360/67 at M.I.T.'s Lincoln Labs—plus, of course, half a dozen or so TENEXes. There were probably others, and I apologize in advance to anybody I've inadvertently left out, but the flavor should be clear: What we were up to was an attempt to get a number of *very disparate* operating systems to "cooperate," not merely to do packet-switched communications between TENEXes. (Note that I'm not blaming BBN for the popular misconception of what the ARPANET was; it just goes to show how widespread the notion is that you learn an art by nose counting—a trait I've seen displayed in any number of ISORM-oriented "Features Analyses.")

If, by the way, you don't know what an operating system is, I hope and trust you're reading this book for the fun of it, rather than to become a "networker."

How did we go about "networking" all those mutually alien systems? Well, the comm subnet was pretty much of a given: BBN got to specify how you interfaced to an IMP because they built the IMPs. (That was a year or more before I got involved, so I don't know to what extent they played *IM*B games with it.) Borrowing from traditional Communications, the way you interfaced became known as "the protocol." (Confusingly enough, the same document—

BBN Report 1822—specified both the hardware attachment/protocol and the software attachment/protocol; I'll have more to say about that soon.) So if the Hosts were going to have things to say to each other over the comm subnet, the next step was "obviously" to invent a Host-Host protocol. That, of course, leaves out a year or two of deep thought which I wasn't privy to and haven't really been able to reconstruct, despite several chats with people who were privy to it—which should serve as a useful reminder about Futility, and as an excuse to do a crude segue into a more appropriately named section.

Protocols

As Chapter 4 will attempt to convince you, I believe quite strongly that what really matters in Intercomputer Networking is the protocols. Neither Chapter 4 (nor Chapter 5) is particularly intended to spell out what protocols are, however, so let's try a different level of abstraction here, starting with a few attempts at (I claim Non-Rigorous) definitions of the term.

First, the old reliable one, coming from one of the 1970 SJCC papers which introduced the ARPANET to that fraction of the world which happened to be noticing (unless it comes from the follow-up session at the '72 SJCC . . . well, ARPA used to have nifty booklets reprinting both sets, and if you're a Serious Scholar you ought to have them already):

> *When we have two processes facing each other across some communication link, the protocol is the set of their agreements on the format and relative timing of messages to be exchanged. When we speak of a protocol, there is usually an important goal to be fulfilled. Although any set of agreements between cooperating (i.e., communicating) processes is a protocol, the protocols of interest are those which are constructed for general application by a large population of processes in solving a large class of problems.*

> *Crocker, et al.*

Next, let's look at one from the first doctoral dissertation known to me to come out of the ARPANET troops (it's also used in a paper which of course I can't find, but honest, Serious Scholars, you *can* trust me to have quoted it accurately):

> *The ways in which processes organize their cooperation are called* protocols. *Webster defines the word* protocol *in one way as a "rigid long-established code prescribing complete deference to superior rank and strict adherence to due orders of precedence and precisely correct procedure."* [Oh. No wonder the ISORMites are the way they are! —MAP] *We use the word to refer to a set of agreements among*

communicating processes relating to (1) rendezvous, (2) format, and (3) timing of data exchanges.

Metcalfe

(Yes, the Father of Ethernet was one of Us.)
Finally, let's try:

They're just appropriate Common Intermediate Representations.

Padlipsky

Note that what they have in common (even the last, though it's utterly implicit there) is this notion of "process." Note also that "process" is a technical term in Computer Science. Note further that there are lots and lots of definitions of "process." Note still further that I'm not going to help you much if you don't already know what a process is by saying that the definition I prefer is that of an address space in execution. Note finally that, just as with "operating system," if you don't know what a process is you're reading this book for fun rather than for real. (Not, by the way, that there's anything wrong with reading it for fun. It's just that I never agreed to throw in a tutorial on Computer Science. Hell, it took me at least ten years to learn to say "computer science" with a straight face.)

While you're in note mode, please be aware that I not only don't think you now know what a protocol is—based on what you've found here, that is—but I also don't think you've got a chance to know what one is until and unless you go off and read several protocol specifications *and* several source listings of programs which "interpret" those specs. In a spirit of good fellowship, however, I'll give you a sample, simple protocol right away and even show you a header format or two in a while. Just promise you won't run off and take a seat on some ISO committee or another because you think I've turned you into an expert. (On second thought, it probably would be an improvement . . . oh, never mind.)

A Protocol

1. Insert coin(s)
2. Dial number
3. Wait for response
4. If response correct, press Button B
   /* Coin(s) will drop */
5. If response incorrect (or no response) (or circuit engaged, which could have been mentioned between 2 and 3), press Button A
   /* Coin(s) will return */
6. If you got this far, now you can communicate . . . if you can communicate
   /* The object of the game, though we sometimes forget it */

Note that it's (approximately) the protocol for using British pay phones, or was a number of years ago. Note also that if you react to it by saying, "What a dumb way to get around switching problems—they probably use 19 percent more components than necessary," you're almost definitely a Traditional Communications Engineer and are reading this book either for fun, out of masochism, or in search of grounds for a libel suit. (I've never met a T. C. E. who knew what operating systems and processes really are.) (Not that I know what Reed-Solomon Codes really are, myself, of course.)

By the way, truly astute readers will have noticed that the comment on step 6 is extremely pithy. It might help to point out that the "response" expected is the announcing of the number of the phone being answered; but the crux of the matter is that after you've gotten through the "protocol" it had better turn out that the answerer and the caller speak the same language—beyond the level of just mouthing the right number—if there's going to be a conversation on the connection.

The "Natural Hierarchy" of Protocols

It might help to take a closer look at a few Intercomputer Networking protocols. To introduce them, let's agree that, technotheology aside, it makes sense to design protocols as some sort of "hierarchy." In other words, "Layers" and/or "Levels" notwithstanding—because of the connotations those terms will turn out to have in the Great Battle of the Reference Models I've alluded to in Chapter 1 and will be returning to here and in Chapter 5 (and elsewhere, come to think of it)—there are going to be "strata" of protocols, falling out naturally from what protocols are for and some common-sense observations about how you'd like to use them.

From the Intercomputer Networking point of view, the lowest stratum has to do with the interface to the comm subnet processor (CSNP, for future reference), even if you insist, as some do, that it consists of several substrata itself—or even if you think the CSNP is part of the Host, rather than a separate box. (If you insist that the lowest stratum is whatever protocol is in play from CSNP to CSNP, you don't understand what I mean by "the Intercomputer Networking point of view": Sure there's an IMP to IMP protocol [by now it's probably the fourth or fifth such], but from the IN PoV it doesn't matter whether the bits are getting to the other Host over a string between a couple of tin cans.) After all, the builder of the comm subnet owns that particular ball, and even though there might (though I for one doubt it) be a case to be made for standardizing *all* network interfaces at some point in the future, that sure isn't the way the world is structured today; so the interface protocol to the comm subnet has to figure into the natural hierarchy we're sketching here. *But* . . . no sensible protocol designer wants to get "locked in" to the protocol "below" him or her—especially in the early days of Intercomputer Networking, where everybody knew the CSNP wasn't cast in concrete. So when you realize that Hosts are going to have to "say things" to other Hosts if you're going to be able to do Resource Sharing, you realize that the first concern about your evolving Host-Host protocol is to get it *insulated* from possible changes in the Host-CSNP protocol, if only to avoid your having to change things in response to those changes and hence ramify the change up to your own users. (Well, OK, maybe it's not obvious why you know you're going to have users yourself if you're a Host-Host protocol; but it's also not worth the trouble of trying to "derive" it.)

The desire to insulate from possible changes "below" also applies to the Host-Host stratum from the perspective of the stratum "above" it. After all, even though we haven't discussed the properties of the Host-Host stratum yet we can be confident that whatever they are some clever body is going to want to change them sometime. What we've got, then, is the crux of "Layering," arrived at from a rather *a priori* sort of argument: You could tell in advance that whatever protocols you came up with, you'd want them to comprise at least three strata (let's call the top one "Applications" for now), and that the strata should be viewed as in some sense independent of each other in order not to have changes at the bottom of the heap dictate changes higher up.

I'm not convinced that's very satisfying, and I know it's not very rigorous, but it's the best I'm up to right now. Chapters 4 and 5 attempt to make the same point in different ways. It *is* important, in my view. For present purposes, though, I don't want to go any more deeply into the hierarchy/layering/levels/ strata topic for the simple reason that I want to get on to the descriptions of some particular protocols as soon as I can, in the hope that so doing actually will serve something like a conventional tutorial purpose. I wouldn't have even tried the foregoing at all if it weren't for the fact that I wanted to offer some sort of motivation for what was more or less a given when the protocols I'm about to tell you about were being designed.

The Approach

One more little Tiantesque preliminary, since you might like to know what I'm about to try to do. The object of the game is to give a feeling for what Intercomputer Networking protocols look like. Not, mind you, with any thought or implication of being definitive; rather, just to introduce those of you who've never dealt with protocols at first hand to a few, admittedly at second hand. But I can't force you to go out and read specs and listings, so I'll do the best I can.

At this stage, recalling that this is all supposed to be a History, the best I can think of is to go over a few of the early ARPANET/ARM (ARPANET Reference Model, for those with bad memories) protocols—*not* by way of touting them, but because I find them easier to talk about at something like limited length—and offer some suggestions about the general properties one would expect from similar protocols. The approach will at least gratify those who complain that I never show them what the headers look like, and will perhaps help to convince non-hardware types that headers are the last thing you worry about when trying to grok a protocol anyway. (An act of kindness for nonspeakers of Martian: "grok" comes from Robert Heinlein's *Stranger in a Strange Land* and means something well beyond "comprehend the essence of.")

[If you've read something about "networking" in *Computermation* and / or *Dataworld* and are wondering where the Seven-ness is, be patient; we'll get there eventually, but I'd rather try to get you to "know the territory" a bit before the dogma starts.]

An Archetypal Network Interface Protocol

Let's start with the first protocol I know of for interfacing to a communications subnetwork processor. It's the ARPANET Host-IMP Protocol, where "IMP," as I hope you recall, stands for Interface Message Processor, which is the ARPANET packet switch—and if you're worried about "packet switching" versus "circuit switching" and / or "message switching," you'll find a very few words about that sort of thing in Chapter 4. (By the way, I don't know if it was a hack or not, but our bulletin board at Project MAC had for some time a purported copy of a telegram from Senator Ted Kennedy to BBN, congratulating them on the awarding of a contract to build "Interfaith Message Processors." The way things have worked out, maybe somebody Knew Something.)

The protocol was enunciated in a document called BBN Report 1822 and is often called the 1822 Protocol. Actually, it's not that old, but it *was* issued sometime prior to September of 1969, which is when, according to Jon Postel's recollection, the first IMP was installed. A point which is often overlooked is the fact that 1822 specified both the hardware *and* the software interface to the IMP. If you want to learn about the hardware, you'll have to look elsewhere, except for one point I'll have to make later about it. The software, on the other hand, was implied by the sorts of headers that Hosts and IMPs were told they had to expect from one another, plus some descriptive prose. This would probably be a good time to look at Figure 2-1, the 1822 header picture I've managed to dig out of my piling system. (It's actually not the '69 version, but that's no big deal; it's not the current version either—and that's on purpose.)

Now, I don't propose to bore everybody with comments on all the fields, but we should touch a few bases. In the first place, you'll notice the Destination field isn't very big. Actually, the original thought apparently was that there would never be more than 64 IMPs, each of which could deal with up to four Hosts. Oh, well, wasn't it Von Neumann who thought you'd never need more than 8K of memory to program everything? The other field of particular interest is called Message-ID in later versions of the picture. It started life as "Link" and was only eight bits long (four bits got added with the name change), as shown. I haven't bothered to dig up the words elsewhere in the document about the field, in part because as I recall they're fairly fuzzy anyway, and in part because I think it's a stitch that the spec doesn't even cross reference the words in the picture.

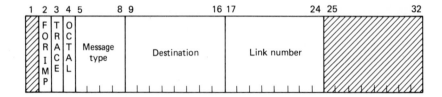

Bit 1   **Unassigned.**

Bit 2   **For IMP**

The For IMP bit, which is designated for debugging, changing IMP parameters, IMP Teletype output, and discarding packets, is discussed in Section 5. The Host should normally set this bit to zero. In particular, the Host should not set this bit on control messages to his own IMP.

Bit 3   **Trace**

If equal to one, the message is designated for tracing as it proceeds through the network so that reports on this message's transit through the network may be sent to a trace destination.

Bit 4   **Octal**

This bit applies only to messages directed to the IMP Teletype. If equal to one, the message will be printed on the Teletype as a sequence of octal numbers, each representing one 16-bit IMP word. If equal to zero, the message will be printed as a sequence of 8-bit ASCII characters.

Bits 5–8   **Message Type**

0.   *Regular Message:* All Host-to-Host communication occurs via regular messages.

1.   *Error Without Message Identification:* The Host program detected an error in a previous IMP-to-Host message and had to assume that the leader was garbled; i.e., the leader had a format error, or the Error flip-flop was set during transmission of the first packet in a message.

2.   *Host Going Down:* A responsible Host should send this message to its IMP before the Host voluntarily goes down. The Host should continue to accept messages from the IMP for a period of 5 or 10 seconds following transmission of this message. This delay will allow the fact of this Host's going down to reach all other IMPs in the network and will allow messages already in the network to reach this Host. Any subsequent message from the Host will signify that the Host is up again.

3.   *Unassigned.*

4.   *NOP:* The IMP will discard this message, which is intended for use during initialization of IMP/Host communication. A simple rule for the Host to follow is to send a few *NOP* messages whenever the Host or the IMP has been down either voluntarily or involuntarily.

5.   *Regular Message for Discard:* A message of this type is handled by the IMP as a regular message (type 0) but is discarded by the destination IMP rather than sent into the destination Host. An

Figure 2-1   Host-to-IMP Leader Format, from 1822 (slightly edited)

incomplete transmission message (type 9) is returned to the source Host.

6. *Unassigned.*

7. *Unassigned.*

8. *Error with Message Identification:* The Host detected an error in a previous IMP-to-Host message after the leader was correctly received; e.g., the message was too long, or the IMP Error flip-flop was set after transmission of the first packet of a multiple packet message but before the end of the message. A message of this type will have a leader whose assigned bits are identical to the assigned bits in the leader of the message in error except that the message type bits will be changed to have value 8.

9. *Unassigned.*

10. *Cease on Link:* This control message is used to stop the flow of messages on a given link. The IMP will specially mark the next RFNM it returns on the specified link for delivery (as IMP-to-Host message type 10) to the Host originating the traffic. That Host is expected to heed this signal and stop sending messages on the specified link. The link will not remain blocked after this notification.

11. *Retract Cease:* The cease on link request for the given link is to be deleted. This message is ignored if no cease is found. A Cease Timeout message will be returned if the deletion occurs.

12-15. *Unassigned.*

Bits 9-16 **Destination**

Identify a destination IMP and the particular Host at the IMP site. Bits 11-16 identify the destination IMP and bits 9-10 identify the particular Host.

Bits 17-24 **Link number.**

Bits 25-32 **Unassigned.**

The leader for all Host-to-IMP messages must be exactly 32 bits, even though some of these bits are presently unused. The IMP will detect any message containing fewer than 32 bits (exclusive of hardware padding) and will return a type 1 error message.

Figure 2-1 (*Continued*)

The gist of the Link notion was that Hosts would be able to use this field to de-multiplex connections. It did work, but we'll see some of its nastier implications shortly. For now, be aware that there wasn't much to the protocol, in some sense, and trust me that you don't really want to see the coresponding IMP-Host header. (Oh, yeah: Notice also that I've been using the more generic term "header" even though the picture says "leader.")

The one hardware point that needs to be made—aside from the observation that one of the real hassles of attaching Hosts to IMPs from the perspective of Host system programmers was getting the "Special Interface" (SPIF) boxes built right—is that the way either party let the other know that it didn't want any bits squirted at it right now was to hold the Ready Line of the SPIF "down." Not a very sophisticated form of Flow Control.

Indeed, not a very sophisticated protocol. But . . . it worked.

Please note well that I'm not defending it by saying it worked, just making a factual observation. The shortcoming of the Destination field had to be remedied in the mid-70s by going to a "Long Leader," and there's still some question in my mind why Uncontrolled messages (not discussed here) were viewed with alarm by BBN, but the major lesson I think we can learn from "1822" is that whatever assumptions comm subnet designers make and build into their interfaces (e.g., what the Host address space looks like, or what the Host demultiplexes on) *will* function as constraints on the "next level up" *somehow*, and the great trick of designing protocols above the Network Interface is to avoid being overconstrained by it. That does *not*, however, make me think that there ought to be only one Network Interface in the world, even if I were given final cut on the design . . . and certainly not if it came from a committee of telephonists. (See, I'm not utterly immodest after all.) What the universalists have got to realize is that Circumstances Alter Cases, and you just can't tell in advance what will be right for a given comm subnet in the future even if you have looked at a lot of current ones. (You also can't—or shouldn't, in my view—cop the plea that you can do what you want in the comm subnet "behind" the interface, unless the interface is awfully general.) Well, more on this when we get to The Windmill.

Properties of Network Interface Protocols

As the years went by, lots of people had a go at building comm subnets. (All too many of them thought they were building networks, but that's another problem.) Let's take a look at the sorts of things you'd expect to find.

A Host-CSNP protocol must, at the very least, allow the Host to express where a given transmission is to be sent, and allow the CSNP to regulate the flow of data into itself from the Host. Depending upon the design decisions taken in the given subnet, this level of protocol may also do more or less elaborate status reporting (on the result of a given transmission) and error checking/reporting; at the minimum, one would expect the local (or "proximate") CSNP to report that the destination CSNP is out of service—although some "Local Area Networks" don't do this sort of thing but instead rely on the presence of some higher level protocol to worry about whether a transmission "got there"—and that a hardware interface malfunction has rendered the Host's most recent trans-mission unintelligible (although that might be conveyed via a subordinate "line" or "link" protocol). More generous designs would attempt to "guarantee" correct receipt of transmissions by the destination CSNP—or even by the desti-nation Host—typically by means of establishing a discernible "connection" (the "virtual circuit" one hears so much about, to oversimplify it). Parsimonious designs would send transmissions on their way as separate items and leave any accountability for/or confirmation of proper receipt to a Host-Host protocol (the "datagram" approach, to oversimplify it). Just how big a transmission can be ("packet size") can vary widely, depending upon all sorts of hardware issues I don't pretend to understand.

In addition, some comm subnets will allow for "broadcast" and/or "multicast" transmissions, and some will offer very "strong" line or link protocols while others will offer relatively "weak" ones. The real point of it all for our purposes is that comm subnets get bits from point A to point B as their designers see fit, and things start getting interesting to intercomputer networkers only when we start looking at what the bits are "saying," no matter how unfair this view is to the serious and responsible engineers who are trying their hardest to build "good" (rapid, reliable, economical) comm subnets. (I don't truly hate engineers, you know—just the ones who lose sight of the fact that they're moving bits for a reason and try to tell me that Reed-Solomon Codes are more important than Host-Host protocols.)

An Archetypal Host-Host Protocol

How's that for a neat segue? Let's do look at a Host-Host protocol (Figure 2–2), without even pretending to do the sort of motivational and philosophical stuff you can find in Chapters 4 and 5 if you're interested.

Following the Approach, we'll look at the original ARPANET Host-Host Protocol, which is often *mis*called "NCP," probably because an early paper said that's what we called the combination of the program that interpreted ("followed"/"obeyed") the Host-Host Protocol *and* the program that interpreted the Host-IMP Protocol *and* the program which served as "device driver" for the SPIF on a given Host. In other words, NCP is Network Control *Program*, not Protocol; we didn't give the Host-Host Protocol a jazzy acronym in the old days, but just to satisfy my lurking purist tendencies, I'll call it the AH-HP here.

The key notion of AH-HP is that there is a Control Link. That is, the good old "1822" header field called Link Number in the last picture was taken cognizance of and a value of it (0 or 1, as I recall, and probably 0 then 1, for some historical reason . . . but it really doesn't matter) was reserved to carry "the protocol," which turned out to be a set of commands that AH-HP protocol interpreters (or "PIs") could exchange. (The commands turn out mainly to deal with what's going over other links.) Before you go off and pore over the picture—which *isn't* the header, because that was simply the Link field and some padding on non-Control Link transmissions and isn't very interesting (other than to very scrupulous Scholars, who can find it for themselves), except for the fact that using the Link field is singularly ill-layered because it's a Network Interface artifact, not a Host-Host Protocol one—you might like to know that somebody decided "connections" should be "simplex." That is, the "sockets" (SKTs) mentioned in the picture were defined as the addressing/demultiplexing entity of the protocol (and chosen to be quite a large field because there was once a notion of encoding process IDs in socket numbers) and a pair of socket numbers (nominally one on each Host, but you could connect to yourself if you wanted to) determined *a* connection, but you needed two of *them* to have a two-way conversation. (If I remembered the rationale, I probably wouldn't waste the ink on

ARPANET Host-Host Protocol

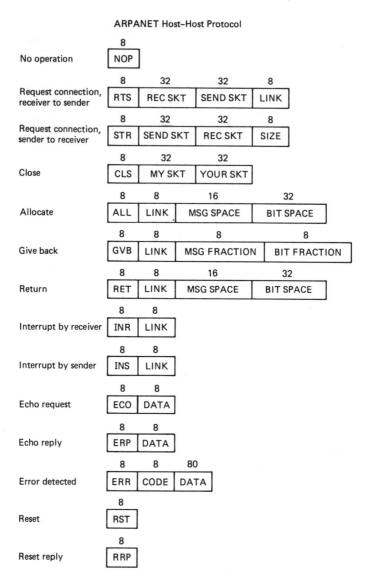

Figure 2-2   Host-to-Host Protocol

it anyway, but I trust you're beginning to get the idea as to why I started this chapter off deploring tutorials; I mean, I really ought to spell all that out, I guess. . . .) It's also interesting that sockets were equated to links by the RTS command, so even though you had 32 bits to name them you couldn't use more than eight bits' worth of them at any given time (less one or two for the reserved Control Link values).

OK, let's assume you've now gone off and stared at the AH-HP commands picture, and that their names are fairly suggestive of what they were for—and even that if you're a serious student of this sort of thing you'll go off and look up the Initial Connection Protocol (ICP) once I tell you there was such a discipline for properly exchanging RTSs and STRs in order to get a "duplex" connection going. The interesting things about the protocol for present purposes are the following: Flow Control (between the sending and receiving Hosts, on a "per socket" basis) was achieved by a rule which held that a sender had to wait for an ALLocate command from the receiver, specifying how much could be transmitted before the next ALL had to be waited for. The Interrupt Commands (INS/INR) achieved the "Out-of-Band Signal" I make so much fuss about elsewhere. The Reset was a nice gimmick when there weren't many Hosts: Whenever an NCP (re)initialized, it sent AH-HP RSTs to all the Hosts it expected to communicate with, so they could know that if they needed to purge their connection tables it was time to do so. And, given ICP, there was a charming notion called "Well-Known Sockets" available, whereby certain values of the socket field were reserved to be the places you could ICP to in order to get a connection to a given service (i.e., to a given Applications protocol).

Again, it worked—by around the end of 1970 as I recall. (Matter of fact, I still remember the fuss some of us made over the ALL mechanism, and as I only got involved toward the end of that year, it must be that the protocol hadn't been finalized 'til then—especially because our Project MAC-wide delegate to the finalizing meeting is still an enemy of mine after the yelling I did at him for giving in on ALL, even though he's been at BBN so long almost nobody else remembers he was once one of the Tech Square contingent.) Chapter 4 even has a few War Stories, about ICP, ALL, INS, and ECO, which might help you understand how even so apparently straightforward a protocol can be difficult to implement properly.

Properties of Host-Host Protocols

I'm starting to feel somewhat guilty about how little justice I've done to "1822" and AH-HP, but I'm determined not to spend a major fraction of the rest of my out-of-the-office life trying to make it possible for serious students to avoid reading specs and listings for themselves, so let's forge ahead. (Cheer up, ARPANET fans, I'll do even less justice to all the hardware manufacturers' idiosyncratic networking efforts soon.)

The previously unstated (or at best glanced over) premise of Host-Host protocols in general is that there are some things you want done in common for *all* processes which are going to want to communicate with each other over an intercomputer network, on a Host-wide basis. (Well, for small values of all, actually.) However, Circumstances Alter Cases, and just what a *given* process-oriented communication path "wants" can vary; so just what you want by way of a Host-Host protocol can vary too. Usually, though, you're concerned with the general case—or your best guess at it, anyway—when you come up with "the" Host-Host protocol for your suite of protocols, so the emphasis here will be on that; but do keep the need to deal with cases other than the general one in mind when you're reading Chapters 5 and 7.

A protocol at this level is, fundamentally, responsible for the maintenance (opening, controlling flow, transmitting over, and closing) of connections between processes communicating via an intercomputer network. Of course, to do that a Host-Host Protocol "protocol interpreter" (PI) must interface on the one hand with a Host-CSNP PI, and on the other hand with user processes or Applications PIs. A somewhat subtle aspect of the maintenance of connections, but one which is customarily expected of an H-HP, is a primitive function— usually called an "out-of-band signal"—which in effect allows the desire to interrupt the process at the other end of the connection to be expressed. Because the opening of a connection involves addressing of the destination Host, another function which can be considered a part of the H-HP is that of dealing with "internetworking" issues, especially in those environments where it is necessary to cause transmissions to Hosts/processes attached to communications subnet-works other than "one's own." Since any number of things are happening in common for communicating processes at this level, many H-HPs will also deal with "reliability" by containing explicit mechanisms such as checksums and/or by taking cognizance of whatever reliability properties the proximate comm subnet (or the internet, if such be the case) offers. Finally, mechanisms for finding particular services/Applications level protocols may "come with" an H-HP, as with the ARPANET Well-Known Socket discipline; it should be noted that in the absence of such a mechanism, a protocol suite must make some other provision for identifying services at a higher level of protocol, and that the presence of such a mechanism does not preclude an additional means (beyond the Well-Known Sockets, that is) for such identification of services.

An Archetypal Virtual Terminal Protocol

If you recall the Creation Myth, you'll realize why the first thing we did "on top of" AH-HP was Telnet (for Telecommunications [or maybe Teletypewriter] Network). We did want to log in on each others' systems after all. While we were at it, we "invented" (or at least independently derived) the notion of Virtualiza-tion, which I probably say too much about elsewhere. Very briefly, the idea is that it's too much to ask each Host/operating system to take cognizance of all the different sorts of terminals that exist out there in Network Land, so instead you come up with a common intermediate representation—or "Virtual Terminal"— that each Host adds to its terminals repertoire. Another way of putting it is that each participating Host maps into and out of the Network Virtual Terminal representation (out of and into some representation "natural" to its preconcep-tions about terminals). Naturally, the streams of bits must be hooked up to native processes; in particular, to the generic "command language interpreter" of a native process. The effect is to let someone "out there" get logged in. (Chapters 3–5 say more about this topic.)

What we did, then, was to declare that socket 1 on a Host was the Well-Known Socket for Telnet. That is, if you ICP to it you get associated with a Logger of some sort which will do what's necessary to get you to a process that's ready to go through the Host's login ritual (if it has one). On the socket pairs (remember AH-HP was "simplex"), Telnet decreed you'd find "ASCII" (American Standard Code for Information Interchange, in case you never knew), and/or "Telnet Control Codes." We used seven-bit ASCII in eight-bit fields, you see, and defined some special meanings for "characters" which had the high-order bit on. The NVT itself "was" an ASCII table with some of the format effector characters left out (because we thought they'd be too hard to deal with). The control codes allowed for such things as hiding input (not echoing at the physical terminal end *or* printing out a "mask" if it was a hardcopy terminal), going into a "raw" mode (if you were physically at a terminal the Host did "know about"), doing the non-AH-HP part of the much-fussed-about out-of-band signalling, and a few other things I don't care to bother remembering for present purposes.

Note that we blithely intermixed control information and data. Note also that it all worked (all = Telnet ⟶ AH-HP ⟶ 1822) for most of the original Hosts by July 1, 1971 (see the true story at the end of Chapter 1).

One somewhat subtle distinction: We spoke of "User Telnet" and "Server Telnet." What we meant was that some aspects of the protocol mattered more to the side of the connection where the terminal was physically attached, while other aspects mattered more to the side where the process doing the work on the user's behalf was. The interface to User Telnet, then, has to be a "human interface." That is, depending on which system's User Telnet you're exposed to, you might have to learn different ways of saying which Host you want to get at, whether you want echoing done by it or by the system managing your terminal, and the like. I only mention it because over the years I've noticed that a number of people whose exposure has been either through "the literature" or via hearsay have failed to grasp the distinction—some even think that the "command language" of the TIP (for Terminal IMP; it's the ARPANET archetype of the generic terminal support machine, or "mini-Host," actually) *is* Telnet. Not so. Indeed, as I make a great fuss about in the new Host-Front End Protocol I'm working on during normal working hours as this is being written at home, *the interface to an interpreter of a protocol is NOT the protocol* in general . . . but that might be a bit far afield for now.

Properties of Virtual Terminal Protocols

Speaking of going too far afield, I think we'll have to give rather short shrift to the topic of VTPs in general, as things get quite complicated quite rapidly when your conceptual model extends beyond the simple scrolling terminal of

Telnet to such things as "data entry terminals," graphics capabilities, and the like. However, based upon my experience with the "New" Telnet (which I *think* was '73, but might have been as early as '72), I'd expect any contemporary VTP to allow the user to control who echoed, to do an out-of-band signal, to express a desire to do specialized functions his terminal or the Host in question can handle even though not all members of each class can ("negotiated options" is the New Telnet name for this sort of thing), and I'd hope it allowed for a generic way of causing the Server side to erase characters and kill lines.

Rather than go any further into that, let's clear up the mysterious reference earlier to IACs. Actually, it does have something to do with VTP properties, because as you might imagine one thing you have to worry about is the differentiation of control and data. Now, as we'll see in not all that many pages, in the ISORM you'd find that sort of thing in a given protocol's header (at least, you would as I read the ISORM—and I hope I'm right, because it's not all that bad an idea). But in the ARPANET style—against my better judgment, I might add—we settled early on letting each top-level protocol set up its own customs for how "the protocol" was expressed; as you already know, in Old Telnet, we just swiped some of the character space. So what IAC is is a single reserved eight-bit value which "says" Interpret As Command (the following character[s]). If memory serves, after losing the battle to go to separate connections for control and data in New Telnet (as we'd done in our first file transfer protocol, FTP), I said something like, "Well, hell, if that's the way you're going to be [everybody else was concerned about "losing synchronicity," which I wasn't convinced we actually had], why don't we stop this foolishness about using up control code values and just go to one value that could mean. . . ." You get the picture, I trust. If not, don't worry about it. (I'm prouder of the generic erase and kill—and interrupt process and abort output—notions, myself.)

A Mini-Essay on Waffles

One reason why I chose to go with the oldest versions of the ARPANET protocols, shortcomings, inelegancies, glitches, and all, is that I wanted to lead up to the following: There's a perhaps-apocryphal Law of Programming attributed to Sutherland (though nobody ever told me for sure whether it was Bert or Ivan) which goes "Programs are like waffles, you should always throw the first one out." Well, that goes double for protocols. That is, we went through two or more passes over every protocol in the ARM suite as we were learning our craft, and there's no reason to suppose we were much dumber than anybody else who might have gotten into the field subsequently, so unless they went to the trouble of learning from our mistakes they ought to expect to have to do a couple of passes themselves. Unfortunately, however, even from the cursory treatment I accord to Other Efforts in what follows, it becomes apparent that not too many of the "new kids on the block" did much learning from what went before—and, I suspect but can't prove, it's possible that employer pressure "to get something out soon" would probably have prevented them from doing as much learning as they'd have liked even if such had been their intention.

What that is, is a round-about way of saying that even if it isn't apparent, we're about to be zipping over the ground that led me to the realization that the It's *My* Ball Syndrome isn't just another one of my little jokes, however much I'd rather it were.

And a Micro-Essay on "Layering"

In case you're wondering how all this stuff fits together, I've done a couple of things which might be helpful: (1) There's a picture called "ARPANET Process Level Protocol Schematic" in Chapter 4; and (2) there's a picture here called "Packet on a String" (Figure 2–3) which gives an idea how layers add headers to transmissions (which their counterpart PIs will interpret and remove at the other side.) What they're meant to suggest is that protocol layers "package" related functions for their users without forcing those users to take cognizance of just how things are mechanized "internally." That's probably still too terse (maybe even cryptic), but you know my views on tutorials by now.

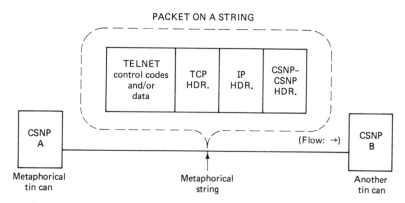

PACKET ON A STRING

NOTE 1: I've snuck IP and TCP in instead of AH-HP in order to supplement Chapter 5

NOTE 2: For our purposes, if there's a link protocol in play between the CSNP's we'll asume its header is part of the CSNP header (or invisible, "to the right") and its trailer, if any, is invisible "to the left"

NOTE 3: If you're wondering where the HOST-CSNP header is, it's way off to the right — on the string between CSNP B and its host ("in place of" the CSNP-CSNP header, and, more accurately, in its guise as CSNP-HOST header)

NOTE 4: The leftmost box in the packet could contain another header or three, depending on what sort of "upper-level" protocols are in play (but if so, there'd better be fields in each "lower" one to lead you to the right "upper" one — just as there's a protocol field in IP to lead you to TCP, and port fields in TCP to lead you to TELNET in the first place and to the right process doing TELNET in the second place)

Figure 2–3 "Packet on a String"

A CURSORY GLANCE AT THE PRESENT

I don't know about you, but I'm getting tired of all this . . . and the "word processor" I borrowed from a friend in order to avoid having to resort to my old electric portable while also avoiding misuse of Government property (because this is a personal undertaking so I can't do it "on the ARPANET") has to get back sometime soon (and neither of the ones I'd be willing to spring for has hit the shelves yet), and I've still got to say *something* about the bloody manufacturers, and then there's The Windmill, and I really do want to do the Future History, and. . . . Well, let's just go into skim mode and see if we can't end the agony soon. Apologies to all whose stuff is about to be slighted, but, after all, you can scarcely avoid running into plenty of propaganda from the manufacturers and the standardsmongers, and if you really want more details about the ARPANET Experience you can clamor at the Publisher for a sequel (and/or the conference papers anthology).

Other NWG (and IWG) Efforts

We don't have to plunge into the other guys' stuff right away, even if we are in a hurry, if for no other reason than that I've got to introduce the Catenet Context picture. (See Figure 2–4). Actually, the most important post-proof-of-concept development to come out of Our Camp is almost certainly "TCP," but there's plenty about it in Chapter 5, so all I'll say for now is that the Catenet Context picture really should have gone into the Conference version of the ARM paper, but I really was already two pages over their length limit. Study the

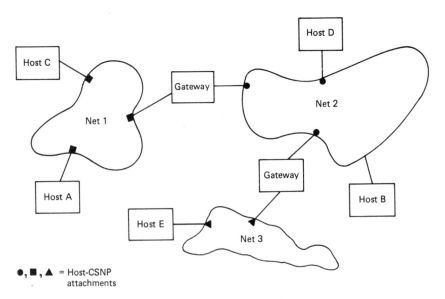

Figure 2-4   Catenet Context picture

picture well; it implies some subtle things we'll be getting back to when we get to The Windmill. (By the way, the "IWG" in the subtitle refers to the Internet Working Group, the NWG's evolutionary successor—and the whole point of the picture is that *all* the Hosts can "interoperate" with each other.)

There's a lot of interesting stuff still going on under ARPA sponsorship, even if it doesn't often hit *Dataworld* and *Computermation* (much less the *Extremely Learned Journal of the Assemblage of Computerscientists Manqué*). There's Packet Radio, and Multi-media, and Wideband (satellite stuff), and there were Graphics, and the Procedure Call Protocol, and for that matter FTP and H-FP (see Chapter 6 for that particular favorite of mine) . . . and there was even an attempt at a Unified User Level Protocol (a.k.a. Common Command Language) I was awfully fond of. (The interesting thing about UULP is that I put in a timorous suggestion, in an appendix, about the possible desirability of having a common editor command, and that's the one part of it which did catch on. Yes, Open System Editor fans, there has been a NETED around for ten years or so.) But this isn't intended to be counter-advertising, just a quick look at what's going on, so I'll leave it at encouraging anybody out there who happens to own a ball but has an immunity to the Syndrome to poke around the ARPA world for some potentially amusing games the rules of which have already been worked out, and get on to the bad stuff.

Whizzing Through Vendorland

Even if you don't ever read "the trades," and hence have been spared all the ads for ThingNet, MyNet, Ournetworkarchitecture, Distributed Whatsis, and the like, you won't be uninfected by all the different vendor-idiosyncratic "networking" stuff that's going on these days unless you also don't ever watch commercial television. Good Lord (or Good Lady [Ada, of course]), even the local phone company's pushing optical fiber gadgets these days! And if you're supposed to be a Protocols Guru, you're expected to know something about all these damn things. Well, I try to know *something*, all right; but I try even harder not to know too much. The reason is that every time I take a look at another vendor's "network" I find idiosyncracy after idiosyncracy, based either on their preconceptions about what it takes to get their own, preexisting operating systems to talk to each other with some degree of comfort, or on their local ball-owners' misunderstandings of what We were up to (or, of course, ignoring of what We were up to). It's so *boring*. [I once spent several hours in a pub in Oxford trying to learn to say that with the proper Oxonian Whine. I didn't quite master it, unfortunately.]

Therefore, I'm going to ignore some probably quite legitimate work at places like Prime and Burroughs and Wang and Data General and Honeywell (the latter despite—not because of, honest—the fact that a guy from there told me the other month that *they* invented Seven-ness), and just say a very few things about the ones most people seem to have heard of. It's more of an "appreciation" than anything else; not, of course, that I'll be saying particularly Good Things about 'em, but rather that it isn't an explication.

But first . . . a crucial distinction. I'm *NOT* saying one damn thing about "networking technologies." I didn't mention BBN or Network Systems or Ungermann Bass or Sytek or New England Tel and Tel (even though Pegasus is a cute name) or whoever else there is out there (and I'm not even pausing to think about whom I've omitted) who just furnishes generic comm subnet processors (or even who mainly furnishes CSNPs, as at least one of the above claims to have come up with higher-level protocols too). The only ones I'm going to do an injustice to by simply not telling you much about them are the ones who are monging Intercomputer Networking approximations, in *my* sense of the term.

First, because I do want to give them pride of place, there's Xerox. *Not* "Ethernet," mind you; "XNS" (which I assume is Xerox Network System, but I won't swear to it—nor will I look it up). The point is that Xerox got involved with a fairly interesting comm subnet technology, having to do with rapidly pumping bits over cable within relatively short distances (even though they did make their Hosts perform what I think of as the CSNP-CSNP protocol, which I dislike because it seems to me that it's wasteful of the resources you're intending to share, but I *can* see some reasons for it in their context), and one thing led to another and they eventually came up with a suite of protocols for doing Intercomputer Networking. But just as the IMPs aren't what I mean when I talk about the ARPANET, Ethernet isn't what I (or they) mean when I talk about XNS. Not that I have much to say about XNS actually, but my understanding is that it's rather close in spirit to the ARM Suite (not surprising, seeing that their Palo Alto Research Center had acquired more than its share of Old Network Boys since the early 1970s). There are even Xerox Hosts attached to the ARPA Internet. Unfortunately, they're attached through our protocol suite, and they do their own suite to their own (other) machines. Also, somewhat unfortunately, because their implicit comm subnet "came with" a broadcast mode of trans- mission, they took advantage of that property to some extent at higher levels, with things like "Name Servers" (i.e., responders to requests for services which were "sent out into the aether"). That's tagged as somewhat unfortunate because it can make it somewhat awkward to "internet" with other flavors of comm subnet (which don't broadcast, that is); but it does work reasonably well in their own island universe, I'm told. At any rate, by all reports, if you want to look at a fairly clean vendor-invented suite, see if they'll let you look at theirs. (They might not, though; I hear the dreaded word "proprietary" has cropped up in their lex- icon when it comes to anything above the Ethernet interface.) At least I haven't run into anybody there who preaches "interoperability" via magical Translating Gateways, though (see Chapter 10); so if I've got to say something about The Vendors, I'll say something about them first.

Of course, the vendor you've probably heard the most about isn't Xerox . . . but I'm saving that one for last. The next one to mention is DEC, if only because I heard about "DECNET" before I heard about "SNA." Indeed, the early words about DECNET were quite promising. They seemed to have done their homework moderately well and were quoting most of the really relevant precepts and principles from our stuff by around '75 or '76. But then I learned they were having "no trouble" with FTP but "a lot of trouble" with Telnet (using both terms as generics, of course; I have no idea what they call their File Transfer and Virtual Terminal protocols). What I *think* went on (based on a couple of very private conversations with friends there) is that each operating system was (maybe/probably still is) a separate fiefdom, and the liege lords didn't want to go to the trouble of making the splices into their systems in order to get the virtual terminal stuff attached to the local processing path (from device driver to command language interpreter to process). They might well have it all working now, but again what's working is Intercomputer Networking between Hosts which interpret *their* protocols. Less informally, what I'm saying is that the vendor-developed protocol suites tend to be prepared only for a greater level of homogeneity among participating Hosts than do the sorts of suites we're interested in here, which are, of course, those designed with heterogeneity in mind.

An important aside, before getting to The Vendor: For some strange reason (perhaps their apparent tangibility), it's the low-level protocols which get most of the attention. When DECNET was announced, people kept asking me whether a particular line or link protocol of theirs called "DDCMP" (if I've even re-membered it correctly) was "better than [some other protocol called] 'HDLC'." For that matter, the Big Question about Ethernet was "Isn't 'contention' wasteful?" So before we get to the part of the forest where "SDLC" reigns supreme, let me observe, as mildly as I can, that I'm not even going to expand any of those acronyms for you, because I'm not all that interested in the labels on the tin cans at the ends of the strings. Provided, of course, that they don't wind up constraining me in some fashion "at the next level up". . . . That is, most Vendors seem to find it natural to incorporate the CSNP-CSNP routing and transmission functionality directly into their Hosts (or sometimes into their tightly coupled "communications front-ends") rather than deal with a separate comm subnet processor. A friend of mine at DEC assures me that this isn't motivated by a desire to sell more powerful CPUs but rather is a consequence of the fact that the Public Data Networks are sufficiently expensive that you don't need all that large a volume of traffic before it becomes cheaper to lease your own lines, so I guess I won't insist on the more paranoid interpretation of why they don't choose to make lighter demands on their Hosts; at least I'll grant they probably didn't try to waste cycles consciously. (I do seem to recall a paper by the Ethernet troops that expressed some concern about how much of their workstation-sized Alto machines was getting chewed up to do the "networking," though.) What I do worry about, however, is that this view of "owning" the comm subnet could have unfortunate consequences when it comes to the design of the protocols that *use* the comm subnet. An example mentioned earlier is the assumption that all transmissions can be broadcast, but I don't want to make too big an issue of particulars here. The real point of concern is the general one of whether assuming you're attached to a comm subnet of specific, known properties (in other words, one that's "end to end") doesn't wind up making it hard to connect such nets to an "internet" (i.e., to a concatenation of heterogeneous, autonomous nets). I think it probably does, but even if I thought I could "prove" it I wouldn't do so in a nominal tutorial. (It would doubtless be too paranoid to wonder further if the Vendors don't *prefer* to make it hard to internet with other Vendors' gear in hopes of selling still more of their own gear . . . wouldn't it?) I didn't want to omit the point, however. One of the problems with venerating Reference Models of any stripe is that they all tend to be overly abstract—a trap I often fall into myself when I say that there "is" a CSNP, rather than that some place has to exist where CSNP-like functions are performed—and that *is* a point I wish both beginners and alleged old hands would take into account. The test of the RM recipe is in the eating of the protocol suite pudding, after all, and not in how pretty a picture you find of it in the cookbook.

Well, why put it off any longer . . . and then there's "SNA." IBM is a large company. It exerts considerable influence. Fortunately, they aren't the whole story, so I don't see why I should have any trepidation about being snotty in their direction. After all, I could probably find somewhere to teach a course in Science Fiction if I were willing to handle enough sections of Freshman Comp for them, so I shouldn't have to worry about starving even if I'm not immodest enough to expect to survive on my royalties. Seriously, though, it is the case that large numbers of people who have some sort of connection with the computer biz feel they should be somehow awed by "Big Blue," and they just might think I'm about to commit lese majesty. So be it.

When it first was announced, "System Network Architecture" struck me (and others) as merely an attempt to recoup from the old IBM tradition of having applications programs be aware of the particular terminal they were being used from by introducing some type of "generic I/O." The "networking" was nugatory; all they did was Communications to a single Host. As the years went by (and my attention was elsewhere), they seem to have at least gotten into Intercomputer Networking—but they still have lots of applications running around "knowing" their terminals, and they do seem to think that *their* Network Interface equivalent *is* "end to end" . . . and they're no less homogeneous in their assumptions than any other vendor, even if statistically they're got better grounds for it. To me, the only interesting point to be made about it all is that the mistake of binding knowledge of the properties of the actual terminal into the application programs is probably the locus classicus for worrying about binding knowledge of the actual properties of the comm subnet into your Host-Host protocol equivalent (much less into your Applications protocols). Having just fussed about a very similar point in the context of Vendors generally assuming it's *their* CSNP, I won't bore you with another digression on this one, but do think about how much trouble you have to go through when you eventually find you need to use some *other* artifact (terminal or subnet) if awareness of the peculiarities of the "old" gadget is embedded in large numbers of programs. It may well be too cryptic, but let's leave it at "Layering *is* a Good Thing," and move on.

(I hope you at least now dig the in-joke earlier about leaving the Buddha out.)

The Low Standards

If I've been short with the vendors, I'm going to be downright curt with the Public Data Networks. Almost all I have to say about the present state of the world of the PDN's is to be found in Chapter 9. (Ooops. I should also mention that I do have more to say about the vendors, in Chapter 8, actually.) Again, a lot of people think "all there is" is the comm subnet, so they think there's something special about "X.25" because it's supposed to be a standard for interfacing to comm subnets. Again, they're wrong. There is one point I want to make about comm subnets, though. There's been a lot of fussing going on about "datagrams" versus "virtual circuits." Indeed, both Chapter 9 and its Prefatory Afterthoughts do their share of fussing. The one thing I think gets obscured in all of it is that it's a false dichotomy, if you define terms aright. That is, if you look at things functionally, datagram mode is the one where you don't worry about whether the packet (of bits) "got there," and virtual circuit mode is the one where you do worry. That's OK, except for the fact that some people think you've always got to worry. *But* . . . if you look at things mechanistically, worrying about whether things got there *doesn't* mean that the things *can't* contain destination addresses within themselves. So the popular mechanization of a virtual circuit as a shorthand notation (a VC number, with no address explicitly conveyed in the messages after the set-up phase) isn't *necessary*, and probably merely reflects a shortsighted desire to "save bits." (It also leads to a line of reasoning that results in the conclusion that X.25 nets don't do packet switching, which I might not even have the strength to go over in the P.A.s to Chapter 9.)

Whoops! That's not very tutorial, is it? Semi-sincere apologies. I had to say it somewhere, though, and even if it's utterly obscure, here's as good a place as any, because I really don't want even to pretend to be "surveying" the PDNs. I imagine you can find what most of you need in *Computermation* or *Dataworld* if you're interested in this sort of thing. Let the record show that one of the many factors in today's "networking" games is the fact that there does exist some sort of protocol for using a Public Data Network in a "standard" fashion, and let it go at that.

The High-Rises (a.k.a. The Windmill)

Here we are, at last. In case anybody hasn't figured it out long ere now, The Windmill I've been planning to tilt at is the Open System Interconnection Reference Model of the International Standards Organization, which I call the ISORM. In the mid- to late-'70s, all the stuff I've just shamelessly skimmed over was in full flight, and somebody noticed that it would probably be a good idea to try to have some Standards for Intercomputer Networking. (In reality, lots of bodies noticed, but we'll focus on just one of them.) I can't speak with much authority about ISO, as I wasn't there. But they managed to capture a good deal of attention, and as I've discussed elsewhere in the book are now in the position of appearing to be "all there is" to newcomers to the field. You should already know what I think of that. However, I'm going to attempt to be as un-"judgmental" as I can here, so that newercomers can gather some facts by which to judge the opinions they'll find in abundance elsewhere. (I know in advance I won't keep that implicit promise to the letter, but I'm going to give the spirit of it my best shot.)

A digression on scholarship. The ISORM was proposed, propounded, and/or promulgated in either 1978 or 1979. I have two apparently reputable journal articles in my piling system which give each of those years. Since then, a number of real and imagined experts have jumped on, toward, at, and/or all over the bandwagon. I'm about to be quite unfair to the ISORM, myself, because I find it impossible to sort out what's "official" from what "everybody knows" about it; there's just been too much noise during the last few years for me even to pretend that what I'm doing is Scholarship, even if I weren't associated with a different camp. I'd feel better, however, if you understood that point better, so I'll try saying it differently: All I'm up to in this subsection is a quick and dirty sketch of a fairly complicated and subtle area. There are doubtless several errors of omission and of commission in what I have to say about the ISORM (I'm aware of a few myself); I *know* I'm doing it an unjustice, but (1) if you're a serious student of this sort of thing, you'll already be up on it, so *you* shouldn't care what errors I've made (providing they weren't malicious, which I assure you they're not); (2) if you're the technological equivalent of a religious zealot on one side or the other (and statistically the odds are about 9 to 1 it's the other), nothing I say is going to change your position anyway, so *I* shouldn't care what errors I've made; and (3) if you really are just "getting up to speed" on/in Intercomputer Networking, it's not going to give you anywhere near as much as you need anyway, so *nobody* should care what errors I've made. (Besides, so many ISORMites—and even a few ISORMists—manage to convey the impression that the IN field didn't exist before they started "working it" that I don't really feel, down deep, much of a compulsion to be all that much more scrupulous than my *bêtes noires* have been. I mean, I wouldn't have even bothered with this whole chapter if I hadn't been talked into it.)

[I'd manage to come a lot closer to feeling guilty about the rather cavalier refusal to "do my homework"—a trait I deplore in others, in most contexts (i.e., whenever it's *not* based on a refusal to eat entire rotten eggs)—were it not for the fact that the target moves around so much. That is, on several occasions, I've been bellowing cheerfully about some ISORM flaw or another only to be told, usually with a patronizing grin, "Oh, we've changed that; you don't seem to have read the *latest* version." It's gotten so bad that my friend Arouet is threatening to write one of his little letters to the International Court of Justice at The Hague, demanding a Consent Decree banning pre-announcements of protocols, and even "reference models," just as soon as he can find out what the legalistic grounds were for getting IBM to stop pre-announcing products/gadgets. So you see that even had I been more inclined by nature to be extremely scrupulous I probably wouldn't have succeeded . . . not that I've tried to be *un*scrupulous, mind you.]

[An historical analogy comes to mind: The situation is somewhat akin to the period when the U.S. Constitution was being debated. That is, what was binding was the document itself, not the Federalist Papers' glosses on it; however, in that time, I seem to recall reading that the F.P.'s were taken into account in subsequent Supreme Court decisions, so I think it's legitimate to fear that "what everybody knows" about the ISORM will indeed influence designs of particular protocols to/for it despite what the Draft Proposal, or whatever it comes to be called (perhaps, *shudder*, the Standard?), says or doesn't say to the contrary.]

Leaving aside the philosophy of "reference models," what I understand the ISORM to look like is depicted in the picture I've called "The Real One" (Figure 2–5). We'll get to what the words in it are supposed to mean shortly, but I want to

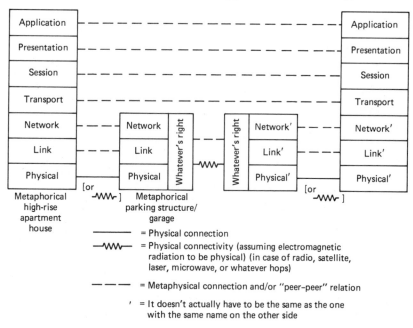

Figure 2-5   "The Real One"

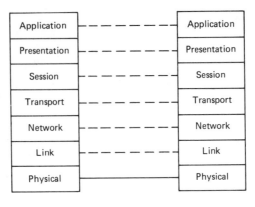

——— , — — — per The Real One picture

NOTE: Some call Application "Applications", and some call Link "Data Link"

Figure 2-6 "The Wrong One"

get the other picture, which I've called "The Wrong One" (Figure 2-6), out of the way first. The difference is the presence or absence of the little boxes that look rather like parking structures between the big boxes that look rather like high-rise apartment houses. [This is a good place to observe that I've gotten the inspiration for the pictures—and, indeed, for the whole discussion—from a number of sources: talks at conferences, articles in trade and learned journals, conversations with ISO advocates, and at worst a year-old (or maybe a two-year-old) version of a document that *says* it's an ISO document right on its cover. In other words, don't bug me about how I've misquoted the very latest "official" ISORM; I'm not claiming to be quoting it at all, I'm claiming to be representing the popular view of what it is, which is also why I'm not going to bother talking about Levels 3A–3C, which I heard about from an ISORMist semi-friend in a supermarket the other month.]

Why do I say there have to be parking structures? Simple. Because if you don't have CSNPs in your conceptual model and if you do think protocols between "peers" have to be "end to end" (a commonly held view of the ISORM; in fact, one I've run into among half a dozen or so serious and responsible networking neophytes within the last year or less), then you're going to have to deal with the problem that you're assuming a contrary-to-fact view of the world in your very conceptual model. That is, whatever they mean, if the "Physical" and "Network" layers *are* taken to be end to end, you must be positing either a single communications subnetwork or a "universal" one, neither of which accurately describes the state of the comm subnets world. Of course, you could say that you're not assuming it's *the same* Levels 3–1 everywhere, so it's not assuming one and only one comm subnet, but the problem is that you'd be in a very small minority if you made such a claim. Almost all of The Vendors who have come up with their own approaches to networking (almost all of whom pay some sort of lip service to the ISORM) seem to have fallen into the trap of *relying* on the presence of *their* "network" at both the local and the destination Host. The point is that if Layering means anything—and Layering *is* a professed axiom of the ISORM—it must mean that you can't posit "The Wrong Way" picture's implication of end-to-endness at the lowest three levels.

[You might well think it's rather presumptuous of me to sit here and tell Them what Their pictures should look like, especially if you're aware that they actually have both flavors of picture in their "DP." Well, I don't think there's anything particularly sacred about a document that represents the results of the deliberations of a number of committees—in a number of languages—and I don't think it makes sense to have both flavors of pictures *unless* you have an explicit "Internet Protocol" in your conceptual model. That is, if the claim were that the Network Interface Layer really was meant to be a virtualization of the interfaces to any and all comm subnets, then maybe you could leave the parking structures out of your pictures, but They don't seem to care for IP (or didn't until L3A-C got snuck in—sometime after the ISORMites were trumpeting The Answer), so . . . It does get awfully complex—and admittedly borders on the technotheological—but we might as well let it go at that for now, as long as we realize that the deep problem of casual reference to misleading pictures is one of the characteristic external stigmata of the ISORMite. (For more on my view of committee designs in general, do take a peek at the Cover Cartoon for Chapter 9; and if you've heard from any ISORMites that TCP is a camel itself, consider that it has an even number of humps and legs—and was *meant* to be good at crossing deserts.)]

Again, that might violate the letter and the spirit of Tutoriality, but it needed to be said somewhere. . . .

Onward. Before quoting the good words about the Seven Levels, let's take note of a few "rules" about the way the model works. In the first place, the levels all seem to come into play on each transmission. There may be "null layers" someday, but there weren't as of the day I wrote this. Also, each "protocol entity" is supposed to "talk" only to its "peer" (i.e., I think, another PI of the same protocol), although it talks to it "through" the entity immediately below itself, which in turn is talking to its peer, in turn through the one below it. . . . The way you talk to your peer is in terms of "data-units," which do contain your control information and may contain (your user's) data. (Note that your user may well be another protocol entity.)

In fairness, let's digress for a moment about "rules." The early words in the document I have which comes closest to being "official" (INWG note 283, ISO/DP 7498, ISO/TC 97/SC 16 N 719, and other numbers elsewhere on the cover page) *are very scrupulous* about insisting that the Reference Model isn't meant to dictate implementations. (*The page also contains*, by the way, the legend "THIS DOCUMENT IS STILL UNDER STUDY AND SUBJECT TO CHANGE. SHOULD NOT BE USED FOR REFERENCE PURPOSES." So let the record show that I wouldn't think of using it for reference purposes; all I'm doing here is giving the best snapshot conveniently available of their thinking at that point in time: that is, **I wouldn't dream of holding them to it** . . . if it were up to me, of course [and I'd much rather quote the public domain DP than either of the articles I have that say the same things—without, as I recall, bothering to cite said legend—which would require still another bloody Permission].) It's just that later in the document, I think, and in the minds of its readers and explicators, I'm certain, principles get treated and/or restated as rules, and people start having to abide by them or play some other game. The underlying problem is similar to that of learning how to play bridge well: Good bridge players know that the *rules* of the game have to do with the necessity to follow suit, what to do after a bid out of turn, and the like; the rest, whether it be when to take a finesse, or should you pass an opening two-bid, or even how many "points" it usually takes to make game (high-card points, that is; it takes 100 or more real points to make game . . . on the scoresheet) aren't rules at all, they're principles. So if you think it isn't "fair" for me to treat what they *say* are meant as principles, in my sense of the term, as rules, you might well be right; what I'm worried about, though, is that you and I (and a very few of Them) are the only ones aware of the distinction—and when people start claiming that the "Reference Model" *is* a Standard itself, as some have, we're all in trouble.

[Speaking of "Principles," there are some very nice ones tucked away in the back of the DP I have a copy of. I can't resist quoting three of them, even though it's going to make it impossible for me to stay nonjudgmental. (They are, by the way, "The principles used to determine the seven layers in the Reference Model" according to the line/section heading marked 6.2.) "P1: do not create so many layers as to make the system engineering task of describing and integrating the layers more difficult than necessary," would be more believable to me if seven weren't two and a fraction times three. "P5: select boundaries at a point which past experience has demonstrated to be successful," would be more believable to me if I'd seen any awareness of Our past experience reflected in Their discussions. "P13: allow bypassing of sublayers," would be more believable to me if sublayers hadn't been tabbed "for further study" earlier in the document—and, for that matter, would be delightful to me if the "sub" string hadn't been present.

[I know that's a somewhat dirty trick, but at least I haven't really gone below the belt and quoted some of the alleged definitions of things like "service-access-points" and/or "protocol entities" (which we'll return to, I fear) earlier in the document.]

To continue doing a bit of an injustice to what really and truly is a subtle and complicated topic, let's pretend I'm writing for one of the trades and push ahead with the good words about the layers (which is the term the ISORM seems to be using, even though most casual discussions use "levels"). What I'll do is just copy out some of the Purpose words for each, without much comment or interpretation, so that we can finally get to the Future History (which is all that's been keeping me going for some time).

> *The purpose of the Application Layer is to serve as the window between communicating application-processes* [earlier defined as possibly meaning human users; i.e., *not* the CS sense of the term, necessarily] *using the OSI environment to exchange meaningful information.*

> *The purpose of the Presentation Layer is to represent information to communicating application-entities in a way that preserves meaning while resolving syntax differences.*

> *The purpose of the Session Layer is to provide the means necessary for cooperating presentation-entities to organize and synchronize their dialogue and manage their data exchange. To do this, the Session Layer provides services to establish a* session-connection *between two presentation-entities, and to support their orderly data exchange interactions.*

> *The Transport Layer exists to provide the transport-service in association with the underlying services provided by the supporting layers.*
> *The* transport-service *provides transparent transfer of data between session-entities. The Transport Layer relieves the transport users from any concern with the detailed way in which reliable and cost effective transfer of data is achieved.*
> *The Transport Layer is required to optimize the use of the available network-service to provide the performance required by each communicating transport user at minimum cost. . . .*

[You didn't really think I could keep out of this forever, did you? Do note that the cost business is either none of Their business (if the user *wants* maximum speed and is *willing* to ignore the cost), or is a mere pious—and circular—platitude (if "the performance required" can include damn the cost, full speed ahead).]

> *The Network Layer provides the means to establish, maintain and terminate network-connections between systems containing communicating application-entities and the functional and procedural means to exchange network-service-data-units between transport-entities over network connections* [sic, though probably what's meant is "network-connections"].

> *The Data Link Layer provides functional and procedural means to establish, maintain and release* data-link-connections *among network-entities. A data-link-connection is built upon one or several physical-connections.*

The Physical Layer provides mechanical, electrical, functional and procedural characteristics to activate, maintain and deactivate physical connections [cf. above] *for bit transmission between data-linked-entries possibly through intermediate systems, each relaying bit transmission within the Physical Layer.*

So there.

Well, maybe just a *teeny* bit of editorializing, even though most of it merely anticipates Chapter 5. First, I assume that in trying to play fair and quote the primary source, even if it's not the very latest, I'll probably get into some level of trouble because what I got from INWG isn't somehow the "real" DP, or something. Tough. (I tried to play fair, anyway.) Second, I still think the Application Layer is fuzzy, and I'm far from encouraged by the rumors I've been hearing that it's going to be chock-full of "Management functions." Third, I still feel that the Presentation Layer is a roundabout way of talking about Virtualization, and I still think you don't always want or have to Virtualize. Next, it still seems to me that L5–7 *don't have to be separate layers.* Also, I'm encouraged that there's evidence my view of the parking structures issue is the correct one by the reference to "intermediate systems" in the Physical Layer words; I just wish they weren't down there. (That is, I think they belong in the Network Layer description—but I'm probably missing some subtle point by continuing to equate their stuff to ours, down deep in my heart.) Finally, if anybody thinks I haven't played fair by having chosen not to copy all those "definitions" (or even all those other words about services and the like), I don't agree. Without yielding to the temptation to be snotty about the quality of the definitions, I'd just mildly observe that all I was trying to do was be *pro forma* courteous, not follow the lead of so many popularizers and heap so much pious prose on you that you decide it must be a Good Thing because nobody would waste so much ink on a Bad Thing.

[Did anybody notice I fell into a classic trap over the last several pages? Don't be ashamed if you didn't; it took me three days after finishing the first draft to become aware of it myself. What just happened, though, is that I spent all my time talking about the "Reference Model" itself, and none on the proposed protocols which are supposed to be being designed to and/or for it. There are several reasons for this lapse, and I don't want to bore you much more than I already have, but let's just note that (1) if the Model has flaws—as I believe it does—they certainly should be expected to cause flaws in the resultant protocol suite; and (2) there aren't all that many proposed protocols around in a sufficiently evolved state to be worth saying much about anyway. (Chapter 8 does make a few points, however.) Besides, when there's a 36-or-so page section in the DP called "Concepts of a layered architecture" it does seem fair to infer that They attach a good deal of importance to such things Themselves. . . .]

So much for that.

FUTURE HISTORY

I know, I know. That wasn't much of a tutorial. Well, I tried to warn you. Anyway, I have some hopes that some readers learned some things from it. As I've said, I only took a bash at it because the Publisher insisted. What's sustained me through it all, though, and what I hope might have sustained you as well, has been the thought that at the end I'd get to address Future History. So here goes.

To undestand my view of the future of Intercomputer Networking, we've got to start in the Fourth Century of the Common Era. If you'll cast your minds back, you'll recall (or trust me) that the burning issue amongst Christians had to do with the debate over ὁμοούσιον vs. ὁμοιούσιον. OK, OK, I always hated that sort of thing myself. The debate was over whether the nature and/or substance of The Son was "homoousian" or "homoiousian"—that is, the same as, or "similar to," respectively, that of The Father. The reason why it always stuck in my mind is that the difference between the two words is only an *iota*, and I always thought it would be charming if the real origin of "it doesn't make an iota of difference" turned out to be akin to "it's not a Federal case." (You see, they really did have big battles over the doctrinal point.) Unfortunately, I've yet to find a reputable etymologist to support my view.

But we digress. Back to the Fourth Century. Another thing that was going on, was that the Christians were busily co-opting many older religions' sacred days and figures—particularly from the Mithraists. (Mithra[s] was born on December 25, it's said; Mithraists also had some sort of symbolic eating of "flesh" and drinking of "blood"; I won't bother to go look up the other points.) Indeed, at one point in time (361-3, actually) the regnant Emperor (Flavius Claudius Julianus [331–363]) decided that he disapproved of the whole exercise so strongly that he made a concerted effort to restore the Old Religion. If he'd succeeded, of course, those who have heard of him today wouldn't know of him as Julian the Apostate . . . but at least anybody who was puzzled by my Dedication now knows what the first half of it was about. [It's extremely tempting to leave the second half as an exercise for the student, but my guilt over not having been tutorial enough earlier in the chapter impels me to tell you that my greatest undergraduate paper wasn't my thesis ("More Than Pulp: Science Fiction and the Problem of Literary Value"), even if it was the first known (to me, anyway) academic treatment of SF as Literature. No, it was "Offender of the Faith"—about Voltaire's war on the Church (motivated by his reaction to how the Inquisition treated the Hugenots, as I recall). Guess I'll never be a real poet after all, since poets never tell, but it did seem gratuitously cruel to make either of you who'd noticed the Dedication and didn't pick up on the allusion have to worry about it.]

So the questions we should be asking ourselves are the following: *Is* there "only an iota of difference" between the ARM and the ISORM, and Is the ARM actually Mithraist rather than Taoist? That is, Is the dispute between Us and

Them "really" on fine points of doctrine similar to that between the Athanasians and the Arians (there *are* a number of similarities, after all), and/or Will the newer, more vigorous belief adopt what it likes from the older one and ignore the fact that it's done so, so that the older one will eventually be more or less totally forgotten, regardless of what you and I might prefer?

Maybe.

For that matter, maybe in ten years or so we'll look around and discover that "ARM versus ISORM" was more like the Zoroastrians' co-opting of the Mithraists a millennium before the Christians' co-opting than anything else, and—oh, dear—SNA will turn out to be the parallel to Christianity and "conquer" both. (We can hope it turns out to be some still unknown mysticism, though.) As I said somewhere else entirely, crystal balls aren't the only kind you need for doing "technology forecasting" . . . but let's try a couple of scenarios anyway. The first is the Idealistic one and the second is the closest I could come to a Realistic one.

What I really do hope is that the quasi-religious undertones of what should be a legitimately open technical debate *won't* drown out the technical debate, and that if there *are* valid, technical grounds for choosing both a superior framework for networking *and* superior realizations of the framework, that's what'll happen—through the workings of "the marketplace of free ideas" and/or "free and open debate."

But that's not what I think will happen. Too many ISORMites, and even some ISORMists, have smugly told me that if I have any objections to raise, I should feel free to join them in free and open debate . . . by which they mean come to their meetings, which would scarcely be neutral territory even if they weren't so organized as to preclude my attendance. (Remember, you've got to be sent by a Voluntary Standards Organization.) So if Abstract Truth probably won't prevail, what's the alternative?

The insight as to what the future *will* look like came to me in the following circumstances: The last session I went to at INFOCOM '83 was a "Futures" panel. The premise was that the panelists were to talk about what they thought things would be like when hardware was cheap enough that everybody (for reasonably large values of everybody) had enough "compute power" at home. The interesting part is that they were all into Networking and/or Communications on the panel. During the ensuing discussion, the metaphorical coin dropped for me and I had the following Vision (which, I must confess, I made so bold as to share with the audience during a few minutes of nonquestion time from the floor—motivated, I should mention, by the fact that some friend of mine hadn't made it to the panel, so I felt entitled to his five minutes, "to keep it in the family"):

Given enough "compute power," what will happen is that the techno-theology can and will become moot: Nobody will have to give up his or her favorite approach to Intercomputer Networking, nor will anybody have to give up on the sunken investment in current networking software, nor will somebody have to come up with something that really does border on the magical by way of Translating/Mapping Gateways. No, what will happen is that when you want to get at a particular resource you'll just go off to it *in its "own" protocol suite* . . . because you'll have an Outboard Processing Environment (see Chapter 6) available to you, on that cheap and plentiful enough hardware, which is capable of interpreting all reasonable (and some unreasonable) suites "in parallel," so it doesn't really matter much—except to technicoaestheticians—which suite is "best."

I'd like to think that's the way it will be, actually; it's so attractively Ecumenical.

[Though I must confess to a lingering fear that the suites which do assume end-to-endness of the Network level could still foul things up. . . .]

CHAPTER 3

The Elements of Networking Style

ABSTRACT

Early attempts at intercomputer networking—many of which are still operational—often relied on an emulation *approach to communications between dissimilar systems. The limitations of this networking style are exposed and a superior, readily available style is discussed: "Virtualization" of network resources is the approach which evolved in the ARPANET, and is at present serving as the basis for the network protocols chosen and documented for the Department of Defense.*

PREFATORY AFTERTHOUGHTS

In retrospect, the main thing I *don't* like about "The Elements of Networking Style" is that it still had to be written as recently as a couple of years ago. No, I take that back: I like even less the fact that it will probably still need to be read a lot more than a couple of years from now. The trouble is, Emulation appeals to the shortsighted. (It apparently feels like a hardware sort of solution, which appeals to EE types; the trouble with that is that if you want to do *real* Intercomputer Networking you have to transcend—or, better still, have grown up without being exposed to—the hardware mentality.) As I've said in passing elsewhere, though, the main features you look for in an operating system to ease the necessary integration of Intercomputer Networking software are interprocess communication, explicit process creation, and ease of adding new devices, and many, if not most, modern operating systems come with these features; so perhaps in time system proprietors will get systems they're not afraid to "change," and the Emulation Style will wither and die.

I do wish I didn't know so much about the sunken investment in applications software for obsolescent—but not, more's the pity, obsolete—operating systems, though.

*   *   *

Still, I think it's a convincing paper, on the whole—even if it's best understood by those who don't need to be told. Maybe I could have been a bit nastier about what it takes to understand it, however. Hmmm . . . wonder if it'll play better coming as it now does after Chapter 2? (Notice, by the way, that if Open System Interconnection means anything, it must mean that both the ISORM style and the ARM style are what I call the virtualizing style here. See, there *are* grounds for Ecumenicism, aren't there?)

After visiting a number of sites to gather facts about the key computer systems that will comprise a particular new Department of Defense inter-computer network, I noticed certain similarities in their current "style" of interacting with other systems. The common style is to send the remote system "what it already expects to see" in its native mode, whether it be a particular type of interactive terminal, a particular representation of a magnetic tape file, or a particular data base inquiry or job control "language." This style of *emulation* apparently developed because it seemed to offer an expedient means of communicating with dissimilar systems, and it does "work"—in its own fashion, and with its own limitations.

In this very informal paper, I attempt to expose some of the limitations of the emulation style of networking, not to censure those who chose to employ it but rather to demonstrate that there is a superior style readily available. There is a sense, it must be acknowledged, in which this sort of exercise should be considered as "beating a dead horse." After all, the alternative style has been employed to excellent effect in the ARPANET, serves as the basis for the current efforts to achieve international standardization (even though those efforts have certain defects), and, in the arena which gave rise to this paper, has been mandated by the DoD. Unfortunately, however, having been out in the field recently, I have seen that the horse is still alive and kicking, and it seems to me that an exercise of this sort is needed both for abstract tutorial purposes and for the practical purpose of getting key people who are involved with making decisions about intercomputer networks, but who aren't as well grounded as they might be in the state of the art, to be willing to saddle up and ride on the new, livelier horse.

Some of the forthcoming discussion will be in the abstract, and some will be on quite practical grounds; the hope is that if the one treatment doesn't "work" for a given reader, the other will. At any rate, the intent is to make the chosen style plausible, if only because the alternative is clearly worse. (As almost anyone who has taken—or taught—a course in Composition will realize, people take their styles very personally. In an attempt not to "get personal," I elect not to cite what I take to be examples of "bad style" by name; this means that the reader is implicitly asked to trust my inductions on the data I've looked at. Some people don't like that sort of thing either, but I feel the alternative would not only be worse in some abstract sense, it would also make the paper longer and less nearly readable.)

THE PRACTICAL CASE AGAINST EMULATION

Suppose you have a computer in, say, Washington, D.C., and suppose you have somebody in, say, Hawaii you'd like to have use that computer. Suppose further that you have a packet-switched communications network available between the points in question, that there's a suitable entry point into the network "out there," and a suitable terminal as well. Even if "suitable" is given a fairly broad definition (the computer at the Washington end "knows" the terminal type and the Hawaii entry machine can support it), do you want to just hook up the pieces and go to it?

Well, suppose instead that you have three or four different computers in Washington (let's call them "Hosts"), where by "different" we mean that each Host runs a different operating system, comes from a different manufacturer, and "expects" a different type of terminal when used locally. You could buy all the different types of terminals and use each with the Host that expects it, of course. But that would get expensive, and besides you might have more users wanting to use a particular Host at a particular time than you have suitable terminals. Also, you'll have to alter the local Hawaiian machine to be able to support more kinds of terminals as you add more types of remote Hosts in Washington with their differing expectations. So straight physical matching of terminals to Host expectations isn't a good idea.

What about taking whatever terminals you happen to have and somehow making them "look like" what the Hosts expect? This approach of emulating known devices seems straightforward, and even if it isn't easy "locally" for some reason, it will clearly have the advantage of not making anybody have to tinker with the remote Hosts' operating systems. Let's consider the problems that arise if our conceptual model is one of emulation, though, to get an idea of the price we have to pay for avoiding that sort of tinkering.

First, let's expand our set of suppositions: Suppose that there are also Hosts in Hawaii that users in Washington want to get at. Suppose, indeed, that there are Hosts all over the country, 40, 50, 60 of 'em, and users all over the country (sometimes where there are Hosts, sometimes not), 500, 1000, 1500 of them, and you want all the users to be able to use all the Hosts. So you might have 100 machines (Hosts and other "suitable entry points into the communications network"—which we'll call Terminal Support Machines, or TSMs) where users might have terminals attached for the purpose of using, say, 15 to 20 different *types* of Host.

Now, what happens when you change one type of Host? That is, either you replace it with a new machine type or its manufacturer adds a new terminal type, and some application program you'd like to be usable from afar "expects" that new terminal, or whatever. You now have to make suitable changes in most (or maybe all, if the changed host is one of a kind) of the other 99 terminal-bearing machines to emulate "the right things" for the changed Host. This maintenance can be very expensive. It can also take a lot of time before everybody's changed over and can proceed as before. This sort of thing might be attractive to the companies that get paid to do all the work, but it's not very wise for the bill payers.

So you decide to be judicious about Host changes in order to avoid this "ripple effect." Okay, let's assume you can get away with that position, even though it will hinder "progress." What other problems arise from the decision to emulate known devices? For one thing, your TSMs are going to have to be fairly big and expensive if they have to be prepared to cope with all these emulations (at least one terminal type for each Host type, and more than one for some Hosts). Well, hardware's getting cheaper all the time. What else? Well, for another thing, some features of terminals aren't easy to emulate. (For that matter, emulation in general isn't all that easy—especially when you consider that the real experts on the device are the system programmers on the Host that expects it, who aren't of course the TSM and other Host system programmers.) A good example of a hard feature to emulate is the "Attention" or "Interrupt" button on many terminals. The problem here is that when such a terminal is attached directly to a Host, such a button causes a line condition to be generated, not a normal character code, so if you want to "push" such a button remotely you've got a real problem if your Host is connected in the normal fashion to a packet-switched network, which is after all strictly digital.

That "out-of-band signal" problem is only embarrassing for some kinds of Hosts and terminals, though, and we can probably live with it. What else might be wrong with emulation? How about the fact that some Hosts send fairly large chunks of data to their terminals all at once and sometimes the communications network isn't ready to accept such a big chunk, and at other times the TSM or other Host (where the user's terminal is) isn't ready either? The network can be made "bigger" with respect to buffering, perhaps, and the other machines as well, to solve such Flow Control problems, but it's already beginning to look as if maybe we're paying too high a price "everywhere else" just to preserve the advantage of not making any changes to the Hosts' software.

Another problem: Most Hosts have tables that contain entries for each terminal which can possibly be in use, and most of these tables have size limits. Under the emulation approach, local and remote users would have to contend for these limited "slots." Even worse, if the physical attachment to the remote Host is, for whatever reasons (but it does happen that way in practice) on a line-by-line basis—that is, the network "looks like" a bunch of terminal modems to the Host—you not only have obvious limitations on the number of network connections available, but you also have problems making connections *from* the Host *to* the net unless the Host can deal with dialout modems in its native mode. And you wind up looking like a milking machine* to top it all off.

Still another problem, and this one's pretty severe: You don't only want users to be able to "get in" to the remote Hosts, you also want files to be

---

*Acknowledgment to Vic DeMarines for the simile.

transferred. Well, have the sender of a file invoke an editor command on the Host and let it fly. But some sorts of files have internal structures different from the one you get with an editor. Okay, we'll write a little user program for each Host to take the files in. But then each sender (person or program) has to know what that program's called on each Host. So we'll give it the same name. But different operating systems invoke programs differently, and the senders would still have to know that. So they'll have to know that. But the simple little TSMs we started with are becoming as big as Hosts. Well, hardware's getting cheaper all the time.

Assuming you somehow resolve the last problem, you're still going to have to deal with a fascinating sidelight. Suppose you're transferring files with emulated terminals on both sides. That is, you've got a user at a terminal at a TSM using Host A and sending a file from Host A to Host B, with Hosts A and B "thinking" only terminals are involved. This might not be easy in the first place, especially when you realize that we haven't really talked about how you get out *from* a Host *to* another Host if the Host "thinks" the network is just terminals. . . . Now consider what might happen when the system operator at Host A sends an allusers message (sometimes called a "blast" command) to warn of an impending shutdown. Well, if Host A really thinks it's sending the blast to one of its own terminals, out it goes . . . to the file on Host B!

Now, you might try to "look out for" such messages in your once "little" program that's taking the file in on Host B, but that's clearly a bad idea, because there are at least 15 different Host types out there and not all of them have mechanically recognizable blast formats anyway. So perhaps you try to prevent it on the Host A side. After all, some operating systems let you turn off messages from the operator (and, for that matter, from other users), and we haven't really figured out how the "outgoing" connection gets made yet, so maybe there's some magic to be done there. Congratulations, you've just gotten to make operating system changes to all Hosts that don't already let you prevent such messages. But weren't we trying to avoid operating system changes in the first place with the emulation approach? Well, maybe we'd better not transfer files. Okay, but are you sure it wouldn't be cheaper just to make phone calls and "talk" directly to the remote Hosts if all you're doing is letting people log in from afar? And what happens when you'd like a particular program to talk to more than one user "out there" but your operating system "knows" that each of its jobs (tasks/processes) can only talk to one terminal at a time?

(The alternative of using RJE station emulation to deal with files might seem appealing at first glance. The problem is that some systems *only* put RJE input into their equivalent of a "sysin" jobstream, so there's no general solution. For that matter, not all systems support RJE stations. And if RJE emulation *were* introduced, you'd be stuck with two emulations unless you could convince yourself that interactive terminal traffic could be faked in somehow on the RJE path. So it really looks as if emulation is only good for "incoming" terminal traffic *to* a Host.)

A SOMEWHAT MORE ABSTRACT CASE
AGAINST EMULATION

With apologies to any readers who found the foregoing too "breezy" for their tastes, let's turn to a view of the problem that some readers may well find too "academic" for *their* tastes. With any luck at all, one view or the other will wind up satisfying just about everybody.

Although it is sometimes overlooked, there is a distinction between what has been called "resource sharing" and what should be called "remote access." Unfortunately, many people use the term "networking" to cover both concepts without being aware of the distinction. This can lead to problems when only remote access is provided via a given communications network.

To attempt to define terms: "Remote Access" means that a human user at a physical terminal can use a distant computer system in some fashion even though the distant ("Host") system does not directly control the terminal—contrary to the expectations of the native Host operating system. To achieve remote access, an apparently straightforward solution is emulation; that is, to make the remote terminal "look like" a terminal of a type already known to the Host, so as to avoid making Host operating system changes. "Resource Sharing," on the other hand, means that "processes" ("jobs," "tasks," "programs") on various Host systems can use each other in some fashion even though the Hosts possess different operating systems—and despite the fact that such use is also contrary to the expectations of the native operating systems. To achieve resource sharing, solutions have evolved which hinge on defining appropriate common intermediate representations of those objects the several Hosts represent in idiosyncratic ways, so that each type of Host need not be cognizant of the idiosyncratic representations of all of the other types of Host with which it might "want" to share resources" ("interoperate"). (We assume without discussion that resource sharing is desirable.)

To complicate matters further, the solution to resource sharing just sketched came to be called "protocols." But the term was already in use in the communications field (indeed, it was almost certainly chosen because of the analogy between its use there and its intended use in the new field of *intercomputer* networking for resource sharing). The attempt to use a familiar term in an extended fashion seems to have led to a loss of the intended extension: Many people appear to use the term as if it means precisely the same thing in both intercomputer networking and communications.

What has this to do with the claim that a distinction should be made between resource sharing and remote access? The problem is that if you don't know what you've really got, you don't know what you can really do with it. If, that is, you've got "a network," but it's a remote access style network based on the emulation of known devices, you don't have a resource sharing style network. (We've already seen that there's a serious doubt whether you even *could* have one, given that basis.) If, also, you've got "protocols" but they're communications protocols intended only to get bits from one place to another, you still don't have a resource-sharing network. By hypothesis, though, you want a resource-sharing network, so let's look at why "mere" remote access (and communications protocols) don't fill the bill.

Remote access in the sense we're using the phrase (assuming known device emulation) fails to furnish the appropriate "primitive operations" for resource sharing. As we've seen, flow control is lacking, "out of band signals" cannot be dealt with, number of "slots" is often a problem, outgoing connections cannot necessarily be made, multiple connections cannot necessarily be supported—and so on. The abstract problem seems to be that the "preconceptions" of operating systems, if allowed into the conceptual model, lead to functional deficiencies for at least some Host types. And in addition to functional deficiencies, there are the problems of how to transfer files and the "ripple effect" already discussed which comes into play when a given system is changed and all the emulations of it have to be changed as well. (Another practical deficiency is that "the right people" to program the emulation aren't those likely to be assigned to it.)

What, then, *are* the primitives suitable for resource sharing? After all, if we've put down mere (i.e., emulated) remote access on the grounds that it doesn't lead us to the desired goal of letting programs on heterogeneous Hosts cooperate somehow, what do we take up instead?

THE CASE FOR VIRTUALIZATION

One more strawman needs to be taken care of: If you can't live with emulation, what about "standardization" as a stye of networking? That is, if all your Hosts were the same, you (probably) wouldn't have to emulate (unless you chose the wrong Host to standardize on and it had built-in assumptions that it exercised physical control over all its terminals, the terminals had "quit buttons" that operated nondigitally, and so on). Well, even if you could come up with a Host suitable to standardize on, you'd have to throw out all those awfully expensive applications programs you've developed over the years to run on your current mix of dissimilar Hosts and do them over for the standard Host. Now, maybe there's a way of achieving that sort of "software transferability" in acceptable time at acceptable cost, but I don't know what it is. Even if it did exist, we are entitled to look at another alternative if only out of intellectual curiosity. And if, as we probably almost all agree, standardization really is "too hard," we look at that other alternative out of necessity as well.

I'm calling the style of networking that leads to resource sharing "virtualization," for parallelism with "emulation" and "standardization," and for lack of a better term. I'll try to make it clear what I mean by it, but I concede without argument that I don't expect to convince everybody that it's the "right" label for the style of networking I'm trying to describe.

Let's try another supposition. Suppose you want to make it possible for remote users to log in to Hosts as if they were local, and you decide for whatever reasons that you *won't* emulate terminals already "known" to the Hosts. Further suppose that you rule out *making* the new terminals known to the Hosts because you don't want to wind up in a situation where *n* types of Hosts have to know about *m* types of terminals, as that's too hard to manage (as well as too much work). You then come up with the bright idea that you could define a single "virtual terminal" that each Host would add somehow to its repertoire, so that if everybody pretended to be at a virtual terminal "on the way in" to the Host and expected to "see" a virtual terminal "on the way out" of the Host, the only thing you'd have to add to the Host would be a program that changed the virtual terminal representations of data and control characters into those representations already expected, and did the reverse trick in the other direction. (This trick assumes an underlying environment that we'll get to in a while.)

Example: Some Hosts expect the code for "carriage return" will also activate a "line feed" at the physical terminal. Some, however, send both codes when they want a "new line" because the carriage return without a line feed allows for overstriking. The virtual terminal to be agreed upon must take cognizance of these differing treatments and specify a "common intermediate representation" for "new lines" that doesn't lose the overstriking functionality for everyone, even though some Hosts don't offer it in their native modes. (The exact solution chosen gets rather involved, especially because it has a great deal to do with interpretations of "standard" character sets.)

Another, simpler, example: Some Hosts expect 6-bit character codes, some 8-bit, some 7-bit, some 7-bit in 8-bit fields, and so on. The virtual terminal must define both the common field size and the common code set, and each Host must map out of and into the common representation as appropriate.

To virtualize, then, is to represent in a defined, common fashion entities that are represented differently in various native states. That's a bit of a leap, but I'm already worried about gilding the lily here, so I'll let it go at that.

If you use virtualization rather than emulation as your conceptual model, you eliminate the practical problems of ripple effects, knowledgeability of implementers, and the like. *But you pay a price.* The price is that you introduce code into your operating system that "does the right thing"—that is, that preserves the illusion that the common representation is acceptable to the rest of the operating system. Sometimes this will require considerable effort. Suppose, to continue with terminals, your native terminals *do* possess analog "quit buttons." Then in order to allow the user "at a virtual terminal" to "have a quit button," you need the following: a common intermediate representation (CIR) of the quit button and an internal mechanism to "tell" the process operating on the user's behalf (on your system) that the quit button's been hit. The CIR isn't hard; putting a marker code in the input stream and using the Host-Host protocol's Interrupt (or Urgent) command would do—if we can leave out for now the implications of all *that*. The interesting point for present purposes is, What if you don't have an "interprocess signal" mechanism of some sort to stimulate the process to behave as if a local terminal's physical quit button had been hit? Answer: Build one.

There's one little issue we've been delaying for which the time has finally come: What about that cryptic "Host-Host protocol" reference? What, for that matter, about these "primitive operations" touted earlier? To do justice to those questions would require a paper about as long as this one. For present purposes, let's just observe that, in order to support a virtualized style of doing applications (terminals, files, "electronic mail," user-user "conversations," RJE, graphics, common data base query langue, common time-sharing system command language, and/or "distributed data bases") you really need a separate *layer* of protocol that allows the processes on the several Hosts (which are performing the virtualized protocols that allow all those desirable applications to happen) to "communicate." The communication has to deal with Flow Control, out-of-band signals, initiation (and identification) of "connections," multiple connections to/from the same process, and the like—in general, that is, the sorts of primitive operations you *don't* get when you emulate. The layer that does those things was historically called the "Host-Host protocol"; later it came to be known as an "End-to-End" or "Transport" Protocol. In any case, it's there to support the spectrum of applications protocols based on the virtualizing style that we have been sketching. (Indeed, it may even be viewed as being itself a virtual interprocess communication mechanism, but that is probably too Computer Science-y for our context.)

However we characterize it, the Host-Host Protocol layer "comes with" the virtualizing style. As a matter of fact, doing a generic "Network Control Program" (which includes a Host-Host protocol "interpreter" and a Host-Comm Subnet protocol "interpreter"—where an interpreter is a program that performs the actions required by the protocol) for a given Host is clearly harder than doing a remote emulation of that Host's expected terminals. But having a generic NCP furnishes "the right sort" of primitive operations *for the whole range of applications protocols*, which are what we're really concerned with. (And besides, there's a clever trick you can play so as to avoid putting the whole GNCP "inside" each Host.) So by handling even the terminal-to-Host aspect of remote access in a fashion compatible with resource sharing, once you have remote access you also have the conceptual model and a lot of mechanisms for doing other kinds of resource sharing—even though there's "more to" that mechanism than you might like.

We see, then, that virtualization isn't a free lunch. The main claim in its favor though—aside from the fact that it lets you avoid the pitfalls of emulation—is that there is enough commonality of functions among Host operating systems that the need for adding major new mechanisms is not too onerous, especially when the protocols have been developed by knowledgeable system programmers from diverse Host backgrounds with an eye toward minimizing such needs. But it isn't a free lunch.

"Is the price worth it?" is, of course, the final question we should worry about. The answer could take a very long time, if it's supposed to be a "proof." However, to return once again to the arena that started all this, although it's abundantly clear that the particular network in question is only one of many intercomputer resource-sharing networks in the same boat, a short-cut argument that should suffice is that the virtualized style of networking is what's used in the ARPANET, and the ARPANET does the sorts of things these nets want to do (more accurately, Hosts using the ARPANET's style of protocols do what Hosts that will use the recommended protocols want to do), so there you go.

CONCLUSIONS

To go much deeper than the foregoing seems to be a waste of time; "rigor" after all isn't the object of the game here. The case against emulation should be clear. Readers who need more convincing should take a look at the very similar case of "rigid" versus "flexible" attachment strategies in network front-ending in Chapter 6. The case *for* virtualization might well not be quite so clear.* Readers who need more convincing might get something out of Chapters 4 and 5, but probably should invest the time and effort to examine closely the ARPANET specifications of, say, TCP and Telnet (which happen to be, respectively, the recommended Host-Host and virtual terminal protocols). In any event, virtualization is not only the recommended style, but also the state of the art style and should be accepted as such.

*This is not mock modesty; rather, it's based on conversation after conversation with people who have been exposed to the supporting abstractions but for some reason haven't "internalized" them.

CHAPTER 4

A Perspective on Intercomputer Networking

PREFATORY AFTERTHOUGHTS

As usual, I'm not even convinced "A Perspective on Intercomputer Networking" hits the right level of abstraction myself. On this one, there's external evidence as well: After all, maybe we'd all have been spared the ordeal of Chapter 2 if I'd managed to be enough less abstract, more nearly tutorial in a conventional fashion here. Sigh. Perhaps pictures of headers *would* have helped. . . .

*   *   *

In terms of content, the major deficiency I'm aware of is that more should have been made of the interprocess communication axiom. It *is* profound. To cop a plea, I wrote it shortly after having wasted hours and hours trying to get a superannuated "system engineer" to realize that neither of the Fortran programs he'd written qualified him for entry into my particular Mystery, and I summarily decided that the appeals to "job" and "task" ought to be enough for anybody reasonable. Ah, well. (Have another look at Chapter 2, or wait till Chapter 5 if you prefer.)

*   *   *

It should be noted that the perspective here is in essence a *pre-*internetting one. That doesn't make it untrue or invalid, mind you, it just makes it several pages shorter than it might have been, and lets me keep the old ARPANET Host-Host Protocol in mind rather than TCP/IP. As the original version was supposed to have been written for a company vice president, it's probably too long as it is, so I don't feel all that bad.

*   *   *

No surprise, I trust, but let the record show that the Trailer Cartoons, illustrating the "war stories," were *not* part of the previously published version.

INTRODUCTION

Despite its popular success, intercomputer networking has not been particularly well understood. Perhaps what is needed is some perspective on networking. At any rate, this paper will attempt to furnish *a* perspective on intercomputer networking—not only where it is, but also where it's going—based on a particular set of assumptions as to why networking is attractive and another related set of assumptions as to how it should be accomplished. The stress on "a" perspective is significant: the views offered here stem from experience with the development of the ARPANET, from the "inside." That is, there is almost certainly a system programmer's bias present. This is probably a good thing, for familiarity with the actual workings of intercomputer networks should lead to a heightened sense of realism about their current and potential utility. However, the probable bias should not go unnoted, for it is clear that other perspectives on the field are tenable.

MOTIVATIONS

Rather than contrive an abstract definition of an intercomputer network, let's just say that a network in our sense involves an unspecified (but greater than one) number of computers that communicate with one another via some unspecified medium (or media), and address the reasons why it is desirable for them to do so. Note, though, that the assumption of more than one computer rules out "mere" communications networks for single machines.

Economics

It is tempting, though almost certainly historically inaccurate, to imagine that intercomputer networking started like this: Once upon a time, the director of the Advanced Research Projects Agency's Information Processing Techniques Office said to himself, "I keep getting requests for funding for projects that require computers. But I've already funded dozens of computers around the country, and I'm sure they're not all fully utilized. So if only there were a way of getting at the ones already around without costing more for phone calls than it would just to keep scattering new ones around, we'd be that much better off. Hmmm. What about an ARPANET?"

However whimsical the foregoing, it must be acknowledged that a primary motivation for developing a computer network (though not necessarily an intercomputer network) is the simple ability it confers to allow users *remote access* to computing resources. The economics of communications dictate multiplexed use of communications media, so the need for a computer-based communications subnetwork becomes clear. Is networking then merely a case of calling in the queuing theorists and the electrical engineers, deciding on the right computer to do the multiplexing, and letting users around the country have access to in-place large-scale systems?

Increased Capabilities

Clearly, it's not that simple, even if we're willing to ignore the very hard work the communications subnetwork entails. Economically desirable though remote access might have been in the late '60s, the prospect of cigarbox-sized PDP-10s was even then remotely visible. And given cheap computing power, who needs expensive communications, even if multiplexed? The answer is that from the outset* there was acknowledged a second major motivation for networking: the new capabilities achievable through what has been called *resource sharing*.

Recalling our pseudo-history, it is important to note that ARPA is, after all, in the research business. Thus, it is not surprising that the ARPANET, which is the archetype of "modern" intercomputer networks, should have had theoretical goals as well as practical ones. Granted, there is research interest aplenty in the designing of an appropriate communications subnetwork to achieve "good" remote access, and that by itself might well have justified the ARPANET; but once large-scale ("Host") computers are connected to the subnet, the really interesting thing is that they can communicate with each other as well as with communications subnet processors and geographically dispersed users. At least, that seemed to be the really interesting thing to many of the system programmers from the several ARPA-sponsored Host sites who comprised the Network Working Group, and "resource sharing"—or the uses of the ability to communicate—will be the dominant theme of what follows.

Program Sharing

Aside from such one-of-a-kind hardware resources as ILLIAC IV, where remote access is the key, the resources that networks make sharable are of two sorts, programs and data. To see the increased capabilities derivable from the ability to share programs, first, let's go back to the cheap PDP-10 in a cigarbox that will eventually upset the initial economic rationale: There are some known problems that are too "big" for a single machine. Even given : ally cheap machines, there are limits to how effectively they can be lashed together as multiprocessor systems, because (unless a major breakthrough occurs in operating system architecture) there will always be critical resources that must be dealt with serially and contention for these resources will hamper throughput. So the techniques evolved in a network context to allow programs in geographically distributed machines to communicate and cooperate can still be beneficial when all the machines are in the same room, in the sense that at least informal "parallel processing" will be desirable for the foreseeable future.

That's all rather abstract, though. For a somewhat more concrete instance, suppose you have a breadbox-sized 370 to go with your cigarbox-sized PDP-10. Now suppose someone's already solved a particular problem on one of them, but not on the other, and another problem's been solved on the other, but not on the first. The solution to a third problem requires the solutions to both previous

---

*The lead published paper on the ARPANET in the 1970 Spring Joint Computer Conference , was called, as a matter of fact, "Computer Network Development to Achieve Resource Sharing" (by the then head of ARPA IPTO, L. G. Roberts, and B. D. Wessler).

problems. . . . Now, you could reimplement one or the other for whichever machine has more capacity to spare, but "software transferability" is a nasty, expensive problem in and of itself—and besides, what if neither system has any capacity to spare? Again, techniques evolved to deal with such "distributed processing" problems in an intercomputer network will still be beneficial even when dramatically decreased machine costs allow communications costs to be largely avoided.

Still more concretely, consider the case that will probably continue to apply in the real world for some time to come, where computing resources are still noticeably expensive. It would be nice to be able to perform "load sharing" amongst systems that are necessarily geographically dispersed, in the sense of causing jobs waiting to be run at a currently busy site to be run on a currently not-busy machine "elsewhere." Although this application clearly has a great deal to do with the particular operating systems at hand (can they even tell how "busy" they are?), the medium through which they communicate when they have something to communicate will be a network.

A final instance of the desirability of program sharing, and the most concrete of the lot, lies in the area of "common command language." That is, networks of heterogeneous Hosts right now make quite diverse resources available to users. Even though it is easy to overlook users in our zeal to address grander topics like distributed processing, parallel processing, and even load sharing, it turns out to be rather frustrating to be told that you have more than a dozen different operating systems at your fingertips on the ARPANET and then realize that to use them you're going to have to memorize a dozen different command languages. For example you have to learn which one wants you to say "list," which "directory," which "listc," which "listf," which "ls" which "l," and which merely "files" just to find out what files are accessible in the current machine and context. You'd much rather learn a single command language for generic functions and let the individual systems' foibles be taken care of for you. Besides, a common command language could also play a role in doing some of the more sophisticated distributed processing jobs as well, if it addresses the problems of coordinating the application of preexisting commands as well as merely invoking them in a uniform fashion.

Data Sharing

Turning to the other sort of resource that networks make sharable—data— the main new capability that can become available is what is sometimes called the "distributed database." Prompted by either administrative necessity, the desire for redundancy, or even the costs of centralizing, there are contexts in which locally discrete databases are maintained which, from some perspective, would be better viewed as aspects of a single epi* database. Techniques for achieving such geographically dispersed databases lie in the area of data sharing.

*In the sense of "above" or "upon."

Actually, two broad classes of techniques for data sharing are envisioned: On the one hand, it is relatively straightforward to extend the program sharing techniques already sketched in order to achieve a common query language to deal with geographically dispersed, free-standing database management systems in a (user-) convenient fashion. On the other hand, the research community is already addressing the more challenging issue of creating a true distributed database, in the sense of allowing not only queries, but also updates to be performed remotely. It is clear that in the area of data sharing, technical capabilities will have to be tempered by appropriate policies. At least there is some solace to be derived from the consideration that doing a distributed database via a network allows for the possibility of local control over what data will be made available externally. But for good or ill, data sharing is indeed an area of large potential.

Summary

All the increased capabilities that intercomputer networks *can* lead to might well have come off sounding rather vague. One hopes that is only because the potentials haven't as yet been realized, which makes it difficult to be very specific. Rather than pursue the theme of increased capabilities further, though, this seems to be a good point to recall why we went off on it: The contention is that the economic advantages of being able to access remote computing resources in a multiplexed fashion over various media (phone lines and satellite communication links being two prominent examples) represent but one motivation for intercomputer networking—and the less interesting motivation, at that.

Because simply achieving remote access was difficult, however, and because the problems addressed in that area are far from uninteresting themselves, the resource-sharing aspects have taken a back seat to the remote access ones in most of the literature. The foregoing might redress the balance a bit; at any rate, it sets a background for the forthcoming.

TECHNIQUES

With some feeling for why networking is desirable, we turn to how it is accomplished. For expository purposes, it is possible either to take the goals and suggest a "top-down" design for achieving them, or to continue the sort of pseudo-history already begun and suggest a "bottom-up" route to the goals. Although top-down might be more fashionable, bottom-up is more convenient, for with it we can see both how remote access has been accomplished and what the available primitives are for eventually building the increased capabilities cited. Therefore, we begin the discussion of networking techniques at the lowest level of abstraction, the communications subnetwork itself, and will go on from there to progressively higher levels of abstraction, as embodied in various "protocols" (defined later).

Communications Subnetworks

It is an article of faith with some networking veterans that "the bits could be transmitted over a moist string, what matters is the protocols."* Although this slight overstatement has its appeal, it must be acknowledged that there are indeed fundamental problems involved in getting the bits from one Host to another, irrespective of what interesting things the bits are "saying." Indeed, from the telecommunications point of view the major initial impact of the ARPANET was its employment of a *packet-switched* communications subnetwork as opposed to the more conventional "circuit-switched" approach.

Without getting into such fine points of telecommunications as "message switching" versus "packet switching"† and the varieties of "virtual circuits," from an intercomputer networking point of view the key to packet switching is that it allows more efficient use of transmission media than circuit switching—both in terms of cost and of time-responsiveness. Further, the transmission speed promotes interactive use of remote computers, and the cost considerations and connection speed promote short—even single-transmission—"conversations" where desirable for particular applications.

Doing an injustice to a complicated area, let's accept packet switching as a good idea and proceed to look further at how intercomputer networks are put together. It might be pseudo-history again, but it is at least plausible that the desire to take advantage of packet switching as a concept led to the perception of a need for a dedicated computer to manage the routing of packets across leased phone lines and to manage retransmission of packets damaged in transmission. To have the Hosts perform these tasks would not only require too much of their computing capacity but would also complicate the administrative issue of dealing with the phone company. The dedicated communication subnet computers are called IMPs (Interface Message Processors) in the ARPANET, and will be referred to generically as CSNPs (Communications Subnet Processors). Of course, once CSNPs are introduced, they must also manage a hardware and software interface to the several Hosts that are connecting to the network through them. And, recalling that remote access is a major goal, it is natural to make suitable additions to the CSNP to manage local terminals directly, so that users need only have access to, in ARPANET terminology, a Terminal IMP ("TIP") to have access to all the Hosts on the network. (Generically, the TIP is a Terminal Support Machine, and there is no necessity for a TSM to "be" a CSNP as well.)

It is important to note that, with the possible exception of the TIP's dual terminal support plus packet switch role, the CSNP functions of achieving rapid,

---

*Recently available information suggests that perhaps the string should be waxed instead of moistened.

†A dichotomy that many would hold is more significant than circuit switching versus packet switching.

error-free transmission of data through some medium or media while presenting a manageable interface to the Hosts are *not* ARPANET-specific. Rather, they are functions which must be performed at the lowest level of abstraction in any "flavor" of intercomputer network, and the reliance on ARPANET as an example should not be construed as an unqualified endorsement. Indeed, performing the generic CSNP function on a single LSI chip is a reasonable goal.

Even if we were to limit ourselves to ARPA-like packet-switching networks, not all the communications subnet issues are resolved. Open questions include: optimum packet size; "best" routing algorithm(s); the handling of communications satellite links; the desirability of hybrid circuit- and packet-switched networks for particular applications; and the topological and/or queuing theoretical sorts of issues having to do with configuring additional Hosts in. But going beyond the confines of "ARPA-like networks" (at the communications subnet level anyway) there is also an array of open issues having to do with such apparently "different" technologies as rings, coaxial cables, fiber optics, or what have you. Fortunately, it is by no means clear that we need concern ourselves with any of these problems here, for regardless of how the bits are transmitted from computer to computer, we still have to consider what the bits represent. In other words, what's on the other side of the CSNP-Host interface?

Protocols

Not surprisingly, what's on the other side of the interface between a Host and a communications subnet processor is a CSNP-Host protocol interpreter. That is, for *any* intercomputer network the CSNP will, among other things, (1) require particular addressing and data-blocking formats; (2) demand a particular discipline be followed in regard to the flow of data to and from itself; and (3) have some sort of error-handling discipline to cover CSNP-Host interface problems at least, and in some instances to cover subnet problems as well (e.g., the Host may be required to buffer transmissions until the communications subnet informs it of successful delivery). The codification of all these factors comprises the CSNP-Host protocol, and implicit in such a protocol is a noticeable fraction (but by no means all) of the functionality of the given network—for where and how rapidly bits may be moved clearly impacts the feasibility of "higher level" applications and/or functions.

Definition

Before turning to the higher levels of functionality and the sorts of protocols they entail, it is appropriate to deal with protocols in the abstract a bit more. The notion of "protocols" in networking is an extremely powerful one, as may be inferred from the number of times it has been mentioned thus far. Indeed, it is even customary to refer to the transactions between the CSNPs themselves as the IMP-IMP Protocol in the ARPANET. Unfortunately, however, the term can cause confusion because it was borrowed from the traditional communications world, where its connotations are far less sweeping than they are in the intercomputer networking world. When we refer to a protocol, then, what we mean is perhaps best conveyed by the following quotation (from one of the early ARPANET papers):

> *When we have two processes facing each other across some communication link, the protocol is the set of their agreements on the format and relative timing of messages to be exchanged. When we speak of a protocol, there is usually an important goal to be fulfilled. Although any set of agreements between cooperating (i.e., communicating) processes is a protocol, the protocols of interest are those which are constructed for general application by a large population of processes in solving a large class of problems.* *

The emphasis on "cooperating processes" is significant, and gives the intercomputer network use of the word "protocols" a rather different flavor from the communications sense of the term. (We will have more to say about processes later.) This view at least explains—and, it is hoped, justifies—the earlier refusal to delve into areas that focus exclusively on management of transmission media; "line protocols" are important, but they don't in and of themselves confer the ability even to do remote access, much less resource sharing.

Host-Host Level

There are several reasons why a level of protocol "above" the CSNP-Host level is necessary, even from the sort of "bottom-up" analysis we're performing: The flow rates acceptable between Hosts and Hosts or Hosts and terminals will differ from those between Hosts and CSNPs (unless the CSNPs are so slow as to be uninteresting). Depending on the communications subnet at hand, transmissions may get out of sequence (e.g., from alternate routing). The kind of addressing information Hosts use to convey *logical* destinations is unlikely to fit into the format CSNP's need to decide on physical destinations. For these and other reasons, some sort of Host-Host protocol which is at least in part independent of the CSNP-Host protocol is necessary.

The issue of how independent the Host-Host protocol is from the CSNP-Host protocol brings us to an extremely important point. For whether it was discovered to be a good idea in the evolution of the ARPANET because the IMP-Host protocol was a "given," or whether it was imposed because it seemed like a sound design principle in the abstract, when the ARPANET's Host-Host protocol was designed, it was consciously made logically independent from the IMP-Host protocol. Indeed, it is an axiom of the style of networking we're discussing that protocols are "layered." The principle of layering is perhaps best stated as an insistence that control information at a given level of protocol must

---

*S. D. Crocker, J. F. Heafner, R. M. Metcalfe, and J. B. Postel, "Function-Oriented Protocols for the ARPA Computer Network," AFIPS Conference Proceedings, SJCC, 1972, Montvale, N.J., 1972.

be treated and conveyed as data by the next "lower" level of protocol. Although related to the traditional programming precept of "modularity," layering turns out to be easier to recognize and/or mechanize. (The necessity of proper function assignment remains major, of course.) The value of the layering axiom applies in two ways: With the management of logical connections (Host-Host protocol) in a separate layer from the management of physical connections (CSNP-Host protocol), a total change in the physical transmission level leaves the logical transmission level intact, so that improvements in communications subnet technology do not invalidate work at "higher" levels; and if, on the other hand, the Host-Host protocol itself changes for some reason, the "lower" level CSNP-Host protocol need not. Further, once layering has been thought of, any protocols evolved for using the logical connections will also be layered, so the changes at the Host-Host level can in their turn leave the "higher" (process level) protocols unimpacted.

Logical Connection Approach

In retrospect, the notion of a logical connection has about as profound a philosophical impact as layering on the style of intercomputer networking we're describing. To appreciate this, a final axiom must also be introduced: the notion that a Host-Host (or End-to-End) protocol is "really" an interprocess communication mechanism. Now there might well be more definitions of "process" by reputable computer scientists than there are reputable computer scientists, and what we're up to here isn't particularly meant to be computer science anyway. But whether you think of a process as a program or an address space in execution, or a job or a task on your favorite operating system, when you recall the resource-sharing goal for intercomputer networking it should be evident that to achieve it you'll have to make it possible for processes on different systems to communicate. (It is striking that some systems which were attached to the ARPANET only conferred the ability to communicate on *local* processes after the systems were networked.)

Further reflection leads to the realization that because processes are so disparate on heterogeneous operating systems, the "best" way for them to communicate is "over" very abstract entities known as logical connections rather than, say, as if they were "talking" to locally known terminals. So although it is sometimes argued that generality costs, in the context of intercomputer networking it was decided early on that particularity costs even more. Again, it's pseudo-history, but the decision to adopt the interprocess communication model with logical connections can be justified by the consideration that to have employed the obvious alternative of pretending to be terminals would have caused N different *kinds* of Host machines to have cognizance of the peculiarities of M different *kinds* of physical terminals. (See also the discussion of the virtual terminal concept in the following section.) Figure 4–1 attempts to depict the model, and Figure 4–2 presents a stylized interface to the sort of Host-Host Protocol under discussion.

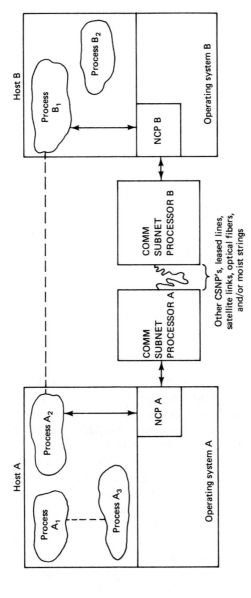

Figure 4-1 Interprocess Communication Model

OPEN	(Local-socket, mode, [type,] foreign-socket, index, code)*
WRITE	(Index, buffer, length, code)
READ	(Index, buffer, length, code)**
SIGNAL	(Index, type, code)
CLOSE	(Index, mode, code)
[STATUS	(Index, buffer, code)]

*Might be separate listen, connect primitives
**Might offer block/no block option; might permit
flow control policy to be influenced

Figure 4-2   User Interface Schematic

Process Level

Given the Principle of Layering, the notion of logical connections, and the interprocess communication model—and, of course, Host-Host and IMP-Host protocol implementations based on them—it is relatively straightforward to see how remote access can be done in a heterogeneous Host environment such as the ARPANET (which is the more interesting context because it requires general mechanisms that in turn are conducive to resource sharing). Note, by the way, that the combination of Host-Host and IMP-Host protocol interpreters came to be called a Network Control Program (NCP) in the ARPANET; for convenience, the terminology will be retained, despite the fact that other networks assign a different meaning to the term.

We are now at the process, or applications, level. Using simple remote access as the example, we see that, in the first place, the Host must be able to associate a request for logical connection (through its NCP) with a desire to do remote access ("log in"). Still following ARPANET terminology, conventionally we detect this desire by a Host-Host protocol request to establish a connection over a particular logical connection (literally, "socket" 1 in ARPANET, where sockets are the logical connection entities in that Host-Host protocol), the logical connection in question being defined to be associated with a "logger" service appropriate to the Host (e.g., dialup line handler or the like). Note that this step can be a distinctly defined Initial Connection Protocol, or it can be implicit, depending on the particular Host-Host protocol at hand; in most cases, though, the activity is referred to as "connecting to a well-known socket." The actual terminal's character set and control discipline must be dealt with somewhere. Transmissions (both input and output) over the logical connection must be associated with the process (job, task) created in response to the appropriate connection request. These functions are accounted for in a protocol which was called "Telnet" (for Teletypewriter Network) in the ARPANET; functionally, at least, other networks would have Telnet protocol analogues.

One particular technique of the ARPANET Telnet protocol bears separate mention: the notion of a "virtual terminal." It was observed that having each of N Hosts, needing to be aware of the characteristics of each of M types of terminal was undesirable; so rather than confront an "N × M problem" it was decided to define a generic, or "virtual" terminal and require mapping into and out of the virtual terminal's set of characteristics by particular systems from and to their local equivalents. Note that this allows physical control of the actual terminal to be exercised "where it belongs"—at the system to which the terminal is physically connected. The virtual terminal approach has received a certain amount of favorable publicity, and appears to deserve it. Figure 4–3 attempts to depict how Telnet happens. (The "1822 interface" comprises both hardware and software, as specified by the developers of the IMP, Bolt Beranek and Newman Corp., in their Technical Report #1822. Also, each Host's NCP must contain code to manage the IMP interface device hardware.)

Model

At any rate, we now have a model for doing remote access in a heterogeneous network: A CSNP-CSNP protocol gets the bits from place to place, a CSNP-Host protocol gets the bits to the transmission medium, a Host-Host protocol manages logical connections over which bits are passed, and a process-level protocol defines how the bits are to be interpreted. In each case, that which is data to the next "lower" level is control information to the "higher" level. Whether or not a given network layers these protocols in modular fashion does not alter the expectation that the cited levels will have functional counterparts in "any" network. However, failing to layer is often accompanied by failure to avoid operating system dependencies in the protocols developed for particular networks, which is undesirable in view of the greater functionality believed possible from general mechanisms.

To do resource sharing, it is reasonable to assume that protocols will have to be worked out just as they had to be to do remote access. The ARPANET File Transfer Protocol may be taken as an instance of a resource-sharing protocol, but its details are not as interesting as the fact that architecturally it is "just another process-level protocol," in the same sense that Telnet is a process-level protocol. (That it happens to subsume the Telnet protocol for its control connection is true, but not relevant.) So rather than describe more protocols as they now exist, let's turn briefly to what makes for "good" protocols in the abstract.

THE NEED FOR APPROPRIATE COMMON INTERMEDIATE REPRESENTATIONS

From the perspective of a Host in a heterogeneous network, protocols may be viewed as common intermediate representations of (logical) objects that local Hosts are at liberty to represent differently (or not even possess) internally. Even

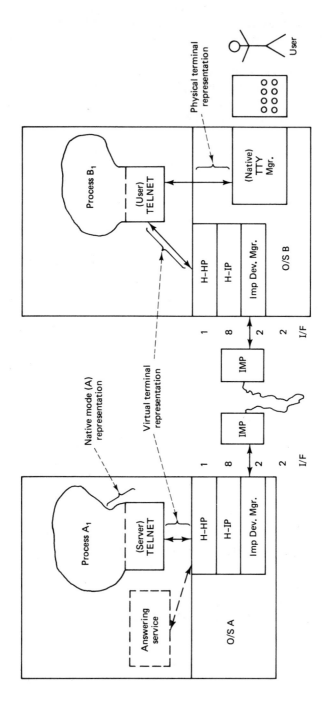

Figure 4-3 Process Level Protocol Schematic

in a homogeneous network, though, it is reasonable to take that view, for not all logical objects dealt with in the network necessarily have counterparts in native software. The reason for being concerned with the reformulation of what a protocol "is" is to focus attention on two apsects of network protocols which might otherwise be overlooked: The objects represented by a protocol (e.g., virtual terminals, actual files, or even the logical communication paths themselves) must confer the necessary functionality, of course, but on the one hand the representations are/can be *intermediate* forms and on the other hand they are to be used *in common* by several types of Host. So when considering the appropriateness of particular protocols, it is legitimate to include such questions as

1. Are the right functions performed/performable?
2. Has the most efficient/economical form been chosen?
3. Are any Hosts discommoded by particular formulations, where alternative formulations (still satisfying the first two) would mitigate matters?

Questions 1 and 2 may jointly be viewed as a concern for efficacy; 3, a concern for equity.

Some real-life examples* should help to explain why so much concern over protocols has been expressed here.

Example 1: ARPANET Flow Control

In the ARPANET Host-Host Protocol, the rate at which one Host may send another data over an open connection is governed by the receiving Host's pre-allocating quotas to the sending Host, via an ALL(ocate) command. This approach allows the receiver to keep the sender from overrunning whatever buffers have been assigned to the connection, and does "work." In practice, however, metering of the NCP on the M.I.T. Multics system showed that well over 90 percent of all the commands processed were ALLs. At the time, each one required explicit invocation of the process which executed the NCP, thus engendering considerable execution-time overhead. The cause of the excessive traffic was rapidly ascertained to be that the smaller systems on the net were granting allocations of 2–8 characters at a time in order to conserve very scarce buffer space. As processing the ALLs was not performed by explicitly scheduling a process on many of the systems on the network, and as it is difficult to coordinate changeovers in protocol implementation even where there is consensus as to the desirability of the change, the inefficiency had to be dealt with by those systems which were strongly affected, by the expedient of restructuring NCP

---

*The examples draw upon the author's personal experience. Because of this, the Multics system is mentioned frequently. For readers unfamiliar with Multics, it should be pointed out that the system is a large-scale, general-purpose Server; it was the first major virtual memory operating system, and was conceived of as a prototype "computer utility," which should explain the concern with accounting and authentication that plays so large a role in several of the examples.

implementations to process ALLs "at interrupt time" (i.e., without paying the penalty of explicit process scheduling). Note, though, that interrupt-time processing consumes system computational resources that would otherwise be shared by *all* users—not just network users—so the network protocol in a sense dictates a local inequity.

There are two important lessons to be learned from this example: On the one hand, correct protocols do not automatically turn out to be efficient ones. On the other hand, once installed, protocols are difficult to alter.

Example 2: PWIN "Generic Sockets"

The Prototype WWMCCS Intercomputer Network (PWIN) was intended to be an adaptation of ARPANET technology to the World-Wide Military Command and Control System (WWMCCS) environment. During its design, the ARPANET Initial Connection Protocol was perceived to be overly complex, and an attempt to simplify matters was made by introducing a notion of "generic sockets." The high-order 16 bits of the 32-bit socket space were reserved, to contain fixed numbers which designate specific "server" processes such as the "Logger" for remote terminal login (Telnet). When a request for connection was made to such a generic socket, the response would furnish a "tag" in the low-order bits and the entire generic socket/tag entity represented the socket or logical connection over which to converse. An unforeseen consequence of this approach, however, is that it removes the ability (highly desirable in such contexts as file transfer) to associate more than one logical connection with a particular created process/job in a straightforward way (tags are supplied consecutively, for one thing, and for another, the further subdivision of the tag field into process and connection subfields would lead to quantitative constraints on one or the other of the subfields). At last reports, the generic socket view was being reappraised.

Rather than belabor this example, let us merely observe that it is evidence for the general contention that "improvements" to working protocols should be performed very circumspectly.

Example 3: ARPANET "Mail"

The next case to be cited involves "mail" (the transfer of files containing messages to named users at foreign Hosts) on the ARPANET. Originally part of the File Transfer Protocol, the command "MAIL ID" caused the receiving ("Server") Host to pass forthcoming data to the identified user, either according to local mail conventions or via a separate mechanism for "net mail." The protocol, however, contained an ambiguity which was not noticed until implementation had been completed: The mail service was prescribed to be free (i.e., not charged for), which led many Hosts to implement it without an explicit login to their system. At a higher level of abstraction in the protocol, though, was a provision that any Server could require a login for any file transfer activity; this was at the behest of those Hosts that were concerned with their access control mechanisms—and viewed authentication as separable from accounting. That is, mail could be free, but should be preceded by a login on a no-charge account. To complicate matters further, on the Host most concerned (Multics), following the majority practice and not requiring the explicit login would have required an entire new mechanism to pass the recipient's ID from the system's "Answering Service" process to the process created to handle the mail. The potentially conflicting requirements were resolved by a gentleman's agreement that replaced the "official" protocol, and net mail sending programs began furnishing an explicit login with an agreed-upon fictitious name when the response to "mail" was the code for "login expected."

This case, which excited considerable controversy in the ARPANET Working Group before it was resolved, is illustrative of the importance of the "don't discommode the Hosts" principle mentioned earlier: Revising the closely held Answering Service process on Multics would have been a very painful exercise. It also serves to introduce an observation that has rather direct bearing on the design of intercomputer networks: In practice, the only technique that has proven fruitful when it comes to proving the correctness of protocols has been traditional "debugging," despite the existence of a growing body of literature on the topic. The example also has a great deal to do with the care that must be exercised in specifying protocols; you see, unfortunately, the original specification had said "mail should be free (*i.e.*, not require a login)" when it was meant to say "*e.g.*"

Example 4: ARPANET Initial Connection

Turning to implementation-related examples, we recall with some embarrassment that the initial Multics "User Telnet" command expected that the Server Host would open *both* (simplex) sockets at once during its execution of the Initial Connection Protocol—on the grounds that "no rational programmer would expect me to code for going to sleep on each, no matter what loopholes the spec might contain"—while the (first available) UCLA SEX System Server Telnet expected acknowledgment that the first socket of the pair had been successfully opened before initiating the second—on the (later learned) grounds that "no rational programmer would expect me to open both at once, no matter what loopholes the spec might contain."

This contretemps bears, of course, on the specification issue. Its primary impact, though, appears to us to be that implementations—even by reasonably good programmers of extremely good will—can only be validated operationally.

Example 5: ARPANET NCP "ECO"

Our final example for present purposes has to do with the time one of the TENEX system programmers decided to send out Host-Host ECO (echo) commands to each Host every minute. Again, the Multics NCP, in its reluctance to "waste interrupt time," employed a specific process wake-up to handle the command. When the network bills tripled one week, the cause soon became apparent—all those ECOs. Now even though it is not germane to detail just how much trouble this one caused before it was finally resolved, the point for present purposes should be clear: Even after protocols are properly designed, documented, and implemented, problems can be engendered by their use in ways not conceived of by the designers.

TRAILER CARTOONS

Example 1:

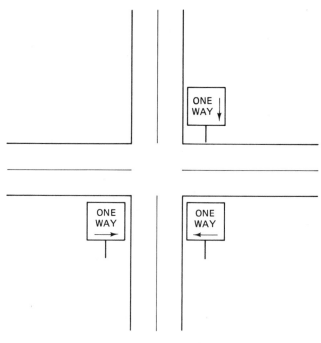

Flow Control Depiction
(AKA "Welcome to Massachusetts")

Example 2:

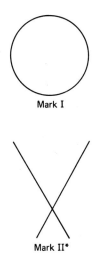

Mark I

Mark II*

Reinvention

*In case you don't know the word, "travois" is the
name of the crossed sticks certain wheel-less
Indians dragged behind them.

Example 3:

Making Mail Free

Example 4:

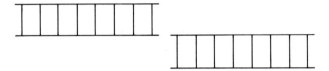

The Golden ICP Spike

Example 5:

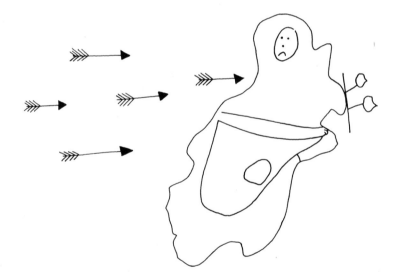

The ECO Story as Seen by
St. Sebastian Multics

CHAPTER 5

A Perspective on the ARPANET Reference Model

ABSTRACT

The paper, by one of its developers, describes the conceptual framework in which the ARPANET intercomputer networking protocol suite, including the DoD standard Transmission Control Protocol (TCP) and Internet Protocol (IP), was designed. It also compares and contrasts several aspects of the ARPANET Reference Model (ARM) with the more widely publicized International Standards Organization's Reference Model for Open System Interconnection (ISORM).

PREFATORY AFTERTHOUGHTS

Does it sound *too* snotty to say that I think of "A Perspective on the ARPANET Reference Model" as my *magnum opus?* Well, I'm not even sure I do, so don't get too fussed. It is, however, by many measures an important paper. It's also the most polished of the lot, in the sense that the previously mentioned "handkerchiefing" process involved several rather astute individuals' helping a great deal with refining the content (as well as the form, to the extent I let them).

Of course, it's still probably at too high a level of abstraction. It's one of the two papers here (the other being Chapter 11) that were consciously aimed at an audience of specialists. On the other hand, given the number of people who have told me it's the funniest conference paper they ever read, it would appear that my distaste for Emulation carries over as far as making me unable to do a very plausible emulation of a Scholar even when I semi-try. Gee, fond as I am of them, maybe I should have chucked the Architectural Highlights; then they might have just called it the wittiest. . . .

Actually, I still regret not having been even nastier about the ISORM-ites (i.e., if you didn't bother to read the Preface, those advocates of the ISORM who are professional panacea pedlars); unfortunately, I *was* quite aware of the fact that there hadn't yet been anything in the "open literature" about the ARM *per se,* so I tried to maintain some semblance of Respectability. I only wish that I, or somebody, had written about the ARM years earlier. We really were too polite about the ISORM. "All networkers together, striving for the same goals" didn't pan out, though: I sometimes suspect They thought that taking cognizance of Our ricebowl would lead to distracting attention from Their ricebowl . . . but it was likely just another instance of Spurning Naismith.

* * *

The redness/smoothness image is still one of my all-time favorites. If it doesn't grab you, do think about it.

Do read the footnote on p. 94—and, for that matter, the Session Chairman's Introduction I've tucked away in Appendix 1. The story in it about the *post hoc ergo huis causa* fallacy is perfectly true, perfectly appalling, and in its own quirky way quite central.

* * *

Some regretted omissions. The Catenet Context picture from Chapter 2 would have gone well here, as would further explication of the distinction between Prescriptive and Descriptive (see Chapter 1, though). I probably should have said a bit more about "protocols" too. The problem was that I had to put both RM pictures on the same page to stay only two pages over the Proceedings' length limit.

* * *

An omission that bears separate mention is that of the Architectural Highlight which appeared in several earlier versions called "24-Hour Guard Service." As you might suppose, it dealt with Security—which I think We (pretty much) have and They don't. Trouble is—and this is one of those junctures at which I sometimes wish the DoD didn't indirectly pay my salary these days—We can't say much about Security in public, and one of the volunteer handkerchiefers convinced me that it would be a rather cheap shot to say that They don't have it, but I can't tell you what we do have in a conference paper. That was convincing for the conference; in my own book, however. . . .

* * *

Further to the topic of why I can't abide the ISORM's rigid/strictly hierarchical view of layering, a delightfully esoteric point occurred to me recently. Even though it might come under the heading of how many pinheads can dance on the corpse of a reference model, consider the following: The one feature I've heard of for "Session" functionality that I find appealing is "multicasting." That is, at L5 you could split (or clone) off multiple instances of the same L4 connection to associate with various local processes (on the way "in" to a Host) for, say, teleconferencing. Unfortunately, however, it would seem that you'd then have to waste the cpu cycles to devirtualize *each* L5 connection in L6 (the "Presentation" functionality). In other words, here's a situation in which you'd rather have L6 happen *before* L5 on the way into a Host and after L5 on the way out (to virtualize only once), but you can't if you're constrained by the n/n-1 business. That may be somewhat obscure to nonspecialists, but if you think about it for a while it should at least help explain why I keep talking about "ISORM Level [sic] 5–7": it would be much better in my view to achieve functional modularity without imposing an ordering on the modules.

(It's an altogether unworthy thought, but in the spirit of true Constructive Snottiness I do wonder if the reason I haven't heard anything about multicasting in recent "Session" proposals is that They noticed the implication too. . . .)

* * *

Still another charming subtlety is the following, even if it does get too metaphorical for anybody but me (and Arouet): If you don't make the integration of the programs that interpret your protocols into the various operating systems that comprise your Hosts a major concern (which the ISORM doesn't appear to do), you all too easily fall into the Emulation/ Rigid Attachment trap fulminated against in Chapters 3 and 6. Another problem, then, of the ISORM "architecture" is that it encourages ISORM-ites to get so fascinated by the interior decoration of each Seven Story High-Rise that they lose sight of the fact that the Highrises *aren't actually freestanding buildings*, they're really more like tall tie corridors between skyscrapers. If, that is, Open System Interwhatever means anything sensible, the Hosts/skyscrapers are the objects of interest, and the protocols/tie corridors are how things get from one to another. Viewing the "highrises" as things-in-themselves, though, can turn tie corridors into mere outhouses with respect to the skyscrapers if you're not careful. Indeed, I ran into a guy at a conference once who claimed to be an internal expert/ teacher on/of "OSI" for the usual *major* manufacturer who wound up looking even blanker than most when I innocently asked him how they were planning to manage to wedge virtual terminals into one of their operating systems I knew from previous experience would be a problem given the vagaries of one of their Access Methods; I mean, it just hadn't occurred to him that the Sacred Seven had to be interfaced to something real, he thought they just *were*.

As I said, that might be more metaphorical (and/or cryptic) than anybody who isn't a Protocols Poet can be expected to appreciate, especially since literal tie corridors aren't as closely integrated with their buildings as Applications protocols should be, but I keep running into networking neophytes whose only exposure is ISORMite propaganda, and they keep betraying ignorance of the facts that FTPs have to read and write Hosts' files/file systems and NVTs have to become I/O source/sinks for Hosts' command language interpreters, and I'm not up to writing another chapter even if the Publisher were willing to increase production costs, so while I knew I had to say something, that's the best I could come up with. As usual, the real moral is Think About It.

* * *

Finally, a central technical issue. As I've indicated, one of the things that irks me the most about the ISORM is that you have to traverse every Level every time. Several ISORMites of my acquaintance—and even one or two ISORMists, which, in case you skipped the Preface, is my term for friends who are involved with the evolving of the ISORM—have assured me that my objections will be answered soon by the introduction of "null layers" into the Model, as indicated cryptically in the "Elevators" section. What even I thought was too snotty for a conference paper but still feel quite strongly is that "null layers" are the ISORMite equivalent of Epicycles.

* * *

Oh, all right. I ought to make you look it up, but I'll be kind for a change: Epicycles were a mathematical Rube Goldberging of the geocentric cosmology of medieval times. I don't remember—if I ever knew—the details, but the gist of it was that to preserve the hypothesis that everything revolved around the Earth, they posited some really weird orbits for the Sun and the planets. As I recall, I first heard about Epicycles in the context of Occam's Razor, in the sense of being a classic example of "multiplying entities needlessly." Do look it up if you're curious. For present purposes, however, I'd observe that the new classic example of needless multiplication of . . . heh, heh . . . entities is The Seven Story High-Rise.

Now let's just hope I don't get into as much trouble as Galileo for challenging the Authorized View . . . although, what could they do? Not invite me to their meetings? They never have anyway. And I've been very scrupulous not to violate the Koch-Goldwater Act (if that's the right one) by refraining from using any of the Government-funded computers ordinarily at my disposal to get all this new stuff typed, so I guess I'm safe.

And even if I'm not, it still moves.

INTRODUCTION

Despite the fact that "the ARPANET" stands as the proof-of-concept of intercomputer networking and, as discussed in more detail below, introduced such fundamental notions as Layering and Virtualizing to the literature, the wide availability of material which appeals to the International Standards Orga-

© 1983 IEEE. Reprinted, with permission, from INFOCOM '83, April, 1983, San Diego, CA, pp. 242–253.

nization's Reference Model for Open System Interconnection (ISORM) has prompted many newcomers to the field to overlook the fact that, even though it was largely tacit, the designers of the ARPANET protocol suite have had a reference model of their own all the long. That is, since well before ISO even took an interest in "networking," workers in the ARPA-sponsored research community have been going about their business of doing research and development in intercomputer networking with a particular frame of reference in mind. They have, unfortunately, either been so busy with their work or were perhaps somehow unsuited temperamentally to do learned papers on abstract topics when there are interesting things to be said on specific topics, that it is only in very recent times that there has been much awareness in the research community of the impact of the ISORM on the lay mind. When the author is asked to review solemn memoranda comparing such things as the ARPANET treatment of "internetting" with that of CCITT employing the ISORM "as the frame of reference," however, the time has clearly come to attempt to enunciate the ARPANET Reference Model (ARM) publicly—for such comparisons are painfully close to comparing an orange with an apple using redness and smoothness as the dominant criteria, given the philosophical closeness of the CCITT and ISO models and their mutual disparities from the ARPANET model.

This paper, then, is primarily intended as *a* perspective on the ARM. (Secondarily, it is intended to point out some of the differences between the ARM and the ISORM.*) It can't be "the official" version because the ARPANET Network Working Group (NWG), which was the collective source of the ARM, hasn't had an official general meeting since October, 1971, and can scarcely be resurrected to haggle over it. It does, at least, represent with some degree of fidelity the views of a number of NWG members as those views were expressed in NWG general meetings, NWG protocol design committee meetings, and private conversations over the intervening years. (Members of the current ARPA Internet Working Group, which applied and adapted the original model to a broader arena than had initially been contemplated, were also consulted.) That

---

*It almost goes without saying that the subtheme is certainly *not* intended to be a definitive statement of the relative merits of the two approaches, although, as will be seen, the ARM comes out ahead, in our view. But then, the reader might well say, what else should I expect from a paper written by one of the developers of the ARM? To attempt to dispel thoughts of prejudgment, the author would observe that although he is indeed an Old Network Boy of the ARPANET, he was not a member of the TCP/IP (the keystone of the current ARM) design team, and that he began looking into ARM "versus" ISORM from the position of "a plague on both your houses." That he has concluded that the differences between TCP/IP-based ARM intercomputer networking and X.25-based ISORM intercomputer networking are like day and night may be taken as indicative of something, but that he also holds that the day is at least partly cloudy and the night is not altogether moonless should at least meliorate fears of prejudice. That is to say, the ISORM has its merits and the ARM its demerits, neither of which are dealt with here, but "A Perspective" really means "My Perspective," and the author really is more concerned in this context with exposition of the ARM than with twitting the ISORM, even if he couldn't resist including the comparisons subtheme because of the one-sidedness of the ISORM publicity he has perceived of late.

might not sound so impressive as a pronunciamento from an international standards organization, but the reader should be somewhat consoled by the consideration that not only are the views expressed here purported to be those of the primary workers in the field, but also at least one Englishman helped out in the review process.

HISTORICAL/PHILOSOPHICAL CONTEXT

Although rigorous historians of science might quibble as to whether they were "invented" by a particular group, it is an historical fact that many now widely-accepted, fundamental concepts of intercomputer networking were original to the ARPANET Network Working Group.* Before attempting to appreciate the implications of that assertion, let's attempt to define its two key terms and then cite the concepts to which it alludes.

By *intercomputer networking* we mean the attachment of multiple, usually general-purpose computer systems—in the sense of Operating Systems of potentially different manufacture (i.e., "Heterogeneous Operating Systems")—to some communications network, or interconnected communications networks, for the purpose of achieving resource sharing among the participating operating systems, usually called Hosts. (By *resource sharing* we mean the potential ability for programs on each of the Hosts to interoperate with programs on the other Hosts and for data housed on each of the Hosts to be made available to the other Hosts in a more general and flexible fashion than merely enabling users on each of the Hosts to be able to log in to the other Hosts as if they were local; that is, we expect to do more than mere "remote access" to intercomputer networked Hosts.) By *the ARPANET Network Working Group*, we mean those system programmers and computer scientists from numerous Defense Advanced Research Projects Agency-sponsored installations whose home operating systems were intended to become early Hosts on the ARPANET. (By *the ARPANET* we mean, depending on context, either that communications network sponsored by DARPA which served as proof-of-concept for the communications technology known as "packet switching," or, consistent with common usage, the intercomputer network which was evolved by the NWG that uses that communications network—or "comm subnet"—as its inter-Host data transmission medium.)

The concepts of particular interest are as follows: By analogy to the use of the term in traditional communications, the NWG decided that the key to the mechanization of the resource-sharing goal (which in turn had been posited in their informal charter) would be *"protocols"* that Hosts would interpret both in communicating with the comm subnet and in communicating with each other.

*Source material for this section was primarily drawn from the author's personal experience as a member of the NWG and from numerous conversations with Dr. Jonathan B. Postel, long-time Chairman of the NWG and participant in the design meetings prior to the author's involvement. (See also Acknowledgments.)

Because the active entities in Hosts (the programs in execution) were widely referred to in Computer Science as *"processes,"* it seemed clear that the mechanization of resource sharing had to involve *interprocess communication;* protocols that enabled and employed interprocess communication became, almost axiomatically, the path to the goal. Perhaps because the limitations of mere remote access were perceived early on, or perhaps simply by analogy to the similar usage with regard to distinguishing between physical tape drives and tape drives associated with some conventionally defined function like the System Input stream or the System Output stream in batch operating systems, the discernible communications paths (or "channels") through the desired interprocess communication mechanism became known as *"logical connections"*—the intent of the term being to indicate that the physical path didn't matter but the designator (number) of the logical connection could have an assigned meaning, just like logical tape drive numbers. Because "modularity" was an important issue in Computer Science at the time, and because the separation of Hosts and Interface Message Processors (IMPs) was a given, the NWG realized that the protocols it designed should be *"layered,"* in the sense that a given set of related functions (e.g., the interprocess communication mechanism, or "primitives," as realized in a Host-to-Host protocol) should not take special cognizance of the detailed internal mechanics of another set of related functions (e.g., the comm subnet attachment mechanism, as realized in a Host-Comm Subnet Processor protocol), and that, indeed, protocols may be viewed as existing in a *hierarchy*.

With the notion of achieving resource sharing via layered protocols for interprocess communication over logical connections fairly firmly in place, the NWG turned to how best to achieve the first step of intercomputer networking: allowing a distant user to log in to a Host as if local—but with the clear understanding that the mechanisms employed were to be generalizable to other types of resource sharing. Here we come to the final fundamental concept contributed by the NWG, for it was observed that if n different types of Host (i.e., different operating systems) had to be made aware of the physical characteristics of m different types of terminal in order to exercise physical control over them—or even if n different kinds of Host had to become aware of the native terminals supported by m other kinds of Hosts if physical control were to remain local— there would be an administratively intractable "$n \times m$ problem." So the notion of creating a *"virtual terminal"* arose, probably by analogy to "virtual memory" in the sense of something that "wasn't really there" but could be used as if it were; that is, a *common intermediate representation* (CIR) of terminal characteristics was defined in order to allow the Host to which a terminal was physically attached to map the particular characteristics of the terminal into a CIR, so that the Host being logged into, knowing the CIR as part of the relevant protocol, could map out of it into a form already acceptable to the native operating system. And when it came time to develop a File Transfer Protocol, the same virtualizing or CIR trick was clearly just as useful as for a terminal-oriented protocol, so virtualizing became part of the axiom set too.

The NWG, then, at least pioneered and probably invented the notion of doing intercomputer networking/resource sharing via hierarchical, layered protocols for interprocess communication over logical connections of common intermediate representations/virtualizations. Meanwhile, outside of the ARPA research community, "the ARPANET" was perceived to be a major technological advance. "Networking" became the "in" thing. And along with popular success came the call for standards; in particular, standards based on a widely publicized "Reference Mode for Open System Interconnection" promulgated by the International Standards Organization. Not too surprisingly, Open System Interconnection looks a lot like resource sharing, the ISORM posits a layered protocol hierarchy, "connections" occur frequently, and emerging higher level protocols tend to virtualize; after all, one expects standards to reflect the state of the art in question. But even if the ISORM, suitably refined, does prove to be the wave of the future, this author feels that the ARM is by no means a whitecap, and deserves explication—both in its role as the ISORM's "roots" and as the basis of a still viable, alternative protocol suite.

AXIOMATIZATION

Let's begin with the axioms of the ARPANET Reference Model. Indeed, let's begin by recalling what an axiom is, in common usage: a principle the truth of which is deemed self-evident. Given that definition, it's not too surprising that axioms rarely get stated or examined in nonmathematical discourse. It turns out, however, that the axiomatization of the ARM—as best we can recall and reconstruct it—is not only germane to the enunciation of the ARM, but is also a source of instructive contrasts with our view of the axiomatization of the ISORM. (Refer again to the footnote on p. 94.)

Resource Sharing

The fundamental axiom of the ARM is that intercomputer networking protocols (as distinct from communications network protocols) are to enable heterogeneous computer operating systems ("Hosts") to achieve *resource sharing*. Indeed, the session at the 1970 SJCC in which the ARPANET entered the open literature was entitled "Resource Sharing Computer Networks."

Of course, as self-evident truths, axioms rarely receive much scrutiny. Just what resource sharing is isn't easy to pin down—nor, for that matter, is just what Open System Interconnection is. But it must have something to do with the ability of the programs and data of the several Hosts to be used by and with programs and data on other of the Hosts in some sort of cooperative fashion. It must, that is, confer more functionality upon the human user than merely the ability to log in/on to a Host miles away ("remote access").

A striking property of this axiom is that it renders protocol suites such as "X.25"/"X.28"/"X.29" rather uninteresting for our purposes, for they appear to have as their fundamental axiom the ability to achieve remote access only. (It might even be a valid rule of thumb that any "network" which physically inter-faces to Hosts via devices that resemble milking machines—that is, which attach as if they were just a group of locally known types of terminals—isn't a resource-sharing network. For a more detailed dicussion of the resource-sharing versus remote access topic refer again to Chapter 3.)

Interprocess Communication

The second axiom of the ARM is that resource sharing will be achieved via an *interprocess communication mechanism* of some sort. Again, the concept isn't particularly well defined in the "networking" literature. Here, however, there's some justification, for the concept is fairly well known in the Operating Systems branch of the Computer Science literature, which was the field most of the NWG members came from. Unfortunately, because intercomputer network-ing involves communications devices of several sorts, many whose primary field is Communications became involved with "networking" but were not in a posi-tion to appreciate the implications of the axiom.

A process may be viewed as the active element of a Host, or as an address space in execution, or as a "job," or as a "task," or as a "control point"—or, actually, as any one (or more) of at least 29 definitions from at least 28 reputable computer scientists. What's important for present purposes isn't the precise definition (even if there were one), but the fact that the axiom's presence dictates the absence of at least one other axiom at the same level of abstraction. That is, we might have chosen to attempt to achieve resource sharing through an explicitly interprocedure communication oriented mechanism of some sort—wherein the entities being enabled to communicate were subroutines, or pieces of address spaces—but we didn't. Whether this was because somebody realized that you could do interprocedure communication (or achieve a "virtual address space" or "distributed operating system" or some such formulation) on top of an interprocess communication mechanism (IPC), or whether "it just seemed obvious" to do IPC doesn't matter very much. What matters is that the axiom was chosen, that it assumes a fair degree of familiarity with Operating Systems, does *not* assume extremely close coupling of Hosts, and has led to a working protocol suite which does achieve resource sharing—and certainly does appear to be an axiom the ISORM tacitly accepted, along with resource sharing.

Logical Connections

The next axiom has to do with whether and how to demultiplex IPC "chan-nels," "routes," "paths," "ports," or "sockets." That is, if you're doing inter-process communication (IPC), you still have to decide whether a process can communicate with more than one other process, and, if so, how to distinguish between the bit streams. (Indeed, even choosing streams rather than blocks is a decision.) Although it isn't treated particularly explicitly in the literature, it seems clear that the ARM axiom is to do IPC over *logical connections*, in the following sense: Just as batch oriented operating systems found it useful to allow processes (usually thought of as jobs—or even "programs") to be insulated from the details of which particular physical tape drives were working well enough at a particular moment to spin the System Input and Output reels, and created the view that a reference to a "logical tape number" would always get to the right physical drive for the defined purpose, so too the ARM's IPC mechanism creates logical connections between processes. That is, the IPC addressing mechanism has semantics as well as syntax.

"Socket" *n* on any participating Host will be defined as the "Well-Known Socket" (W-KS) where a particular service (as mechanized by a program which follows, or "interprets," a particular protocol*) is found. (Note that the W-KS is defined for the "side" of a connection *where a given service resides;* the user side will, in order to be able to demultiplex its network-using processes, of course assign different numbers to its "sides" of connections to a given W-KS. Also, the serving side takes cognizance of the using side's Host designation as well as the proffered socket, so it too can demultiplex.) Clearly, you want free sockets as well as Well-Known ones, and we have them. Indeed, at each level of the ARM hierarchy the addressing entities are divided into assigned and unassigned sets, and the distinction has proven to be quite useful to networking researchers in that it confers upon them the ability to experiment with new functions without interfering with running mechanisms.

On this axiom, the ISORM differs from the ARM. ISORM "peer-peer" connections (or "associations") appear to be used only for demultiplexing, with the number assigned by the *receive* side rather than the send side. That is, a separate protocol is introduced to establish that a particular "transport" connection will be used in the present "session" for some particular service. At the risk of editorializing, logical connections seem much cleaner than "virtual" connections (using virtual in the sense of something that "isn't really there" but can be used as if it were, by analogy to virtual memory, as noted above, and in deference to the X.25 term "virtual circuit," which appears to have dictated the receiver-assigned posture the ISORM takes at its higher levels.) Although the ISORM view "works," the W-KS approach avoids the introduction of an extra protocol.

Layering

The next axiom is perhaps the best known, and almost certainly the least understood. As best we can reconstruct things, the NWG was much taken with the Computer Science buzzword of the times, "modularity." "Everybody knew" modularity was a Good Thing. In addition, we were given a head start because the IMPs weren't under our direct control anyway, but could possibly change at

---

*Yes, the notion of using "protocols" might well count as an axiom in its own right, but, no, we're not going to pretend to be that rigorous.

some future date, and we didn't want to be "locked in" to the then-current IMP-Host protocol. So it was enunciated that protocols which were to be members of the ARM suite (ARMS, for future reference, although at the time nobody used "ARM," much less "ARMS") were to be *layered*. It was widely agreed that this meant a given protocol's control information (i.e., the control information exchanged by counterpart protocol interpreters, or "peer entities" in ISORM terms) should be treated strictly as data by a protocol "below" it, so that you could invoke a protocol interpreter (PI) through a known interface, but if either protocol changed there would not be any dependencies in the other on the former details of the one, and as long as the interface didn't change you wouldn't have to change the PI of the protocol which hadn't changed.

All well and good, if somewhat cryptic. The important point for present purposes, however, isn't a seemingly rigorous definition of Layering, but an appreciation of what the axiom meant in the evolution of the ARM. What it meant was that we tried to come up with protocols that represented reasonable "packagings" of functionality. For reasons that are probably unknowable, but about which some conjectures will be offered subsequently, the ARM and the ISORM agree strongly on the presence of Layering in their respective axiomatizations but differ strikingly as to what packagings of functionality are considered appropriate. To anticipate a bit, the ARM concerns itself with three layers and only one of them is mandatorily traversed; whereas the ISORM, again as everybody knows, has, because of emerging "sub-layers," what must be viewed as at least seven layers, and many who have studied it believe that all of the layers must be traversed on each transmission/reception of data.

Perhaps the most significant point of all about Layering is that the most frequently voiced charge at NWG protocol committee design meetings was, "That violates Layering!" even though nobody had an appreciably clearer view of what Layering meant than has been presented here, yet the ARMS exists. We can only guess what goes on in the design meetings for protocols to become members of the ISORM suite (ISORMS), but it doesn't seem likely that having more layers could possibly decrease the number of arguments. . . .

Indeed, it's probably fair to say that the ARM view of Layering is to treat layers as quite broad functional groupings (Network Interface, Host-Host, and Process-Level, or Applications), the *constituents* of which are to be modular. For example, in the Host-Host layer of the current ARMS, the Internet Protocol, IP, packages internet addressing—among other things—for both the Transmission Control Protocol, TCP, which packages reliable interprocess communication, and UDP—the less well-known User Datagram Protocol—which packages only demultiplexable interprocess communication . . . and for any other IPC packaging which should prove desirable. The ISORM view, on the other hand, fundamentally treats layers as rather narrow functional groupings, attempting to *force* modularity by requiring additional layers for additional functions (although the "classes" view of the proposed ECMA-sponsored ISORM Transport protocol tends to mimic the relations between TCP, UDP, and IP).

It is, by the way, forcing this view of modularity by multiplying layers rather than by trusting the designers of a given protocol to make it usable by other protocols within its own layer that we suspect to be a major cause of the divergence between the ISORM and the ARM, but, as indicated, the issue almost certainly is not susceptible of proof. (We will return to the less structured view of modularity in the next major section.) At any rate, the notion that "n-entities" *must* communicate with one another by means of "$n - 1$ entities" does seem to us to take the ISORM out of its intended sphere of description into the realm of prescription, where we believe it should not be, if for no other reason than that for a reference model to serve a prescriptive role levies unrealizable requirements of precision, and of familiarity with all styles of operating systems, on its expositors. In other words, as it is currently presented, the ISORM hierarchy of protocols turns out to be a rather strict hierarchy, with required, "chain of command" implications akin to the Elizabethan World Picture's Great Chain of Being some readers might recall if they've studied Shakespeare, whereas in the ARM a cat can even invoke a king, much less look at one.

Common Intermediate Representations

The next axiom to be considered might well not be an axiom in a strict sense of the term, for it is susceptible of "proof" in some sense. That is, when it came time to design the first Process-Level (roughly equivalent to ISORM Levels 5.3* through 7) ARMS protocol, it did seem self-evident that a "virtual terminal" was a sound conceptual model—but it can also be demonstrated that it is. The argument, customarily shorthanded as "the $n \times m$ Problem," was sketched on p. 96; it goes as follows: If you want to let users at remote terminals log in/on to Hosts (and you do—resource sharing doesn't preclude remote access, it subsumes it), you have a problem with Hosts' native terminal control software or "access methods," which only "know about" certain kinds/brands/types of terminals, but there are many more terminals out there than any Host has internalized (even those whose operating systems take a generic view of I/O and don't allow applications programs to "expect" particular terminals). You don't want to make n different types of Host/Operating System have to be aware of m different types of terminal. You don't want to limit access to users who are at one particular type of terminal even if all your Hosts happen to have one in common. Therefore, you define a common intermediate representation (CIR) of the properties of terminals—or create a Network Virtual Terminal (NVT), where "virtual" is used by analogy to "virtual memory" in the sense of something that isn't necessarily really present physically but can be used as if it were. Each Host adds one terminal to its set of supported types, the NVT—where adding means translating/mapping from the CIR to something accept-

---

*That is, about three tenths of the possible span of "Session" functionality, which has to do with making up for the lack of Well-Known Sockets, isn't subsumed by the ARM Process-Level protocols, but the rest is, or could be.

able to the rest of the programs on your system when receiving terminal-oriented traffic "from the net," and translating/mapping to the CIR from whatever your acceptable native representation was when sending terminal-oriented traffic "to the net." (And the system to which the terminal is physically attached does the same things.)

"Virtualizing" worked so well for the protocol in question ("Telnet," for TELetypewriter NETwork) that when it came time to design a File Transfer Protocol (FTP), it was employed again—in two ways, as it happens. (It also worked so well that in some circles, "Telnet" is used as a generic term for "Virtual Terminal Protocol," just like "Kleenex" for "disposable handkerchief.") The second way in which FTP (another generic-specific) used Common Intermediate Representations is well known: You can make your FTP protocol interpreters (PIs) use certain "virtual" file types in ARMS FTPs and in proposed ISORMS FTPs. The first way a CIR was used deserved more publicity, though: We decided to have a command-oriented FTP, in the sense of making it possible for users to cause files to be deleted from remote directories, for example, as well as simply getting a file added to a remote directory. (We also wanted to be able to designate some files to be treated as input to the receiving Host's native "mail" system, if it had one.) Therefore, we needed an agreed-upon representation of the commands—not only spelling the names, but also defining the character set, indicating the ends of lines, and so on. In less time than it takes to write about, we realized we already had such a CIR: "Telnet."

So we "used Telnet," or at any rate the NVT aspects of that protocol, as the "Presentation" protocol for the control aspects of FTP—but we didn't conclude from that that Telnet was a lower layer than FTP. Rather, we applied the principles of modularity to make use of a mechanism for more than one purpose—and we didn't presume to know enough about the internals of everybody else's Host to dictate how the program(s) that conferred the FTP functionality interfaced with the program(s) that conferred the Telnet functionality. That is, on some operating systems it makes sense to let FTP get at the NVT CIR by means of closed subroutine calls, on others through native IPC, and on still others by open subroutine calls (in the sense of replicating the code that does the NVT mapping within the FTP PI). *Such decisions are best left to the system programmers of the several Hosts.* Although the ISORM takes a similar view in principle, in practice many ISORM advocates take the model prescriptively rather than descriptively and construe it to require that PIs at a given level must communicate with each other via an "n-1 entity" even within the same Host. (Still other ISORMites construe the model as dictating "monolithic" layers—i.e., single protocols per level—but this view seems to be abating.)

One other consideration about virtualizing bears mention: It's a good servant but a bad master. That is, when you're dealing with the amount of traffic that traverses a terminal-oriented logical (or even virtual) connection, you don't worry much about how many CPU cycles you're "wasting" on mapping into and out of the NVT CIR; but when you're dealing with files that can be millions of bits long, you probably should worry—for those CPU cycles are in a fairly real sense the resources you're making sharable. Therefore, when it comes to (generic) FTPs, even though we've seen it in one or two ISORM L6 proposals, having *only* a virtual file conceptual model is not wise. You'd rather let one side or the other map directly between native representations where possible, to eliminate the overhead for going into and out of the CIR—for long enough files, anyway, and provided one side or the other is both willing and able to do the mapping to the intended recipient's native representation.

Efficiency

The last point leads nicely into an axiom that is rarely acknowledged explicitly, but does belong in the ARM list of axioms: *Efficiency is a concern*, in several ways. In the first place, protocol mechanisms are meant to follow the design principle of Parsimony, or Least Mechanism; witness the argument just cited about making FTPs able to avoid the double mapping of a Virtual File approach when they can. In the second place, we can also argue that implementation decisions belong to implementers. In the author's opinion, the worst mistake in the ISORM isn't defining seven (or more) layers, but decreeing that "*n*-entities" must communicate via "*n*-1 entities" in a fashion which supports the interpretation that it applies intra-Host as well as inter-Host. If you picture the ISORM as a high-rise apartment building, you are constrained to climb down the stairs and then back up to visit a neighbor whose apartment is on your own floor. This might be good exercise, but CPUs don't need aerobics as far as we know.

Recalling that this paper is only secondarily about ARM "versus" ISORM, let's duly note that in the ARM there is a concern for efficiency from the perspective of participating Hosts' resources (e.g., CPU cycles and, it shouldn't be overlooked, "core") expended on interpreting protocols, and pass on to the final axiom without digressing to one or two proposed specific ISORM mechanisms which seem to be extremely inefficient.

Equity

The least known of the ARM axioms has to do with a concern over whether particular protocol mechanisms would *entail undue perturbation of native mechanisms* if implemented in particular Hosts. That is, however reluctantly, the ARMS designers were willing to listen to claims that "you can't implement that in my system" when particular tactics were proposed and, however grudgingly, retreat from a mechanism that seemed perfectly natural on their home systems to one which didn't seriously discommode a colleague's home system. A tacit design principle based on equity was employed. The classic example had to do with "electronic mail," where a desire to avoid charging for incoming mail led some FTP designers to think that the optionally mandatory "login" commands of the protocol shouldn't be mandatory after all. But the commands were needed by some operating systems to actuate not only accounting mechanisms but authentication mechanisms as well, and the process which "fielded" FTP connections was too privileged (and too busy) to contain the FTP PI as well. So (to make a complex story cryptic), a common name and password were advertised for a "free" account for incoming mail, and the login commands remained mandatory (in the sense that any Host could require their issuance before it participated in FTP).

Rather than attempt to clarify the example, let's get to its moral: The point is that how well protocol mechanisms integrate with particular operating systems can be extremely subtle, so in order to be equitable to participating systems, you must either have your designers be sophisticated implementers or subject your designs to review by sophisticated implementers (and grant veto power to them in some sense).

It is important to note that, in the author's view, the ISORM not only does not reflect application of the Principle of Equity, but it also fails to take any explicit cognizance of the necessity of properly integrating its protocol interpreters into containing operating systems. Probably motivated by Equity considerations, ARMS protocols, on the other hand, represent the result of intense implementation discussion and testing.

ARTICULATION

Given the foregoing discussion of its axioms, and a reminder that we find it impossible in light of the existence of dozens of definitions of so fundamental a notion as "process" to believe in rigorous definitions, the ARPANET Reference Model is not going to require much space to articulate. Indeed, given further the observation that we believe reference models are supposed to be descriptive rather than prescriptive, the articulation of the ARM can be almost terse.

In order to achieve efficient, equitable resource sharing among dissimilar operating systems, a layered set of interprocess communication oriented protocols is posited which typically employ common intermediate representations over logical connections. Three layers are distinguished, each of which may contain a number of protocols.

The Network Interface layer contains those protocols which are presented as interfaces by communications subnetwork processors ("CSNP"; e.g., packet switches, bus interface units, and so on). The CSNPs are assumed to have their own protocol or protocols among themselves, which are not directly germane to the model. In particular, no assumption is made that CSNPs of different types can be directly interfaced to one another; that is, "internetting" will be accomplished by Gateways, which are special-purpose systems that attach to CSNPs as if they were Hosts (see also the section "Gateways" to follow). The most significant property of the Network Interface layer is that bits presented to it by an attached Host will *probably* be transported by the underlying CSNPs to an addressed Host (or Hosts) (i.e., "reliable" comm subnets are not posited—although they are, of course, allowed). A Network layer protocol interpreter ("module") is normally invoked by a Host-Host protocol PI, but may be invoked by a Process Level/Applications protocol PI, or even by a Host process interpreting no formal protocol whatsoever.

The Host-Host layer contains those protocols which confer interprocess communication functionality. In the current "internet" version of the ARM, the most significant property of such protocols is the ability to direct such IPC to processes on Hosts attached to "proximate networks" (i.e., to CSNPs of various autonomous communications subnetworks) other than that of the Host at hand, in addition to those on a given proximate net. (You can, by the way, get into some marvelous technicoaesthetic arguments over whether there should be a separate Internet layer; for present purposes, we assume that the Principle of Parsimony dominates.) Another significant property of Host-Host protocols, although not a required one, is the ability to do such IPC over logical connections. Reliability, flow control, and the ability to deal with "out-of-band signals" are other properties of Host-Host protocols which may be present. (See also "TCP/IP Design Goals and Constraints" on pp. 106–110. A Host-Host PI is normally invoked by a Process Level/Applications PI, but may also be invoked by a Host process interpreting no formal protocol whatsoever. Also, a Host need not support more than a single, possibly notional, process (that is, the code running in an "intelligent terminal" might not be viewed by its user—or even its creator—as a formal "process," but it stands as a de facto one).

The Process Level/Applications layer contains those protocols which perform specific resource-sharing and remote-access functions such as allowing users to log in/on to foreign Hosts, transferring files, exchanging messages, and the like. Protocols in this layer will often employ common intermediate representations, or "virtualizations," to perform their functions, but this is not a necessary condition. They are also at liberty to use the functions performed by other protocols within the same layer, invoked in whatever fashion is appropriate within a given operating system context.

Orthogonal to the layering, but consistent with it, is the notion that a "Host-Front End" protocol (H-FP), or "Host-Outboard Processing Environment" protocol, may be employed to offload Network and Host-Host layer PIs from Hosts to Outboard Processing Environments (e.g., to *Network* Front Ends," or to BIUs, where the actual PIs reside, to be invoked by the H-FP as a distributed processing mechanism), as well as portions of Process Level/Applications protocols' functionality. The most significant property of an H-FP attached Host is that it be functionally identical to a Host with inboard PIs in operation, when viewed from another Host. (That is, Hosts which outboard PIs will be attached to in a flexible fashion via an explicit protocol, rather than in a rigid fashion via the emulation of devices already known to the operating system in question.)

Whether inboard or outboard of the Host, it is explicitly assumed that PIs

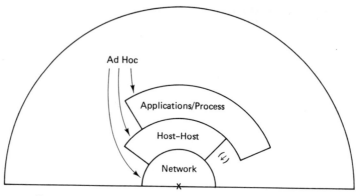

Notes

A. X marks the egress (and the ingress)

B. The whole picture either lives in or is flexibly attached to a Host

C. (↓) indicates it's at least imaginable to use the network layer
   without/in-lieu-of a Host–Host protocol in some circumstances

D. (And if comm subnet processors are present, there will doubtless
   be a CSNP–CNSP protocol in play — which is rendered
   uninteresting for present purposes by Note B.)

Figure 5-1   ARM in the Abstract

will be appropriately integrated into the containing operating systems. The Network and Host-Host layers are, that is, effectively system programs (although this observation should not be construed as implying that any of their PIs must of necessity be implemented in a particular operating system's "hard-core supervisor" or equivalent) and their PIs must be able to behave as such.

Visualization

Figures 5–1 and 5–2* present, respectively, an abstract rendition of the ARPANET Reference Model and a particular version of a protocol suite designed to that model. Just as one learns in geometry that one cannot "prove" anything from the figures in the text, they are intended only to supplement the prose description above. (At least they bear no resemblance to high-rise apartment houses.)

TCP/IP DESIGN GOALS AND CONSTRAINTS

The foregoing description of the ARM, in the interests of conciseness, deferred detailed discussion of two rather relevant topics: just what TCP and IP (the

---

*These figures are very loosely adapted from J. Davidson et al., "The ARPANET Telnet Protocol: Its Purpose, Principles, Implementation, and Impact on Host Operating System Design," *Proc. Fifth Data Communications Symposium*, ACM/IEEE, Snowbird, Utah, September, 1977.

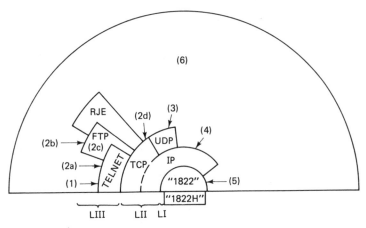

Legend

(1)　Where Terminal–Terminal Protocol would go*

(2a)...(2d)　Where Mail Protocol could go*

(3)　Where muxed packetized speech goes

(4)　Where unmuxed packetized speech could go

(5)　Where you could "pump bits at a peripheral" on a LAN

(6)　Still Ad Hoc Land

　·　"1822" for concreteness only (need not be taken literally)

　·　RJE not endorsed, merely suggestive of using two PLP's
in-support-of/doing-virtualization for a third

*Found via well-known socket

Figure 5-2　ARMS, Somewhat Particularized

Transmission Control Protocol and the Internet Protocol) are "about," and just what role Gateways are expected to play in the model. We turn to those topics now, under separate headings.

　　As has been stated, with the success of the ARPANET* as both a proof-of-concept of intercomputer resource sharing via a packet-switched communications subnetwork and a (still) functional resource-sharing network, a number of other bodies, research and commercial, developed "their own networks." Often just the communications subnetwork was intended, with the goal being to achieve remote access to attached Hosts rather than resource sharing among them, but nonetheless new networks abounded. Hosts attached to the original ARPANET or to DoD nets meant to be transferences of ARPANET technology should, it was perceived in the research community, be able to do resource sharing (i.e., interpret common high-level protocols) with Hosts attached to

---

*See *Proceedings of the 1970 SJCC*, "Resource Sharing Computer Networks" session, and *Proceedings of the 1972 SJCC*, "The ARPA Network" session for the standard open literature references to the early ARPANET. Other source material for this section is drawn from the author's personal conversations with TCP/IP's principal developers; see also Acknowledgments.

these other networks. Thus, the first discernible goal of what was to become TCP/IP was to develop a protocol to achieve *"internetting."*

At roughly the same time—actually probably chronologically prior, but not logically prior—the research community came to understand that the original ARPANET Host-Host Protocol or AH-HP (often miscalled NCP because it was the most visible component of the Network Control Program of the early literature) was somewhat flawed, particularly in the area of "robustness." The comm subnet was not only relied upon to deliver messages accurately and in order, but it was even expected to manage the transfer of bits from Hosts to and from its nodal processors over a hardware interface and "link protocol" that did no error checking. So, although the ARPANET-as-subnet has proven to be quite good in managing those sorts of things, surely if internetting were to be achieved over subnets potentially much less robust than the ARPANET subnet, the second discernible goal must be the *reliability* of the Host-to-Host protocol. That is, irrespective of the properties of the communications subnetworks involved in internetting, TCP is to furnish its users—whether they be processes interpreting formal protocols or simply processes communicating in an ad hoc fashion—with the ability to communicate as if their respective containing Hosts were attached to the best comm subnet possible (e.g., a hardwired connection).

The mechanizations considered to achieve reliability and even those for internetting were alien enough to AH-HP's style, though, and the efficiency of several of AH-HP's native mechanisms (particularly Flow Control and the notion of a Control Link) had been questioned often enough, that a good Host-Host protocol could not be a simple extension of AH-HP. Thus, along with the desire for reliability came a necessity to furnish a *good Host-Host protocol*, a design goal easy to overlook. This is a rather subtle issue in that it brings into play a wealth of prior art. For present purposes, in practical terms it means that the "good" ideas (according to the technical intuition of the designers) of AH-HP—such as sockets, logical connections, Well-Known Sockets, and in general the interprocess communication premise—are retained in TCP without much discussion, while the "bad" ideas are equally tacitly jettisoned in favor of ones deemed either more appropriate in their own right or more consistent with the other two goals.

It could be argued that other goals are discernible, but the three cited—which may be restated and compressed as a desire to offer a good Host-Host protocol to achieve reliable internetting—are challenging enough, when thought about hard for a few years, to justify a document of even more than this one's length. What of the implied and/or accepted design constraints, though?

The first discernible design constraint borders on the obvious: Just as the original ARPANET popularized packet switching (and, unfortunately to a lesser extent, resource sharing), its literature popularized the notion of *"Layering."* Mechanistically, layering is easy to describe: the control information of a given protocol must be treated strictly as data by the next "lower" protocol (with processes "at the top," and the/a transmission medium "at the bottom"), as discussed earlier. Philosphically, the notion is sufficiently subtle that even today researchers of good will still argue over what "proper" layering implies, also as discussed earlier. For present purposes, however, it suffices to observe the following: Layering *is* a useful concept. The precise set of functions offered by a given layer is open to debate, as is the precise number of layers necessary for a complete protocol suite to achieve resource sharing. (Most researchers from the ARPANET "world" tend to think of only three layers—the process, applications, or user level; the Host-Host level; and the network level—though if pressed they acknowledge that "the IMPs must have a protocol too." Adherents of the International Standards Organization's "Open System Interconnection" program—which appears to be how they spell resource sharing—claim that seven is the right number of levels, though if pressed they acknowledge that "one or two of them have sublevels." And adherents of the Consultative Committee for International Telephony and Telegraphy don't seem particularly concerned with resource sharing to begin with.) At any rate, TCP and IP are constrained to operate in a (or possibly in more than one) layered protocol hierarchy. Indeed, although it is not the sole reason, this fact is the primary rationale for separating the internetting mechanization into a discrete protocol (the Internet Protocol: IP). In other words, although designed "for" the ARM, TCP and IP are actually so layered as to be useful even outside the ARM.

It should be noted that as a direct consequence of the Layering constraint, TCP must be capable of operating "above" a functionally equivalent protocol other than IP (e.g., an interface protocol directly into a proximate comm subnet, if internetting is not being done), and *IP must be capable of supporting user protocols other than TCP* (e.g., a nonreliable "Real-Time" protocol).

Resisting the temptation to attempt to do justice to the complexities of Layering, we move on to a second design constraint, which also borders on the obvious: *Only minimal assumptions can be made about the properties of the various communications subnetworks in play.* (The "network" composed of the concatenation of such subnets is sometimes called "a catenet," though more often—and less picturesquely—merely "an internet.") After all, the main goal is to let processes on Hosts attached basically to "any old (or new) net" communicate, and to limit that communication to processes on Hosts attached to comm subnets that, say, do positive acknowledgments of message delivery would be remiss.*

Given this constraint, by the way, it is quite natural to see the more clearly Host-to-Host functions vested in TCP and the more clearly Host-to-catenet

---

*A strong case can be made for desiring that the comm subnets make a "datagram" (or "connectionless") mode of interface available, based upon the desire to support such functionality as Packetized Speech, broadcast addressing, and mobile subscribers, among other things. For a more complete description of this point of view, see V. G. Cerf and R. E. Lyons, "Military Requirements for Packet-Switched Networks and for Their Protocol Standardization," *Proc. EASCON,* 1982.

For present purposes, we do not cite the presentation of a datagram mode interface as a design constraint because it is possible—albeit undesirable—to operate IP "on top of" a comm subnet which does not present such an interface.

functions vested in IP. It is, however, a misconception to believe that IP was designed in the expectation that comm subnets *"should"* present only the "lowest common denominator" of functionality; rather, IP furnishes TCP with what amounts to an abstraction (some would say a *virtualization*—in the ARPANET Telenet Protocol sense of virtualizing as meaning mapping from/to a common intermediate representation to/from a given native representation) of the properties of "any" comm subnet including, it should be noted, even one which presents an X.25 interface. That is, IP allows for the application to a given transmission of whatever generic properties its proximate subnet offers equivalents for; its design neither depends upon nor ignores the presence of any property other than the ability to try to get some packet of bits to some destination, which surely is an irreducible minimum for the functionality of anything one would be willing to call a network.

Finally, we take note of a design constraint rarely enunciated in the literature, but still a potent factor in the design process: Probably again stemming from the popularity of the original ARPANET, as manifested in the number of types of Hosts (i.e., operating systems) attached to it, *minimal assumptions are made about the nature* or even the "power" *of the Hosts* which could implement TCP/IP. Clearly, some notion of process is necessary if there is to be interprocess communication, but even here the entire Host might constitute a single process from the perspective of the catenet. Less clearly, but rather importantly, Hosts must either "be able to tell time" or at least be able to "fake" that ability; this is in order to achieve the reliability goal, which leads to a necessity for Hosts to retransmit messages (which may have gotten lost or damaged in the catenet), which in turn leads to a necessity to know when to retransmit. It should be noted, however, that this does not preclude a (presumably quite modestly endowed) Host's simply going into a controlled loop between transmissions and retransmitting after enough megapasses through the loop have been made—if, of course, the acknowledgment of receipt of the transmission in question has not already arrived "in the meantime."

To conclude with a formulation somewhere between the concise and the terse, TCP/IP are to constitute a means for processes on Hosts about which minimal assumptions are made to do reliable interprocess communication in a layered protocol suite over a catenet consisting of communications subnetworks about which minimal assumptions are made. Though it nearly goes without saying, we would probably be remiss not to conclude by observing that that's a lot harder to do than to say.

GATEWAYS

One other aspect of the ARPANET Reference Model bears separate mention. Even though it is an exceedingly fine point as to whether it's actually "part" of the Model or merely a *sine qua non* contextual assumption, the role of Gateways is of considerable importance to the functioning of the Internet Protocol, IP.

As noted, the defining characteristic of a Gateway is that it attaches to two or more proximate comm subnets as if it were a Host. That is, from "the network's" point of view, Gateways are not distinguished from Hosts; rather, "normal" traffic will go to them, addressed according to the proximate net's interface protocol. However, the most important property of Gateways is that they interpret a full version of IP which deals with internet routing (Host IP interpreters are permitted to take a static view of routing, sending datagrams which are destined for Hosts not directly attached to the proximate net to a known Gateway, or Gateways, addressed on the proximate net), as well of course as with fragmentation of datagrams which, although of permissible size on one of their proximate nets, are too large for the next proximate net (which contains either the target Host or still another Gateway).

Aside from their role in routing, another property of Gateways is also of significance: *Gateways do not deal with protocols above IP*. That is, it is an explicit assumption of the ARM that the catenet will be "protocol compatible," in the sense that no attempt will be made to translate or map between dissimilar Host-Host protocols (e.g., TCP and AH-HP) or dissimilar process-level protocols (e.g., ARPANET FTP and EDN FTP) at the Gateways. The justifications for this position are somewhat complex, but receive more attention in Chapter 10. For present purposes, however, it should suffice to note that the case against translating/mapping Gateways is a sound one, and that, as with the ARMS protocols, the great practical virtue of what are sometimes called "IP Gateways" is that they are in place and running.

"ARCHITECTURAL" HIGHLIGHTS

As was implied earlier, one of the problems with viewing a reference model prescriptively is that the articulation of the model must be more precise than appears to be humanly possible. That the ISORM, in striving for superhuman precision, fails to achieve it is not grounds for censure. However, by reaching a degree of apparent precision that has enticed at least some of its readers to attempt to use it in a prescriptive fashion, the ISORM has introduced a number of ambiguities which have been attributed as well to the ARM by relative neophytes at intercomputer networking whose initial exposure to the field was the ISORM. Therefore, we conclude this not-very-rigorous paper with a highly informal treatment of various points of confusion stemming from attempting to apply the ISORM to the ARM.

(It should be noted, by the way, that one of the most striking ambiguities about the ISORM is just what role X.25 plays in it: We have been informed by a few ISORMites that X.25 "is" Levels 1–3, and we accepted that as factual until we were told during the review process of the present paper that "that's not what we believe in the U.K." What follows, then, is predicated on the assumption that the earlier reports were probably but not definitely accurate—and if it turns out to be in time to help prevent ISO from embracing X.25 exclusively by pointing out some of the problems entailed, so much the better.)

"Customized Parking Garages"

The typical picture of the ISORM shows what looks like two high-rises with what looks like two parking garages between them. (That is, seven layers of protocol per "Data Terminal Equipment," three layers per "Data Circuit Terminating Equipment.") The problem is that only one "style" of parking garage—i.e., one which presents an X.25 interface—is commonly understood to be available to stand beside an ISORM DTE by those who believe that ISO has adopted X.25 as its L1–3. In the ARM, on the other hand, no contraints are levied on the Communications Subnetwork Processors. Thus, satellite communications, "Packet Radios," "Ethernets," and the like are all accommodated by the ARM.

Also, the sort of Outboard Processing Environment mentioned earlier in which networking protocols are interpreted on behalf of the Host in a distributed processing fashion is quite comfortably accommodated by the ARM. This is not to say that one couldn't develop an OPE for/to the ISORM, but rather that doing so does not appear to us to be natural to it, for at least two reasons: 1. The Session Level associates sockets with processes, hence it belongs "inboard." The Presentation Level involves considerable bit–diddling, hence it belongs "outboard." The Presentation Level is, unfortunately, above the Session Level. This seems to indicate that outboard processing wasn't taken into account by the formulators of the ISORM. 2. Although some ISORMites have claimed that "X.25 can be used as a Host-Front End Protocol," it doesn't look like one to us, even if the ability to do end-to-end things via what is nominally the Network interface is somewhat suggestive. (Those who believe that you need a protocol as strong as TCP below X.25 to support the virtual circuit illusion might argue that you've actually outboarded the Host-Host layer, but both the X.25 spec and the ISORM appeal to protocols above X.25 for full L II functionality.) Perhaps, with sufficient ingenuity, one might use X.25 to *convey* an H-FP, but it seems clear it isn't meant to *be* one in and of itself.

"Plenty of Roads"

Based upon several pictures presented at conferences and in articles, DCEs in the X.25-based ISORM appear to many to be required to present X.25 interfaces to each other as well as to their DTEs. Metaphorically, the parking garages have single bridges between them. In the ARM, the CSNP-CSNP protocol is explicitly outside the model, thus there can be as many "roads" as needed between the ARM equivalent to ISORM parking garages. This also allays fears about the ability to take advantage of alternate routing in X.25 subnets or in X.75 internets (because both X.25 and X.75 are "hop-by-hop" oriented, and would not seem to allow for alternate routing without revision).

"Multiple Apartments Per Floor"

As noted, the ISORM's strictures on inter-entity communication within each "high-rise" are equivalent to having to climb downstairs and then back up to visit another apartment on your own floor. The ARM explicitly expects PIs within a layer to interface directly with one another when appropriate, metaphorically giving the effect of multiple apartments on each floor off a common hallway. (Also, for those who believe the ISORM implies only one protocol/ apartment per layer/story, again the ARM is more flexible.)

"Elevators"

The ISORM is widely construed as requiring each layer to be traversed on every transmission (although there are rumors of the forthcoming introduction of "null layers"), giving the effect of having to climb all seven stories' worth of stairs every time you enter the high-rise. In the ARM, only Layer I, the Network Interface layer, *must* be traversed; protocols in Layers II and/or III need not come into play, giving the effect of being able to take an elevator rather than climb the stairs.

"Straight Clotheslines"

Because they appear to have to go down to L3 for their initiation, the ISORM's Session and Transport connections are, to us, metaphorically tangled clotheslines; the ARM's logical connections are straight (and go from the second floor to the second floor without needing a pole that gets in the way of the folks on the third floor—if that doesn't make a weak metaphor totally feeble.)

"Townhouse Styles Available"

Should desirable ISORM Level 6 and 7 protocols eventuate, the "two-story townhouse style apartments" they represent can be erected on an ARM L I–L II (Network Interface and Host-Host Layers) "foundation." With some clever carpentry, even ISORM L5 might be cobbled in.

"Manned Customs Sheds"

Although it's straining the architectural metaphor to the breaking point, one of the unfortunate implications of the ISORM's failure to address operating system integration issues is that the notion of "Expedited Data" exchanges between "peer entities" might only amount to an SST flight to a foreign land where there's no one on duty at the Customs Shed (and the door to the rest of the airport is locked from the other side). By clearly designating the Host-Host (L II) mechanism(s) which are to be used by Layer III (Process-Level/Applications) protocols to convey "out-of-band signals," the ARM gives the effect of keeping the Customs Sheds manned at all times. (It should be noted, by the way, that we acknowledge the difficulty of addressing system integration issues without biasing the discussion toward particular systems; we feel, however, that not trying to do so is far worse than trying and failing to avoid all parochialism.)

"Ready For Immediate Occupancy"

The ARM protocol suite has been implemented on a number of different operating systems. The ISORM protocol suite "officially" offers at most (and not in the U.K., it should be recalled) only the highly constraining functionality of X.25 as L1–L3; L4–L7 are still in the design and agreement processes, after which they must presumably be subjected to stringent checkout in multiple implementations before becoming useful standards. The metaphorical high-rises, then, are years away from being fit for occupancy, even if one is willing to accept the taste of the interior decorators who seem to insist on building in numerous features of dubious utility and making you take fully furnished apartments whether you like it or not; the ARM buildings, on the other hand, offer stoves and refrigerators, but there's plenty of room for your own furniture—and they're ready for immediate occupancy.

CONCLUSION

The architectural metapor might have been overly extended as it was, but it could have been drawn out even further to point up more issues on which the ARM appears to us to be superior to the ISORM, if our primary concern were which is "better." In fairness, the one issue it omitted which many would take to be in the ISORM's favor is that "vendor support" of interpreters of the ISORM protocols will eventually amount to a desirable "prefabrication," while the building of the ARM PIs is believed to be labor-intensive. That would indeed be a good point, if it were well founded. Unfortunately for its proponents, however, close scrutiny of the vendor support idea suggests that it is largely illusory (see Chapter 8), especially in light of the amount of time it will take for the international standardization process to run its course, and the likelihood that specification ambiguities and optional features will handicap interoperability. Rather than extend the present paper even further, then, it seems fair to conclude that with the possible exception of "vendor support" (with which exception we take exception, for it should be noted that a number of vendors are already offering support for TCP/IP), the ARPANET Reference Model and the protocols designed in conformance with it are at least worthy of consideration by anyone planning to do real intercomputer networking in the next several years—especially if they have operating systems with counterparts on the present ARPANET, so that most if not all of the labor-intensive part has been taken care of already—irrespective of one's views on how good the ISORM protocols eventually will be.

ACKNOWLEDGMENTS

Although it has seldom been more germane to observe that "any remaining shortcomings are the author's responsibility," this paper *has* benefited tremendously from the close scrutiny and constructive comments of several distinguished members of both the research community and the (DoD) Protocol Standards Technical Panel. The author is not only extremely grateful to, but is also extremely pleased to acknowledge his indebtedness to the following individuals (cited in alphabetical order): Mr. Trevor Benjamin, Royal Signals and Radar Establishment (U.K.); Mr. Edward Cain, Chairman of the PSTP; Dr. Vinton Cerf, DARPA/IPTO (at the time this was written); Dr. David Clark, M.I.T. Laboratory for Computer Science (formerly Project MAC); and Dr. Jonathan Postel, U.S.C. Information Sciences Institute. Posterity may or may not thank them for their role in turning an act of personal catharsis into a fair semblance of a "real" paper, but the author emphatically does.

CHAPTER 6

The Host-Front End Protocol Approach

[This Cover Cartoon really has to be left to the reader's imagination.]

PREFATORY AFTERTHOUGHTS

I may be willing to kid around a bit about the ARM paper's being my "magnum opus," but "The Host-Front End Protocol Approach" really *is* my most significant contribution to the state of the Intercomputer Networking art. (That might account for the fact that it's the least amusing chapter in the book. Sorry 'bout that.) And I really do feel badly that I never got around to getting it into the "open literature" before now. I just never could figure out which journal or conference it was appropriate for, and couldn't bear the thought that if I picked the wrong one the turkeys might reject it.

* * *

Once you're reminded that the PSTP is the (DoD) Protocol Standards Technical Panel, the following should be nearly self-explanatory:
"Preface to the PSTP Edition"
(Probably should be read after the paper)

Not having the time to reedit the attached paper, I'd like to emphasize a few points in this cover note in order to deal with some common misapprehensions.

1. The whole point of the H-FP Approach is that you integrate the Host-side software, which is meant to be very compact, in precisely the same fashion as you would a "Generic Network Control Program"—in our case, TCP/IP, a Host-Comm Subnet Processor protocol, and whatever device manager/driver code you need for the CSNP hardware interface—so as to be doing real networking. You only lose functionality with the Rigid Attachment Strategy argued against in the paper. (That's the one that looks like a milking machine.)

2. The particular hardware connection between a Host and its NFE/ OPE (for Outboard Processing Environment) is meant to be at the Host's convenience. Use DMA if you've got it. Use HDLC or good old 1822 or even pretend to look like a tape drive if one of them is convenient. What matters is that the Host-side protocol interpreter of H-FP and the NFE/OPE-side PI of H-FP (which two-thirds of the self-professed ISO experts at the last meeting would call the "H-FP entities"... I think) are (a) there, and (b) able to get bits to one another *reliably*.

3. I'd be just delighted to have the NFE/OPE-side H-FP PI "live in" the Comm Subnet Processor; that's where I wanted it to go in 1971, after all. And please note that in a LAN, the BIU—or whatever you want to call it—*is* the CSNP.

4. H-FP has always been meant to be a distributed processing mechanism for relieving Hosts of having to deal with the particularities and pe-

culiarities of Intercomputer Networking protocols to the maximum extent feasible. Unfortunately, not enough people pay attention to the difference between NFEs and conventional comm front-ends; that's why I'm trying to popularize the OPE label nowadays. (Yes, OPEs can, and probably should, consist of multiple microprocessors.)

5. Finally, please note that just because when I wrote this originally I couldn't have told you I knew of anyone who had offloaded Process/Applications Layer protocols (ISO Level [sic] 5–7, for those who insist) doesn't mean that it isn't part of the intent of the approach, at least to the extent of doing the bit-diddling parts in the OPE—and always remembering that, just as in number 1, you will have to integrate "what's left" of the P/ALPs' functionality into the Host properly.

*   *   *

It would be remiss of me to omit mention of one particular dark cloud on the otherwise bright horizon of Outboard Processing: Some knowledgeable networkers (ARMorers, perhaps?) have reservations about the approach, based on their belief that inboard networking software *can* be made "optimal," with enough work, but outboard software just never can be "optimal." I have a great deal of respect for a couple of those who take this position, and a certain amount of sympathy for their viewpoint as well. An analogy comes to mind: I have an outboard Jacuzzi machine on/in my bathtub. It's nowhere near as good as a real Jacuzzi pool/"hot-tub"/ "spa." The catch is that I don't have room for the latter (they're also rather pricey, but whatthehell), whereas I do have room for the former—and it *is* a lot better than an ordinary bath.

That's not the whole story, of course. In the first place, it's not only Hosts where inboard software "doesn't fit" that benefit from OPEs. An OPE might, for example, be a nifty way of adding buffering for a Host that needs to clear out its main memory as soon as possible for other uses when, say, a big file transfer is going on. For that matter, a change in comm subnet or even Host-Host protocol might require vast effort to re-"optimize" inboard (especially summed over a number of Hosts/operating systems, which is a concern intercomputer network proprietors have to worry about even though it might not seem all that significant to those who only worry about their own Hosts), but it can be done "once, for all" outboard. And so on. In the second place, it's not even clear that the apparent "extra step" in interpreting H-FP (in two places) as well as all the other protocols *necessarily* leads to worse throughput (which seems to be what my ARMorer friends mean when they talk about optimality): Microprocessors are getting faster and faster after all and may just outstrip some Hosts in speed soon.

What I think it all boils down to is: If it works good (in your particular context) do it (outboard).

* * *

For those who find this Outboard Processing stuff new and intriguing, keep your eyes peeled. I'm working on a new proposed standard H-FP (for the DoD, nominally, but any number can play) these days, which I think will be a goody, because it's based on the implementation experience of half a dozen or so different H-FPs over the last eight years. As an added inducement, if you find the document when it comes out, its first paragraph will tell you the true story of how I invented Host-Front End protocols.

BACKGROUND

While Network Control Programs were still in the final phases of checkout on the ARPANET, it was observed that had the original Interface Message Processor been a more powerful machine, the Network Working Group could and would have specified a Host-Host protocol that divided labor more equitably (from the Host's point of view) between the Host and the IMP. Areas for real-location included flow control, bit-shifting, retransmission, and, in general, those aspects of the Host-Host Protocol that did not concern the NCP's primary role of associating sockets with processes. Another way of putting the issue is that Hosts would "like" to be able to conserve their CPU cycles and their main memory space. Indeed, those who subscribe to the resource-sharing view of intercomputer networking would hold that the Hosts' CPU cycles and memory are the resources being shared; thus, anything that liberates more of these resources to be shared—i.e., that decreases "overhead"—must be quite desirable. As early as 1971, then, a desire existed for some sort of Host-Front End Protocol which would allow common functions of what was known as "the" NCP to be performed *outboard* of the Host. (Figure 6–1 attempts to depict the inboard NCP versus outboard NCP situation.)

By 1974 "ARPANET technology" had demonstrated its utility to the point that numerous organizations wanted to attach diverse Host systems to "ARPA-like nets." Unfortunately, it had been learned that an ARPA-like NCP was a relatively difficult implementation task for operating systems that could not merely adopt (or at worst adapt) NCPs from like operating systems already attached to the original ARPANET. Again, a protocol that allowed outboarding of significant fractions of the NCP seemed attractive. As it had been observed that a Network-oriented front-end (or a highly intelligent packet switch) could also be of utility in (1) "offloading" selected aspects of such process-level protocols as Telnet and File Transfer; (2) localizing access to Hosts into an environ-

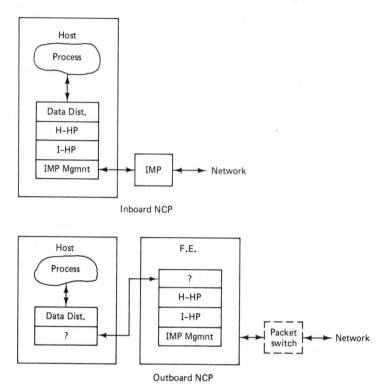

Figure 6-1 Inboard vs. Outboard NCP

ment that could be made certifiably secure much more readily than *n* kinds of Hosts—or even than *n* instances of one kind of Host; (3) shielding the Host from changes in communications subnets and/or Host-Host Protocols; and (4) serving as a terminal-support "mini-Host" to facilitate access to Hosts where (and/or when) a local Host was not available, the need for "a protocol" became overwhelmingly clear to various members of the networking community. In the fall of 1974, an ARPANET Request for Comments was issued, containing a proposed Host-Front End Protocol (H-FP), which was "cosigned" by over a dozen ARPANET developers.*

Before turning to the nature of H-FP and then to its current state of evolution, the question "why a *protocol*" must be briefly addressed. That is, it has also been observed that most Hosts already "talk" to device controllers, and almost all Hosts talk to some sort of devices, so why not just simulate/emulate a "known device" in a front-end, let the front-end talk to the net, and be done with it? There are two broad answers to the latter question: It's too hard and it's not worth it, It's too hard to do a "rigid" attachment strategy because for each and every de-

---

*M. A. Padlipsky, et al., "A Proposed Protocol for Connecting Host Computers to ARPA-like Networks via Directly-Connected Front-End Processors," NWG RFC #647, November 1974.

vice simulated, either experts on the device are going to have to learn to work in the alien environment of the front-end machine, or experts on the front-end are going to have to become experts on the particular device/controller in question. It's not worth it because if anything beyond terminal access to the Host is desired, ad hoc protocols will have to be evolved for *each* Host-Front End pairing to allow connections to be opened from the Host to the net (at the very least a foreign Host address and socket number must be conveyed to the NCP in the front-end—over what "looks" like a line to a terminal), and because even file transfer will require the cognizance of some kind of network-oriented software in the Host (which is, after all, where the file system is). Granted that artifices may be envisioned for transferring files by simulating an RJE station; yet if "the system" thinks it "knows" about the device in question it will, unless it's a very untypical system, be sending messages to it which (a) are not part of the contents of the files being "transferred," and (b) must be separted/segregated from those contents. (This has been called "the poltergeist problem," and no general solution to it is known.) So to answer the question as originally formulated, "one protocol is easier to deal with than *n* protocols" or, more philosophically, "an explicit protocol is necessary to a resource-sharing network, even if it seems more than sufficient for a communications network."

THE NATURE OF THE H-FP

Rather than further belabor the issue of why have an H-FP, let's turn to the issue of what "is" an H-FP. In the broadest sense, an H-FP is a distributed computation mechanism. That is, it consists of conventions and formats that allow a program in a Host computer to manipulate on its behalf a program (the generic NCP or some other resource available through the front-end) in a front-end computer. Another way of viewing it is as an idealized user interface to a generic NCP (which happens to live in another machine). Still another way of viewing it is as a set of primitives that are necessary and sufficient to allow a Host to attach to a resource-sharing network with minimal incursions of network-oriented code into the Host itself.

At any rate, the H-FP does the following: It assumes as little as possible about the hardware connection between the Host and the front-end so that attachment by use of preexisting Host software and hardware (if available) can be effected. It allows processes on the Host to establish (logical) connections to processes "elsewhere" (including on the Host itself), to read, write, and terminate the connections, and to send "out-of-band" signals associated with the connections—if the Host-Host Protocol to which it is interfacing supports such signals. It imposes a simple discipline on the flow of data both to the Host and to the front-end. It also furnishes a mechanism for invoking routines in the front-end that will offer aid to process-level protocols (such as translating from the Host's character set to the virtual terminal's character set, for Telnet connections). It does all this by interpreting commands that represent the generic functions "any" Host-Host Protocol would or should offer, and it offers "escape hatches" to deal with unanticipated future Host-Host and process-level protocols that do not conform to the model assumed by the generic functions, just in case.

Not surprisingly, the exact formats, conventions, and commands to do all of the foregoing in the "best" fashion constitute a topic that engenders considerable debate among concerned designers. However, it is important to stress one further point under the heading of "the Nature of the H-FP": Most of the informal group which had those debates over such issues as whether you'll get a tighter implementation of an H-FP interpreter in a particular Host or front-end (or, preferably, in any Host or FE) by right- or left-justifying the "ready" bit in its byte/field, felt very strongly that if at all possible there should be a single, standard version of the H-FP. The motivation is one of maximizing utility. For, given an appropriate "common" H-FP, it is straightforward to extend the application range of H-FP bearing systems in striking ways. If they "talk the same H-FP," for example, front-ends which were evolved independently, to manipulate different Host-Host Protocols, could be connected "back-to-back" and become what the literature calls "Gateways." Or, as another example, two dissimilar Hosts (similar Hosts are trivial) with H-FP modules could be turned into a "loosely coupled multi-processor" by the simple expedient of connecting their H-FP modules back to back. For that matter, it appears that, at the cost of a 10 to 20 percent larger H-FP implementation, you could "talk H-FP over the net" (i.e., use a modified H-FP as the Host-Host Protocol). Finally—at least of the currently conceived examples—it is commonly held that the front-end is, after all, "only a mini" and many are concerned over whether it can "do all that and still support a reasonable number of terminals" . . . and then the inevitable thought occurs, "Why not front-end the front-end with a terminal concentrator?" Add to that the notion that the "best" front-end for the original front-end might not be a cheaper version of the first one, and again the picture of two H-FP modules connected to each other comes to mind. Therefore, to preserve all these attractive options, it is extremely desirable that any organization front-ending to the H-FP model endeavor to front-end with "the" H-FP.

"FLEXIBLE" VERSUS "RIGID" ATTACHMENT STRATEGIES

The advantages of an explicit, software attachment strategy as opposed to an implicit, hardware-simulation attachment strategy deserve further discussion. The strategies are respectively characterized as "flexible" and "rigid"—the latter term being applied because the front-end must conform rigidly to the expectations of preexisting Host device I/O software. Figure 6–2 attempts to depict the rigid versus flexible attachment strategy situation. Before discussing the advan-

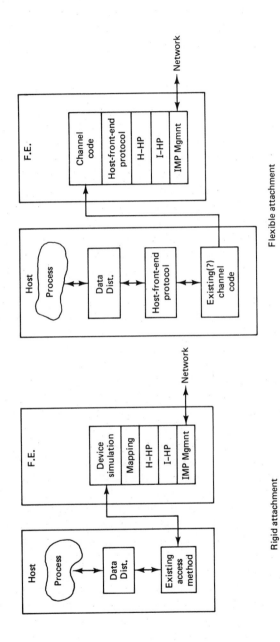

Figure 6-2 Flexible vs. Rigid Attachment

123

tages and disadvantages of these two strategies in detail, one extremely important consideration should be noted. If the generic Network Front-End (NFE) requirement of supporting heterogeneous Host types is interpreted strictly, a "flexible" attachment strategy is virtually the mandatory choice provided only that such a strategy is technically feasible, for a "rigid" strategy would entail a major new implementation effort in the front-end for each new Host (to simulate known I/O devices, and to invent ad hoc protocols for each Host type in order to allow processes on the Host to initiate network connections). Aside from the sense in which a flexible attachment strategy wins by default, other, more direct advantages are also derived from the flexible strategy.

Ability to Perform All Network Functions

Whereas a "flexible" attachment strategy allows processes on the Host to perform all necessary network functions such as opening and closing connections, performing I/O over them, and sending interrupt signals to remote processes, a "rigid" strategy does not. If the network "looks" to the Host like a group of local terminals, these devices will typically be addressed by a "one-dimensional" address (a device number); but to refer to both a foreign Host and a socket on it requires a "two-dimensional" address—and if you're "internetting" you need still another dimension to express the foreign network. Thus at the very least a "rigid" attachment strategy must, in order to open a connection *to* the network, provide for the conveying to the front end of more information than a Host would normally convey to an actual device under its control. So although known device simulation may work for connections coming *from* the network, there must be cooperating software in the Host for "outgoing" connections. (Also, if the Host does not support "dialout" to terminals as a standard capability, a new I/O primitive must be added for this purpose anyway.)

Another function that the "flexible" approach facilitates but the "rigid" approach may obviate is that of multiple connections to/from a process, as in the ARPANET File Transfer Protocol (FTP), where commands are sent over one connection and data over another. If the Host's native I/O system does not allow more than one terminal to be attached to a process, this useful capability is denied by the "rigid" strategy. For that matter, how *are* files to be transferred? Perhaps by simulating Remote Job Entry (RJE) stations, but this leads to other problems in turn, such as how to separate system messages from data intended for the file (the aforementioned Poltergeist Problem). Further, many systems have built-in assumptions as to where input from specific devices goes (e.g., terminal input to a command processor, RJE input to a batch monitor) which can make it difficult for a process to "get at" the data coming in from the network. Each of these problems can probably be either avoided or solved for given Hosts, but the dominant consideration is that they need not even be addressed if a "rigid" attachment strategy is avoided.

Difficulty of Implementation

In addition to the per-system design effort at the protocol level, a "rigid" attachment strategy also entails more work at the device handler level for the front-end implementers, for simulating known devices to the satisfaction of the Host is clearly more complex than simply sending and receiving bits through a hardware interface. When a "rigid" approach was attempted in the ARPANET (using ANTS to simulate a "200UT" user terminal station on a CDC 6600 at Ft. Belvoir), the simulation required four to six months of "top system programmer time" according to the Ballistic Research Laboratory for whom the work was done. Note that even to attempt such an approach requires personnel who are expert both in the Host's I/O system and the front-end's programming environment, in addition to being expert in the Host-to-Host protocol of the network in question; such personnel are probably an even scarcer commodity than the space in the front-end which would be occupied by the simulation code. A "flexible" strategy, on the other hand, vests the Host-specific programming in the more reasonable place: the hands of programmers expert in the Host's operating system.

Costs

Hardware to simulate known devices and attach to the front-end machine as well must in general be newly designed and fabricated on a per-Host basis, which adds to the costs of the "rigid" approach. The "flexible" approach, however, makes no assumptions about the connection hardware; thus, when "off-the-shelf" hardware exists, it can be employed, and where it doesn't it can be as simple as possible because it doesn't have to "fool" preexisting Host software. Estimates of the software costs on the two models tend to cancel each other out (that is, a known device simulation in the front-end appears to take as much work as a "flexible" protocol implementation in the Host) so other differences in hardware costs appear to dominate.

Flow Control

Although apparently not a problem with some Hosts, it cannot simply be assumed that *all* Hosts will have avoided the trap of implicit flow control to the devices they "know." That is, if a particular system were faced by a "rigid" FE, it might not send bits faster than the 75 to 9600 bits per second rate it "knows" the terminal it's told is out there can accept, which would considerably slow throughput. Alternatively, too high a rate might be assumed by the Host (thus flooding the front-end) if the simulation were of a mini-computer device handler. Care must also be taken not to flood a Host. Again, the important point is that a "flexible" approach with its explicit protocol provides explicit flow control, while a "rigid" approach must make do with what the systems already offer or invent a new treatment for each system.

Number of "Lines"

Another difficulty with the "rigid" approach is that when devices are simulated there are usually system limits on the number of connections supported. For example, the University of London node on the ARPANET includes an IBM 360/195 that is front-ended by a PDP-9 simulating an IBM 1130; the real 1130 only supports up to five interactive terminals, which becomes the limit on the total number of incoming and outgoing connections on the 195 from/to the network. Different systems would impose different limits, but a "flexible" connection strategy would avoid the whole messy issue.

Throughput

The final point is that the device simulation code, of unknown extent, in the front-end must require more time to execute (and more space to reside in) than the code that would be necessary to drive a nonsimulated interface; thus, the "rigid" strategy might well lead to inferior throughput compared to the "flexible" strategy. Depending on actual implementations, only microseconds might be added to the processing, but it is clear that the processing will take a measurably longer time.

Interim Conclusion

Even if we defer for the time being those considerations that might lead to the adoption of a "hybrid" strategy in particular cases (wherein terminals would be simulated only for incoming interactive connections from the network to a Host), the case against a "rigid"-only approach based on stated and implied requirements of a Network Front-End is extremely strong. On the other hand, at the price of introducing *some* software into the Host, the "flexible" strategy confers benefits and/or resolves ambiguities in half a dozen cited areas.

"HYBRID" STRATEGY

The foregoing discussion was based upon the assumption that a choice had to be made between a "rigid"-*only* attachment strategy and a "flexible"-*only* one. In such terms, it is clear that the rigid alternative is inadequate. However, it might still be advantageous to employ an approach wherein the NFE simulates known devices for incoming interactive terminal access to the Host ("Server Telnet"), and employs an H-FP approach for all other types of connection. This has been called the "hybrid" alternative. The major tradeoff is between the value of freeing the Host of whatever code is necessary to perform the Server aspects of the

Telnet Protocol, against the value of freeing the FE of whatever code is necessary to simulate the known devices. It is natural to believe that the choice between a hybrid strategy and a straight flexible strategy will depend a great deal on the particular operating system under consideration.

A major advantage of the hybrid strategy is that it can eliminate the need for a certain amount of code in the Host, while not leaving the resulting attachment functionally deficient. As indicated earlier, the straight rigid strategy (with no cooperating code in the Host) would lead to functional deficiency; the straight flexible approach would on the other hand, in principle require more code in the Host than the hybrid. Thus, the hybrid strategy would not appear to be desirable for a virtual memory system such as Multics—where "core" is not at a premium; however, in a system such as GCOS, where "core" is at a premium, the hybrid approach cannot be dismissed out of hand.

It must also be noted that some operating systems are so structured internally as to make it extremely difficult to achieve process creation other than by coming through their native terminal handling code. (TSO on the IBM 360 was a striking example of this.) In such cases, in order to avoid major system "surgery" the hybrid approach would of course be appropriate. Indeed, avoiding having to contend with the native operating system to achieve remote access can be viewed as the dominant advantage of the approach in some contexts.

The main disadvantage of the hybrid strategy is that it entails an as-yet unknown additional level of effort in both the design and operation of the NFE. As was noted earlier, implementing a rigid attachment on the ARPANET required about half a man-year of "top system programmer time." No reports have been made available as to how well the ARPANET (Fort Belvoir) simulation performed, but it is said that it is no longer in use.

In summary, for present purposes, it is clear that the hybrid strategy would have a worse impact on the NFE than the flexible strategy, but it is unclear how bad that impact will be. From the Host's perspective, however, the approach can be very beneficial under certain circumstances.

THE CHOICE OF OUTBOARD PROCESSOR

A final prefatory point: In response to the original H-FP RFC, the question was sometimes asked, "Why a *front-end?*" Since the H-FP approach was initially conceived as a function that should have been performed by what was then called the High-Speed Modular IMP, the question is a natural one. Further, because a free-standing front-end inserts an additional processing locus (or two) into the path between a process on one Host and a process on another Host, reliability and throughput considerations also must be taken into account. It turns out that there are at least three answers to the question: In the first place, none of the organizations known at present to be employing the H-FP approach owns a network consisting solely of PLURIBUS IMPs or their equivalents; therefore, the degree of freedom of having somewhere (other than a free-standing front-end) to put the outboard software is absent. In the second place, it is prudent to employ off-the-shelf hardware and software to the fullest extent possible in the sort of implementation effort H-FP constitutes; therefore, the availability of seasoned NCPs and User Telnets in several PDP-11 operating system environments coupled with the availability of interface hardware for PDP-11s to several types of Hosts led to a natural H-FP vehicle, at least initially. (It should be noted, however, that experience has shown the PDP-11 to be a less than ideal architecture for a sophisticated NFE. Indeed, recent thinking suggests that a virtual memory microprocessor would be more attractive in the long run, especially given large amounts of "real" memory.) And finally, nobody ever said that the PLURIBUS IMP and/or the AUTODIN II packet switch couldn't (or shouldn't) offer H-FP themselves. . . . .

THE CONCEPTUAL MODEL

That which we currently call an NCP is actually a module that performs four distinguishable functions. At the "lowest" level, it manages the IMP (packet switch) interface hardware; that is, it contains an IMP device driver. The next "higher" level consists of interpreting the IMP-Host (software) Protocol—or the equivalent level of protocol in a non-ARPANET. Next, and, confusingly enough, often the only aspect intended when "an NCP" is referred to in the field, is the level at which the relevant Host-Host Protocol is interpreted. Finally, at the "top" level of abstraction, the data to/from the net must be associated with the appropriate processes ("jobs," "tasks," "programs") on the Host. In summary, an NCP "is"

- Data Distribution
- Host-Host Protocol Interpretation
- "IMP"-Host Protocol Interpretation
- "IMP" Device Management

The key observation—on which any H-FP must be based—is that only the data distribution function necessarily requires the Host's cognizance. The other three functions can be performed (advantageously, it is assumed) outboard of the Host, given a means of communication between the data distribution function and the Host-Host Protocol interpreter. That means of communication is a Host-Front End Protocol, as the term is used here. So, on the "flexible" attachment strategy view argued for earlier, both the Host and the FE will contain an H-FP interpreter.

Fundamental to the view of H-FP espoused here is the fact that both the Host and its front-end machine have essentially identical H-FP interpreters. Naturally, their "I/O" modules will differ, but the Host-Front End Protocol per se should "look the same" in either machine. As indicated earlier, given this view, it is straightforward to (1) let the FE "be" a Host, such that it too does I/O from/to processes; (2) let the Host "be" an FE, such that it does I/O from/to some other network's Network Control Program, and (3) let the FE be a terminal support system, such that it does I/O from/to processes local to itself as well as from/to an appropriate NCP. It is also, at least in principle, straightforward to let the Host-Host Protocol interpreted "be" H-FP. That is, with a relatively small change in the area of connection initiation, it is believed that H-FP can serve as an adequate alternative Host-Host Protocol. The contention is not fundamental to the model, but should it be borne out in practice it will open the door to further interesting applications.

There is, it must be observed, one omission in the simple model: What of "higher-level" (process-level) protocols? Here, the symmetry of the simple model must give way to the demands of practicality. For one of the objects of front-ending is to allow for the offloading of as much network-related software as possible from the Host; therefore, to the extent feasible, provision must be made for the interpretation of most or all of such process-level protocols as (to use the ARPANET terms) "Telnet" and "File Transfer" and the like. That is, the Host-Host protocol level is properly viewed as the level of protocol which establishes logical communication routes between processes (usually called "connections"), but it does not—and by application of the Principle of Layering should not—bear on the interpretation of the bits that traverse the connections. That level of interpretation is reserved for the various process-level protocols. To account for this, our simple model must be iterated.

In H-FP, then, at connection establishment time (and at other times, under certain circumstances) provision is made for specifying what, if any, kind of interpretation should be performed on the bits that will traverse the to-be-established connection. Thus, a Host can cause its FE to, for example, pass only genuine characters in its expected character set over a Telnet (i.e., virtual terminal) connection; or, should the Host have particularly idiosyncratic built-in operating system assumptions about what kind of real terminals the world possesses, it could even indicate that it wants the FE to invoke its per-installation special software that maps from a virtual terminal representation to an emulation or simulation of the expected actual terminal. In like manner, when files are being transferred, a given Host might want a degree of shielding from the particular network's detailed FTP ranging from "complete" (where all the Host wants is the file's name—if that—and the bits in its native format), through "default" (where the Host gets or gives file name, user name, password, and—perhaps—structure descriptor), all the way to "no shielding" (where the Host is prepared to interpret the entire process-level protocol inboard). Clearly, such varying degrees of process-level protocol interpretation will lead to various per-Host mixes of available software components in the FE, in the sense that H-FP modules can invoke different "canned" process-level protocol interpreter "packages" at the Host's behest.

The latter point implies a final interesting observation about the model: Given its inherent flexibility, and its almost obsessive modularity, the H-FP model lends itself quite nicely to inexpensive cross-implementations. At the source code level, only the device drivers are likely to differ for "standard" front-endings. For special cases, new process-level protocol interpreters will be needed—but their skeletons will be dictated by the standard ones. Indeed, even when it comes to device drivers, a modicum of engineering can often save the software costs by mating the half of an interface a given Host "expects" to see with the half a standard front-end "expects" to see.

A second, non-networking, apparent omission in the model will be noted but dismissed: Clearly, a user interface to the Host's H-FP module is necessary in order to use all this wonderful stuff. Less clearly, but by stipulation if nothing else, we could attempt to legislate about that interface. We elect not to do so, for several reasons: Choice of an interface "natural" to a containing operating system is probably best left to experts in that containing operating system; user interfaces are probably the least likely area in the entire field from which matters of taste could ever be eliminated; and, finally, this discussion is probably overlong already. Any organization that elects to adopt H-FP then, is, of course, at liberty to do what it will at the user interface level—in the sense of being relatively safe from being told "we told you so." But be careful: The applications that use the interface will be expensive to redo if you decide to redefine the interface in the light of your own subsequent experience. (And one handy hint: Beware "blocking" I/O primitives.)

A NOTE ON CONTAINING OPERATING SYSTEMS

The foregoing discussion of the H-FP model avoided with some care such operating system issues as pertain to both the various Hosts and (potentially) various front-ends. This is proper because protocols, at least in the ARPANET sense, are supposed to foster implementation under various operating systems, without building in assumptions that make implementation vastly easier for some systems and vastly more difficult for others—and H-FP is, after all, a protocol in the ARPANET sense. There are, however, a few assumptions that were made by those who evolved the protocol which should be shared with potential adopters of H-FP: Of paramount importance is that in the final resolve H-FP designers must be able to behave—when, and one hopes only when, necessary— as if they owned the containing operating system. That is, lack of responsiveness of either partner H-FP module (i.e., the "Host"-side or the "front-end"-side) could essentially paralyze the other—and ramify back to the other systems that the Host-FE pair happens to be communicating with. So H-FP integration into a new operating system should not be performed casually. A second assumption is that for standard front-endings (a real, large Host shielded from a network by a real, minicomputer FE) the primary role of the FE is to get bits from/to the net to/from the Host. That is, it is considered imprudent to bias the FE too strongly toward its (optional) terminal support ("mini-Host") role. Finally, although we know of no points at which it impacts the specification, it should be acknowledged that the parties to the evolution of the current version of H-FP are all more comfortable with, and probably unconsciously assume, the notion that the FE will turn out to bear a virtual memory operating system. This last is largely a purist's point, but for what it's worth be it noted that integration of H-FP into a new FE operating system environment should be pursued with even more circumspection than a new Host. In summary, then, the note to be taken in regard to containing operating systems is simply one of caution.

CONCLUSION

The real point at issue is that while H-FP can allow offloading some two-thirds of the bulk of a typical "inboard" generic NCP and an as-yet undetermined fraction of the process-level protocol interpreter software, it does not pretend to offer a magic wand that eliminates any and all per-system programming. Indeed, as was noted under attachment strategies, for certain systems the "native" software turns out to make such idiosyncratic assumptions about the physical terminals that will "ever" be used on the system that integrating either an inboard or an outboard generic NCP with "Server Telnet" can be so cumbersome that the expedient of simulating/emulating "known devices" can appear to be the better course. A compensating advantage to the necessity of getting "inside" various Hosts at the system level, though, lies in the fact that once the work has been done for one instance of a given operating system, it is effectively done for all instances of that system (provided, of course, that not too much site-specific alteration of the system has been performed). The moral of all this is that H-FP is believed to offer more for less, but certainly not something for nothing. So be it specifically noted that initial integration of an H-FP module into a "new" operating system is likely to be a delicate design task—but, we believe, a worthwhile one.

CHAPTER 7

Slaying the "TCP-on-a-LAN" Woozle

ABSTRACT

The sometimes-held notion that the DoD Standard Transmission Control Protocol (TCP) and Internet Protocol (IP) are inappropriate for use "on" a Local Area Network (LAN) is shown to be fallacious.

PREFATORY AFTERTHOUGHTS

I was so annoyed over agreeing to change the title of "Slaying the 'TCP-on-a-LAN' Woozle" to merely "'TCP-on-a-LAN'" for the corporate Off-White Paper publication that I even missed the fact that somebody had omitted the quotation marks from the cover page. But I still maintain that Woozles are the perfect metaphor for the paper.

*   *   *

One point that should have been emphasized much more strongly: *Most of the worry over whether TCP was "wrong" for a Local Area Network stems from the utterly inappropriate application of the ISORM n ⟷ n-1 Entities dictum/straitjacket to the ARM, where, of course, it doesn't apply.* Keep your eye peeled for it.

*   *   *

Another point that should have been emphasized much more strongly, perhaps even more so than the previous one: *There's a gigantic difference between a Local Area Network and a Localized Communications Network.* (That one deserves red ink.) Think very hard about it when you come across it. And if you're reasonably astute, you won't even need to be told that if you're only putting in an LCN initially, you'd still be well advised to pick one that phases up cleanly to a LAN when, as it almost invariably happens, you come to realize that you want more than just letting local terminals get at local Hosts. (Oh, yeah: When you do go to a "real" LAN, go back and reread Chapter 6 a couple of times—'cause you'll be ripe to fall into the old Rigid Attachment Trap in your embarrassment over having settled for mere communications originally.)

Speaking of "real" LANs and Rigid Attachment (and/or the Emulation style of Chapter 3), by the way, it's important to realize that the "right" way to come into your Hosts is by way of a virtual terminal protocol. This means that the appropriate L III protocol (and L II and L I protocols below it) must be interpreted on behalf of the terminal *somewhere* (because the PIs in the Host or in its Outboard Processing Environment, in the sense of Chapter 6, expect to be talking to their counterpart PIs). So if it's too expensive to acquire a (generic) Bus Interface Unit for each terminal on your LAN that "comes with," say, User Telnet and TCP/IP, what you should do is use ordinary BIUs for the terminals but have them go directly to (generic) Terminal Support Machines (a.k.a. TIPs, TACs, NTCs, and sometimes mini-Hosts, among other things) on what amounts to a separate terminal net, rather than directly to the Hosts (where you'd need to go in by Rigid Attachment) on "the" net; User Telnet on the TSM talks to Server Telnet on the Host, and everything's clean. Also, if your terminals are actually "intelligent terminals" (a.k.a. workstations) you should be worried about the ability to do a file transfer protocol as well as a virtual terminal protocol and it won't be easy to let the TSM get at the workstation's file system, so what you should do in that case is treat the workstations as if they were Hosts in their own right (and either give them OPEs of their own or spring for implementing the protocol suite "in" them).

(I wouldn't have bothered with that last paragraph if I hadn't been shown so many pictures of putative LANs lately wherein the terminals were depicted as being on the selfsame "net" as the Hosts were. Gee, do you suppose it's related to the characteristic ISORMite obliviousness to integration? Hmmmmmmm. Well, I can't "prove" it, but it's certainly worth dangling here as a parenthetical provocation: maybe ISORMites have a religious prohibition against paying attention to Context. [You wouldn't be thinking that was a foul if you'd spoken to the presenters of the pictures and realized that all they knew was what they'd heard about the ISORM. I have.])

*   *   *

One other point to be emphasized: If you have to use one particular suite of protocols to do internetting (e.g.—and, in my humble but dogmatic opinion, i.e.—the ARMS), it *is* rather wasteful to go to the trouble of maintaining a parallel suite to do localnetting . . . until and unless the Future History of Chapter 2 comes to pass, of course.

*   *   *

As this is written, by the way, there are altogether too many system proprietors in the DoD who haven't grasped any of the three extra-emphasis points here. That bothers me a great deal, even though it does mean I should be able to find gainful employment for years to come—oops! unless, of course, this book is too effective. Ah, well, probably not much chance of *that*.

* * *

Although it doesn't really deserve extra emphasis, the point about header size does bear a slight amount of amplification: If you don't believe me (and Dave Clark) that "bandwidth is free on LANs," consider two things: (1) the ISORM already has at least seven layers, at least five of which have headers, traversing comm subnets, and (2) some of them have sublayers, which also presumably have headers. (If that's too subtle, consider that you're almost certainly going to be carrying more excess baggage bits if you go ISORM Suite than if you go ARM Suite. What a good thing we don't worry about header sizes, eh?)

For that matter, you might also want to give some thought to the fact that all these incredibly Reliable LANs you've been pitched still have to get bits into their reliable clutches through some sort of interface to/from the Hosts—and then give some thought to just how Reliable those interfaces are. (Unfortunately, I'm too lazy to track down a recent rumor that some LANs turn out to be capable of getting into states where they generate lots of undetected errors, but that shouldn't deter you from also thinking about how much you want to bet that your pet LAN "technology" is really all that reliable in any case.)

* * *

If, by the way, you ever run into an ISORMite who tries to convince you that I'm rotten to the core, you can at least offer the following as evidence that I'm not also rotten to the veriest peripheral: I did spring for around $130 (some of it's in pounds sterling, so I can't be precise until I figure out how to get it there) for permissions to quote the material about Woozles here and Heffalumps in Chapter 10 in order to save you the trouble of having to look it up, so I can't be all that bad a guy . . . can I?

THESIS

It is the thesis of this paper that fearing "TCP-on-a-LAN" is a Woozle which needs slaying. To slay the "TCP-on-a-LAN" Woozle, we need to know three things: What's a Woozle? What's a LAN? What's a TCP?

WOOZLES

The first is rather straightforward:

> One fine winter's day when Piglet was brushing away the snow in front of his house, he happened to look up, and there was Winnie-the-Pooh. Pooh was walking round and round in a circle, thinking of something else, and when Piglet called to him, he just went on walking.
> "Hallo!" said Piglet, "what are you doing?"
> "Hunting," said Pooh.
> "Hunting what?"
> "Tracking something," said Winnie-the-Pooh very mysteriously.
> "Tracking what?" said Piglet, coming closer.
> "That's just what I ask myself. I ask myself, What?"
> "What do you think you'll answer?"
> "I shall have to wait until I catch up with it" said Winnie-the-Pooh. "Now look there." He pointed to the ground in front of him. "What do you see there?"
> "Tracks," said Piglet, "Paw-marks." He gave a little squeak of excitement. "Oh, Pooh! Do you think it's a—a—a Woozle?"*

Well, they convince each other that it *is* a Woozle, keep "tracking," convince each other that it's a herd of Hostile Animals, and get duly terrified before Christopher Robin comes along and points out that they were following their own tracks all the long.

In other words, it is our contention that *expressed fears about the consequences of using a particular protocol named "TCP" in a particular environment called a Local Area Net stem from misunderstandings of the protocol and the environment*, not from the technical facts of the situation.

LANs

The second thing we need to know is somewhat less straightforward: A LAN is, properly speaking† a communications mechanism (or subnetwork) employing

---

*A. A. Milne, *Winnie-the-Pooh*. (See Acknowledgments.)

†The LAN description is based on D. D. Clark, et al., "An Introduction to Local Area Networks," *IEEE Proc.*, 66, no. 11 (November 1978), 1497–1517, several year's worth of conversations with Dr. Clark, and the author's observations of both the open literature and the Oral Tradition (which were sufficiently well thought of to have prompted The MITRE Corporation/NBS/NSA Local Nets "Brain Picking Panel" to have solicited his testimony during the year he was in FACC's employ.)

[In all honesty, as far as I know I *started* the rumor that TCP might be overkill for a LAN at that meeting. At the next TCP design meeting, however, they separated IP out from TCP, and everything's been all right for three years now—except for getting the rumor killed. I'd worry about Woozles turning into roosting chickens if it weren't for the facts that: (1) People tend to ignore their local guru; (2) I was trying to encourage the IP separation; and (3) All I ever wanted was some empirical data.]

a transmission technology suitable for relatively short distances (typically a few kilometers) at relatively high bit-per-second rates (typically greater than a few hundred kilobits per second) with relatively low error rates, which exists primarily to enable suitably attached computer systems (or "Hosts") to exchange bits, and secondarily, though not necessarily, to allow terminals of the teletypewriter and CRT classes to exchange bits with Hosts. The Hosts are, at least in principle, heterogeneous; that is, they are not merely multiple instances of the same operating system. The Hosts are assumed to communicate by means of layered protocols in order to achieve what the ARPANET tradition calls "resource sharing" and what the newer ISO tradition calls "Open System Interconnection." Addressing typically can be either Host-Host (point-to-point) or "broadcast." (In some environments, e.g., Ethernet, interesting advantage can be taken of broadcast addressing; in other environments, e.g., LANs which are constituents of ARPA- or ISO-style "internets," broadcast addressing is deemed too expensive to implement throughout the internet as a whole and so may be ignored in the constituent LAN even if available as part of the Host-LAN interface.)

Note that no assumptions are made about the particular transmission medium or the particular topology in play. LAN media can be twisted-pair wires, CATV or other coaxial-type cables, optical fibers, or whatever. However, if the medium is a processor-to-processor bus it is likely that the system in question is going to turn out to "be" a moderately closely coupled distributed processor or a somewhat loosely coupled multiprocessor rather than a LAN, because the processors are unlikely to be using either ARPANET *or* ISO-style layered protocols. (They'll usually either be homogeneous processors interpreting only the protocol necessary to use the transmission medium, or heterogeneous with one emulating the expectations of the other.) Systems like "PDSC" or "NMIC" (the evolutionarily related, bus-oriented, multiple PDP-11 systems in use at the Pacific Data Services Center and the National Military Intelligence Center, respectively), then, aren't LANs.

LAN topolgies can be either "bus," "ring," or "star." That is, a digital PBX can be a LAN, in the sense of furnishing a transmission medium/communications subnetwork for Hosts to do resource sharing/Open System Interconnection over, though it might not present attractive speed or failure mode properties. (It might, though.) Topologically, it would probably be a neutron star.

For our purposes, the significant properties of a LAN are the high bit transmission capacity and the good error properties. Intuitively, a medium with these properties in some sense "shouldn't require a heavy-duty protocol designed for long-haul nets," according to some. (We will not address the issue of "wasted bandwidth due to header sizes. Clark's work cited in the footnote on p. 136, esp. pp. 1509*ff.*, provides ample refutation of that traditional communications notion.) However, it must be borne in mind that for our purposes the assumption of resource-sharing/OSI type protocols between/among the attached Hosts is also extremely significant. That is, if all you're doing is letting some terminals access some different Hosts, but the Hosts don't really have any intercomputer networking protocols between them, what you have should be viewed as a Localized Communications Network (LCN), *not* a LAN in the sense we're talking about here.

TCP

The third thing we have to know can be either straightforward or subtle, depending largely on how aware we are of the context established by ARPANET-style protocols. For the visual-minded, Figures 7-1 and 7-2 might be all that need be "said." Their moral is meant to be that in ARPANET-style layering, *layers aren't monoliths.* For those who need more explanation, here goes: TCP* (we'll take IP later) is a Host-Host protocol (roughly equivalent to the functionality implied by some of ISO Level 5 and all of ISO Level 4). Its most significant

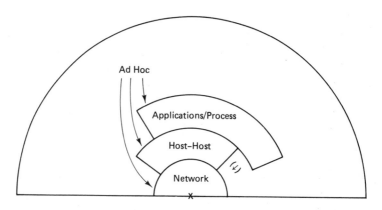

Notes

A. X marks the egress (and the ingress)

B. The whole picture either lives in or is flexibly attached to a Host

C. (↓) indicates it's at least imaginable to use the network layer without/in-lieu-of a Host–Host protocol in some circumstances

D. (And if comm subnet processors are present, there will doubtless be a CSNP-CSNP protocol in play—which is rendered uninteresting for present purposes by Note B.)

Figure 7-1   ARM in the Abstract

*The TCP/IP descriptions are based on J. B. Postel, "Internet Protocol Specification," and "Transmission Control Specification" in *DARPA Internet Program Protocol Specifications*, USC Information Sciences Institute, September, 1981, and on more than 10 years' worth of conversations with Dr. Postel, Dr. Clark (now the DARPA "Internet Architect"), and Dr. Vinton G. Cerf (co-originator of TCP), and on numerous discussions with several other members of the TCP/IP design team, on having edited the referenced documents for the PSTP, and, for that matter, on having been one of the developers of the ARPANET "Reference Model."

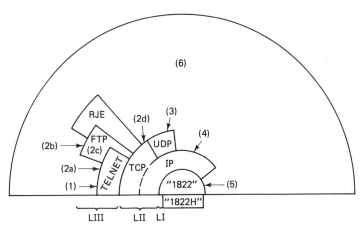

Legend

(1)   Where Terminal–Terminal Protocol would go*

(2a). . . (2d) Where Mail Protocol could go*

(3)   Where muxed packetized speech goes

(4)   Where unmuxed packetized speech could go

(5)   Where you could "pump bits at a peripheral" on a LAN

(6)   Still Ad Hoc Land

·   "1822" for concreteness only (need not be taken literally)

·   RJE not endorsed, merely suggestive of using two PLPs
    in-support-of/doing-virtualization for a third

*Found via well-known socket

Figure 7-2   ARMS, Somewhat Particularized

property is that it presents *reliable* logical connections to protocols above itself. (This point will be returned to subsequently.) Its next most significant property is that it is designed to operate in a "catenet" (also known as the, or an, "internet"); that is, its addressing discipline is such that Hosts attached to communications subnets other than the one a given Host is attached to (the "proximate net") can be communicated with as well as Hosts on the proximate net. Other significant properties are those common to the breed: Host-Host protocols (and Transport protocols) "all" offer mechanisms for Flow Control, Out-of-Band Signals, Logical Connection management, and the like.

Because TCP has a catenet-oriented addressing mechanism (that is, it expresses foreign Host addresses as the "two-dimensional" entity Foreign Net/ Foreign Host because it cannot assume that the Foreign Host is attached to the proximate net), to be a full Host-Host protocol it needs an adjunct to deal with the proximate net. This adjunct, the Internet Protocol (IP) was designed as a separate protocol from TCP, however, in order to allow it to play the same role it plays for TCP for other Host-Host protocols as well.

In order to "deal with the proximate net," IP possesses the following signifcant properties: An IP implementation maps from a virtualization (or common intermediate representation) of generic proximate net qualities (such as precedence, grade of service, security labeling) to the closest equivalent on the proximate net. It determines whether the "Internet Address" of a given transmission is on the proximate net or not; if so, it sends it; if not, it sends it to a "Gateway" (where another IP module resides). That is, IP handles internet *routing*, whereas TCP (or some other Host-Host protocol) handles only internet addressing. Because some proximate nets will accept smaller transmissions ("packets") than others, IP, *qua* protocol, also has a discipline for allowing packets to be fragmented while in the catenet and reassembled at their destination. Finally (for our purposes), IP offers a mechanism to allow the particular protocol it was called by (for a given packet) to be identified so that the receiver can demultiplex transmissions based on IP-level information only. (This is in accordance with the Principle of Layering: You don't want to have to look at the data IP is conveying to find out what to do with it.)

Now that all seems rather complex, even though it omits a number of mechanisms. (For a more complete discussion, see Chapter 5.) But it should be just about enough to slay the Woozle, especially if just one more protocol's most significant property can be snuck in. An underpublicized member of the ARPANET suite of protocols is called UDP—the "User Datagram Protocol." UDP is designed for speed rather than accuracy. That is, it's not "reliable." All there is to UDP, basically, is a mechanism to allow a given packet to be associated with a given logical connection. Not a TCP logical connection, mind you, but a UDP logical connection. So if all you want is the ability to demultiplex data streams from your Host-Host protocol, you use UDP, not TCP. ("You" is usually supposed to be a Packetized Speech protocol, but doesn't have to be.) (And we'll worry about Flow Control some other time.)

TCP-ON-A-LAN

So whether you're a Host proximate to a LAN or not, and even whether your TCP/IP is "inboard" or "outboard" of you, if you're talking to a Host somewhere out there on the catenet, you use IP; and if you're exercising some process-level/applications protocol (roughly equivalent to some of some versions of ISO L5 and all of L6 and L7) that expects TCP/IP as its Host-Host protocol (because it "wants" reliable, flow-controlled, ordered delivery [whoops, forgot that "ordered" property earlier—but it doesn't matter all that much for present purposes] over logical connections which allow it to be addressed via a Well-Known Socket), you use TCP "above" IP regardless of whether the other Host is on your proximate net or not. *But* if your application doesn't require the properties of TCP (say for Packetized Speech), don't use it—regardless of where or what you are. *And* if you want to make the decision about whether you're talking to a proximate Host explicitly and not even go through IP, you can even arrange to do that (though it might make for messy implementation under some circumstances). That is, if you want to take advantage of the properties of your LAN "in the raw" and have or don't need appropriate applications protocols, the Reference Model according to which TCP/IP were designed won't stop you. See Figure 7–2 if you're visual. A word of caution, though: Those applications probably *will* need protocols of some sort—and they'll probably need some sort of Host-Host protocol under them, so unless you relish maintaining "parallel" suites of protocols. . . . that is, you really would be better off with TCP most of the time locally anyway, because you've got to have it to talk to the catenet and it's a nuisance to have "something else" to talk over the LAN—when, of course, what you're talking requires a Host-Host protocol.

We'll touch on "performance" issues in a bit more detail later. At this level, though, one point really does need to be made: On the "reliability" front, many (including the author) at first blush take the TCP checksum to be "overkill" for use on a LAN, which does, after all, typically present extremely good error properties. Interestingly enough, however, metering of TCP implementations on several Host types in the research community shows that the processing time expended on the TCP checksum is only around 12 percent of the per-transmission processing time anyway. So, again, it's not clear that it's worthwhile to bother with an alternate Host-Host protocol for local use (if, that is, you need the rest of the properties of TCP other than "reliability"—and, of course, always assuming you've got a LAN, not an LCN, as distinguished earlier).

Take that, Woozle!

OTHER SIGNIFICANT PROPERTIES

Oh, by the way, one or two other properties of TCP/IP really do bear mention:

1. Protocol interpreters for TCP/IP exist for a dozen or two different operating systems.
2. TCP/IP work, and have been working (though in less refined versions) for several years.
3. IP levies no constraints on the interface protocol presented by the proximate net (though some protocols at that level are more wasteful than others).
4. IP levies no constraints on its users; in particular, any proximate net that offers alternate routing can be taken advantage of (unlike X.25, which appears to preclude alternate routing).
5. IP-bearing Gateways both exist and present and exploit properties 3 and 4.
6. TCP/IP are Department of Defense Standards.
7. Process (or application) protocols compatible with TCP/IP for Virtual Terminal and File Transfer (including "electronic mail") exist and have been implemented on numerous operating systems.

8. "Vendor-style" specifications of TCP/IP are being prepared under the aegis of the DoD Protocol Standards Technical Panel, for those who find the research-community-provided specs not to their liking.

9. The research community has recently reported speeds in excess of 300 kb/s on an 800 kb/s subnet, 1.2 Mb/s on a 3 Mb/s subnet, and 9.2 kbs on a 9.6 kb/s phone line—all using TCP. (We don't know of any numbers for alternative protocol suites, but it's unlikely they'd be appreciably better if they confer like functionality—and they may well be worse if they represent implementations which haven't been around long enough to have been iterated a time or three.)

With the partial exception of property 8, no other resource-sharing protocol suite can make those claims.

Note particularly well that none of these properties should be construed as eliminating the need for extremely careful measurement of TCP/IP performance in/on a LAN. (You do, after all, want to know their limitations, to guide you in when to bother ringing in "local" alternatives—but be very careful because they're hard to measure commensurately with alternative protocols, and most conventional Hosts can't take [or give] as many bits per second as you might imagine.) It merely dramatically refocuses the motivation for doing such measurement. (And levies a constraint or two on how you outboard, if you're outboarding.)

OTHER CONTEXTUAL DATA

Our case could really rest here, but some amplification of the digression on Host capacities is warranted, if only to suggest that some quantification is available to supplement the *a priori* argument: Consider the previously mentioned PDSC. Its local terminals operate in a screen-at-a-time mode, each screen-load comprising some 16 kb. How many screens can one of its Hosts handle in a given second? Well, we're told that each disk fetch requires 17 ms average latency, and each context switch costs around 2 ms, so allowing 1 ms for transmission of the data from the disk and to the "net" (it makes the arithmetic easy), that would add up to 20 ms "processing" time per screen, even if no processing were done to the disk image. Thus, even if the Host were doing *nothing* else, and even if the native disk I/O software were optimized to do 16 kb reads, it could only present 50 screens to its communications mechanism (processor-processor bus) per second. That's 800 kb/s. And *that's* well within the range of TCP-achievable rates (see property 9 on the list). So in a realistic sample environment, it would certainly seem that typical Hosts can't necessarily present so many bits as to overtax the protocols anyway. (The analysis of how many bits typical Hosts can accept is more difficult because it depends more heavily on system internals. However, the point is nearly moot in that even in the intuitively unlikely event that receiving were appreciably faster in principle [unlikely because of typical operating system constraints on address space sizes, the need to do input to a single address space, and the need to share buffers in the address space among several processes], you can't accept more than you can be given.)

CONCLUSION

The sometimes-expressed fear that using TCP on a local net is a bad idea is unfounded.

CHAPTER 8

The Illusion
of Vendor Support

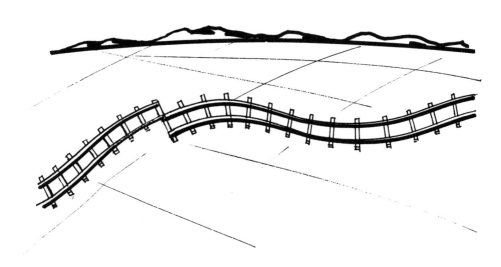

ABSTRACT

The sometimes-held position that "vendor supplied" intercomputer networking protocols based upon the International Standards Organization's Reference Model for Open System Interconnection are worth waiting for, in particular in preference to protocols based upon the ARPANET Reference Model (ARM), is shown to be fallacious.

PREFATORY AFTERTHOUGHTS

The major regret I have about "The Illusion of Vendor Support" is that it's too polite.

* * *

In other words, if you really want to wait a long time for Bad Art, feel free. (Indeed, I encourage you to hold your breath while you're waiting.)

* * *

For more on the "official" relationship between the ISORM and X.25, see the Prefatory Afterthoughts for the next chapter.

* * *

For more on the surprisingly significant, and actually rather subtle, question "Are there parking garages between the high-rises?" see Chapter 2.

* * *

In the spirit of not having to be polite in my own book, I might as well tell you what I said to an acquaintance from, at the time, a presumably major national standards organization, when he suggested that a few modest changes would make X.25 suitable for LAN use at a Local Area Nets conference in '79:

The notion of attempting to take advantage of the close-coupling of a local net environment in order to preserve the X.25 hypothesis is at best a revisiting of those "epicycles" which made medieval astronomy so amusing; at worst, it's on a par with injecting nursing formula at appropriate points on a boar hog's chest in order to pretend to be making use of some artifacts there which otherwise are about as useful as X.25. If *I* had to attach a machine that "came with" vendor-supplied X.25 software to a local net, I'd pay the $2 for the minor surgery and reclaim the buffer space.

I saved it under the heading of "Great Diatribes of Western Man [Number Pending]," but maybe I liked it so much because it was said on my very own birthday.

INTRODUCTION

Even one or two members of the DoD Protocol Standards Technical Panel join with many others (including, apparently, some members of the DoD Protocol Standards Steering Group, and clearly, somebody at the GAO) in expressing a desire to "go with vendor-supported intercomputer networking protocols instead of using our own." The author's view of the implications of this desire should be clear from the title of this paper. What evidence, then, is there to so stigmatize what is clearly a well-meant desire to save the Government money?

SCOPE

First, we must consider what is meant by "vendor-supported protocols." It can't be just X.25, because that only gets you through the network layer whether you're appealing to the International Standards Organization's widely publicized Reference Model for Open System Interconnection (ISORM) or to the unfortunately rather tacit reference model (ARM) to which the ARPANET protocols (e.g., TCP, IP, Telnet, FTP) were designed. It also can't be just X.25 and X.28/X.29 (even with X.75 tossed in to handle "internetting" and X.121 for addressing) because:

1. They don't serve as a protocol suite for resource sharing (also known as OSI), but rather only allow for remote access.*
2. They (coming as they do from the Consultative Committee on International Telegraphy and Telephony—and including one or two other protocols, in reality) don't even constitute the full protocol suite being worked

---

*Chapter 3 attempts to clarify the distinction between "remote access" and "resource sharing" as networking styles.

on by the U.S. National Bureau of Standards, much less the somewhat different suite being evolved by ISO. So it must be a suite from NBS or ISO, and for present purposes we needn't differentiate between them as their Reference Models are close enough to be shorthanded as the ISORM.

TIMELINESS

Realizing that we're being asked to consider an ISORM-related protocol suite as what the vendors are expected to support has one immediate consequence which in some sense can be considered to dominate all of the other points to be raised: That is, the DoD procurement process entails quite long lead times. Yet the ISORM suite is by no means complete at present. Without prejudice to its merits or demerits, only X.25 (as Levels 1–3, and with some ambiguity as to what level X.75 belongs at) is as yet firmly in the ISORM suite (which it will be convenient to refer to as "ISORMS"), and there is even some doubt as to how firmly they're there. (E.g., a British observer at a recent PSTP meeting assured the author that "We in the U.K. don't believe X.25 is officially part of the ISORM.") There are proposals which have been circulating for some time at Level 4, and less far along through the international (or even national, remembering NBS) standardization process, ones at Level(s) 5–7. It must be noted that

1. These are by and large "paper protocols" (that is, they have not been subjected to the test of actual use).
2. Even ISO and NBS's warmest supporters acknowledge that the standardization process "takes years."

So if the DoD is to avoid buying what *might* turn out to be a series of pigs in a series of pokes, it can't wait for the ISORMS.

On the other side of the coin, the DoD is letting intercomputer networking contracts right now. And, right now, there does exist a suite of protocols designed to the ARPANET Reference Model (ARMS, with no pun intended). Implementations of the ARMS already exist for a number of operating systems already in use in the DoD. Now, it is not argued that the ARMS protocols come "for free" in upcoming acquistions (contractors fuss about the style of the available specifications, system maintainers fear incursions of nonvendor supplied code into operating systems, and so on), but it is unarguable that the ARMS can be procured significantly more rapidly than the ISORMS. (It is also unarguable that those who speak of their unwillingness to see the DoD "develop new protocols rather than employ international standards" haven't done their homework; we're not talking about new protocols in the ARMS, we're talking about protocols that have been in real use for years.)

QUALITY OF SUPPORT

The timeliness argument can lead to a counterargument that the ISORMS is "worth waiting for," though, so we're not done yet. Let's look further at what "vendor support" means. Clearly, the proponents of the position expect that vendors' implementations of protocols will be in conformance with the Standards for those protocols. Given the nature of these specifications, though, what can we infer about the quality of support we can expect from the vendors?

There are two problem areas immediately apparent: ambiguities and options. Let's take ambiguities first. The following are some of the questions raised by knowledgeable observers about the present state of the ISORMS:

1. Can an X.25 comm subnet offer alternate routing? (The answer depends on whether "DCEs" are expected to follow X.25 between themselves. The situation is further complicated by the fact that some ISORM advocates don't even include the Data Communication Elements in their depictions of the Model; this leads to the metaphorical question,* "Are there parking garages between the high-rises?") If you can conform to X.25 and not offer alternate routing—which certainly appears to be consistent with the spec, and might even be construed as required by it—the DoD's inherent interest in "survivability" cannot be served by you.

2. Can an X.75 internet offer alternate gatewaying? (The answer is almost surely no, unless the X.75 spec is rewritten.) If not, again the DoD's interest is not served.

3. Does "Expedited Data" have semantics with regard to the L4–L5/L7 interface? (Not as I read the spec, by the way.) If not, the ISORMS lacks the ability to convey an "Out-of-Band-Signal" to an Application protocol. (This leads to the metaphorical question, "What good is an SST if there's nobody on duty at the Customs Shed?")

4. Must all layers be traversed on each transmission? (There are rumors of a new ISORM "null-layer" concept; it's not in the last version I looked at, however, and apparently the answer is yes at present.) If so, the DoD's inherent interest in efficiency/timeliness cannot be served. (This leads to the metaphorical question, "Are there elevators inside the high-rises, or just staircases?")

5. Can an implementation be in conformance with the ISORM and yet flout the prescription that "n-entities must communicate with each other by means of $n-1$ entities"? (Not as I read the spec.) If not, again implementations must be inefficient, because the prescription represents an inappropriate legislation of implementation detail which can only lead to inefficient implementations.

---

*This and other metaphorical questions are dealt with at greater length in Chapter 5.

6. Is each layer one protocol or many? (The point quoted in 5 would seem to imply the latter, but many ISORM advocates claim it's the former except for L1 and L7.) If each layer is a "monolith," the DoD's interest is not served because there are many circumstances in which applications of interest require different L1–3 and L4 protocols in particular, and almost surely different L5 and L6 protocols. (Areas of concern: Packetized Speech, Packet Radio, etc.)

The upshot of these ambituities (and we haven't exhausted the subject) is that different vendors could easily offer ISORMSs in good faith which didn't interoperate "off-the-shelf." Granted, they could almost certainly be fixed, but not cheaply. (It is also interesting to note that a recent ANSI X3T5 meeting decided to vote *against* acceptance of the ISORM *as a standard*—while endorsing it as valuable descriptively—because of that standards committee's realization of just the point we are making here: that requiring contractual compliance with a Reference Model can only be desirable if the Reference Model were articulated with utter—and probably humanly unattainable—precision.)

The area of options is also a source for concern over future interoperability of ISORMS implementations from different vendors. There's no need to go into detail because the broad concern borders on the obvious: What happens when Vendor A's implementations rely on the presence of an optional feature that Vendor B's implementations don't choose to supply? Somebody winds up paying—and it's unlikely to be either Vendor.

On the other side of the coin, the ARMS designers were all colleagues who met together frequently to resolve ambiguities and refine optionality in common. Not that the ARMS protocols are held to be flawless, but they're much further along than the ISORMS.

To conclude this section, then, there are grounds to suspect that the quality of vendor support will be low unless the price of vendor support is high.

NATURE OF THE DESIGN PROCESS

The advantage of having colleagues design protocols leads to another area which gives rise to concern over how valuable vendor-supported protocols really are. Let's consider how international standards are arrived at.

The first problem has to do with just who participates in the international standardization process. The author has occasionally chided two different acquaintances from NBS that they should do something about setting standards for membership on standards committees. The uniform response is to the effect that "They are, after all, *voluntary* standard organizations, and we take what we're given." Just how much significance is properly attached to this insight is problematical. Even the line of argument that runs, "How can you expect those institutions which have votes to send their best technical people to a standards committee? Those are precisely the people they want to keep at home, working away," while enticing, does not, after all, guarantee that standards committees will attract only less-competent technicians. There are even a few Old Network Boys from the ARPANET involved with the ISORM, and at least one at NBS. However, when it is realized that the rule that only active implementers of TCP were allowed on the design team even precluded the present author's attendance (one of the oldest of the Old Network Boys, and the coiner of the phrase, at that), it should be clear that the ARMS enjoys an almost automatic advantage when it comes to technical quality over the ISORMS, without even appealing to the acknowledged-by-most politicization of the international standards arena.

What, though, of the NBS's independent effort? They have access to the experienced designers who evolved the ARMS, don't they? One would think so, but in actual practice the NBS's perception of the political necessities of their situation led one of their representatives at a PSTP (the Department of Defense Protocol Standards Technical Panel) meeting to reply to a reminder that one of the features of their proposed Transport Protocol was a recapitulation of an early ARPANET Horror Story and would consume inordinate amounts of CPU time on participating Hosts only with a statement that "the NBS Transport Protocol has to be acceptable as ECMA [the European Computer Manufacturers Association] Class 4." And even though NBS went to one of the traditional ARPANET-related firms for most of their protocol proposals, curiously enough in all the Features Analyses the author has seen, the features attributed to protocols in the ARMS are almost as likely to be misstated as not.

The conclusion we should draw from all this is not that there's something wrong with the air in Gaithersburg, but rather that there's something bracing in the air that is exhaled by technical people whose different "home systems'" idiosyncracies lead naturally to an intellectual cross-fertilization, on the one hand, and a tacit agreement that "doing it right" takes precedence over "doing it expediently," on the other hand. (If that sounds too corny, the reader should be aware that the author attended a large number of ARPANET protocol design meetings even if he wasn't eligible for TCP; in order to clarify our Host-parochial biases, we screamed at each other a lot, but we got the job done.)

One other aspect of the international standardization process has noteworthy unfortunate implications for the resultant designs. However one might feel on a technical level about the presence of at least seven layers (some seem to be undergoing mitosis and growing "sublayers"), this leads to a real problem at the organizational-psychological level. For each layer gets its own committee, and each committee is vulnerable to Parkinson's Law, and each layer is in danger of becoming an expansionist fiefdom. . . . If your protocol designers are, on the other hand, mainly working system programmers when they're at home— as they tend to be in the ARPANET—they are far less inclined to make their layers their careers. And if experience is weighted heavily—as it usually was in the ARPANET—the same designers tend to be involved with all or most of the protocols in your suite. This not only militates against empire building, it also minimizes misunderstandings over the interfaces between protocols.

"SPACE-TIME" CONSIDERATIONS

At the risk of beating a downed horse, there's one other problem area with the belief that "vendor-supplied protocols will be worth waiting for" which really must be touched on. Let's examine the likely motives of the Vendors with respect to "space-time" considerations. That is, the system programmer designers of the ARMS were highly motivated to keep protocol implementations small and efficient in order to conserve the very resources they were trying to make sharable—the Hosts' CPU cycles and memory locations. Are Vendors similarly motivated?

For some, the reminder that "IBM isn't in business to sell computers, it's in business to sell computer time" (and you can replace the company name with just about any one you want) should suffice. Especially when you realize that it was the traditional answer to the neophyte programmer's query as to how come there were firms making good livings selling Sort-Merge utilities for System X when one came with the operating system (X = 7094 and the Operating system was IBSYS, to date the author).

But that's all somewhat "cynical," even if it's accurate. Is there any evidence in today's world? Well, by their fruits shall you know them:

1. The feature of the NBS Transport Protocol alluded to earlier was an every 15-second "probe" of an open connection ("to be sure the other guy's still there"). In the early days of the ARPANET, one Host elected to have its Host-Host protocol (popularly miscalled "NCP" but more accurately AH-HP, for ARPANET Host-Host Protocol) send an echo ("ECO") command to each other Host each minute. The "Network Daemon" on Multics (the process which fielded AH-HP commands) found its bill tripled as a result. The ECMA-desired protocol would generate four nuisance commands each minute—from every Host you're talking to! (The "M," recall, is for Manufacturers.)*

2. X.25 is meant to be a network interface. Even with all the ambiguities of the ISORM, one would think the "peer" of a "DTE" (Host) X.25 module (or "entity") would be a "DCE" (comm subnet processor) X.25 module. But you can also "talk to" at least the foreign DCE's X.25 and (one believes) even the foreign DTE's; indeed, it's hard to avoid it. Why all these apparently extraneous transmissions? CCITT is a body consisting of the representatives of "the PTTs"—European for state-owned communications monopolies.

3. The ISORM legislates that "n-entities" must communicate through "n-1 entities" Doesn't that make for the needless multiplication of n-1 entities? Won't that require processing more state information than a closed (or even an open) subroutine call within level N? Doesn't anybody there care about Host CPU cycles and memory consumption?

Note particularly well that there is no need to attribute base motives to the

---

*Rumor has it that the probes have since been withdrawn from the spec. Bravo. However, that they were ever in the spec is still extremely disquieting—and how long it took to get them out does not engender confidence that the ISORMS will be "tight" in the next few years.

designers of the ISORMS. Whether they're doing all that sort of thing on purpose or not doesn't matter. What does matter is that their environment doesn't offer positive incentives to design efficient protocols, even if it doesn't offer positive disincentives. (And just to anticipate a likely cheap shot, TCP checksums are necessary to satisfy the design goal of reliability; ECMA four pings a minute is[/was] unconscionable.)

TANSTAAFL

We're very near the end of our analysis. Readers familiar with the above acronym might be tempted to stop now, though there are a few good points to come. For the benefit of those who are not aware: "There Ain't No Such Thing As A Free Lunch." Achieving interoperability among vendor-supplied protocol interpreters won't come for free. For that matter, what with all this "unbundling" stuff, who says even the incompatible ones come for free? You might make up those costs by not having to pay your maintenance programmers to reinsert the ARMS into each new release of the operating system from the vendor, but not only don't good operating systems change all that often, but also you'll be paying out microseconds and memory cells at rates that can easily add up to ordering the next member up in the family. In short, even if the lunch is free, the bread will be stale and the cheese will be moldy, more likely than not. It's also the case that as operating systems have come to evolve, the "networking" code has less and less need to be inserted into the hardcore supervisor or equivalent. That is, the necessary interprocess communication and process creation primitives tend to come with the system now, and device drivers/managers of the user's own devising can often be added as options rather than having to be built in, so the odds are good that it won't be at all hard to keep up with new releases anyway. Furthermore, it turns out that more and more vendors are supplying (or in process of becoming able to supply) TCP/IP anyway, so the whole issue of waiting for vendor support might well soon become moot.

CHAPTER 9

Low Standards:
A Critique of X.25

* -HORSE: DESIGNED BY STANDARDS COMMITTEE

-COMPROMISE BETWEEN DROMEDARY & BACTRIAN FACTION

+ -PLACEHOLDER FOR FUTURE EXPANSIONS

ABSTRACT

The widely touted network interface protocol, "X.25," and its attendant conceptual framework, the International Standards Organization's Reference Model for Open System Interconnection (ISORM), are analyzed and found wanting.

PREFATORY AFTERTHOUGHTS

In fairness to the three or four well-meaning, apparently responsible ISO/OSI advocates who called me up after seeing what was then called simply "A Critique of X.25" (because of the turkeys who complained about the "Low Standards:" part, as griped about earlier) when it was circulated as a separate paper, I feel compelled to begin with the following: .

X.25 IS NOT "OFFICIALLY" PART OF THE ISORM

(until and unless ISO officially says so, which there are rumors will happen when "a few changes" are made to X.25). More accurately, perhaps, the incarnation of X.25 I was talking about wasn't officially part of the ISORM—despite the fact that a number of self-professed ISORM advocates told me (and others) that it was, in public.

More importantly, **X.25 WASN'T ORIGINALLY DESIGNED "TO" THE ISORM**, even if current (1985) efforts to make it "conform" do bear fruit. (I'd even concede that the spec doesn't flat out *say* "DCEs" shouldn't do alternate routing—but it sure encourages that interpretation, what with not having addresses in subsequent-to-the-virtual-call packets, and saying you indicate the virtual circuit has gone away if you get what amounts to an "incomplete transmission.")

* * *

I still don't like it, for the reasons adduced in the paper, and for other reasons which don't seem worth getting worked up over at present, even if I *were* naive enough to think that it would go away if only everybody agreed that it's Bad Art. But I'm not that naive. Honest.

I don't even want to bother to argue too strongly that its roots in Telephony show through all too clearly. Even if I went to the trouble of "proving" it, its advocates would just say they were meant to all the long.

There is, however, one recent development I must take judicial note of: Even though they got 'em somewhat wrong to begin with, that's no justification for *removing* "datagrams"!!! (For those who haven't heard, datagrams are transmission units which contain the target—and usually the source—address in their headers; they're usually presented to a comm subnet without any implicit or explicit agreement that the subnet will get them to their destinations. The idea is that if you care about that sort of thing you'll have a higher-level protocol in play to worry about it, but if you don't you're not burdened by whatever flailing the subnet goes through to attempt to assure delivery.) Just consider: With datagrams out of X.25, the *only* way you can get your bits through a Public Data Net is with *all* the overhead its proprietors choose to load on you. There's no quick and cheap way, really, though some might say the thing they call Fast Connect is a substitute; but it looks to me as if you'd still have to go through all their internal fussing. But *some* users of PDNs might want to do "classical" datagrams because they want their packets to get there in a hurry if at all, for packetized voice, say; and *some* users might want the alternate routing that usually comes with a datagram view; and *some* users might be so concerned with Reliability that they want to assure it with their own heavy-duty algorithms and don't want to pay for you even to bother with your own algorithms . . . so why, oh why, can't there be a "side door"?

Oh, well, I hear it'll all be taken care of in the Integrated Digital Services Network (or maybe it's the Integrated Services . . .).

* * *

I can't resist just one really cheap shot. (After all, how can you say it's an *ad hominem* argument when it's aimed at an institution rather than a person?) Remember that X.25 comes from CCITT, which is made up of "the PTTs," which are Postal, Telephone, and Telegraph state monopolies (of most states except the United ones). Now just consider the following true stories: In 1961, I sent myself a postcard from the main Paris post office to the American Express office a block away, just because I was suspicious about how long other mail was taking. The postcard took a week. (As I recall, there was some reasonable reason to believe that Amex wasn't the culprit.) In 1983, I sent several Par Avion postcards from both the South of France and Paris to friends in the States. The earliest arrival was some three weeks after posting. (I'd remembered the friends' Zip Codes, so I don't think we can blame the USPS for more than one of those weeks.) Moral? Come on, gang, do you *really* want the PTTs "designing" your Intercomputer Networking protocols? I mean, aside from the post offices, the telephone companies are in the act, too!

* * *

OK, OK, that *was* a low blow. However, if you're a serious student of this sort of thing, you really should go to the trouble of looking up Louis Pouzin's critiques of X.25 from a few years back, even if I decide to be spiteful and not give you any citations. And even if you're just a casual reader, you really should join me in doubting the motivations of those ISORMites who try so hard to con people into believing that the ISORM Suite is "nearly here" that for a year or so (half past '81 through half past '82, as I recall) they even had *me* convinced that X.25 "was" L3-1.

* * *

Finally, a bit of Layering theology: I claim that any serious and responsible ISO/OSI advocate who *doesn't* deplore the presence of "DTE"-"DTE" and "DTE"-Remote "DCE" functions in X.25 (that is, functions beyond the necessary Host to Comm Subnet Processor ones) is merely making what he or she thinks of as a necessary gesture of political accommodation. In other words, even though I resisted my friend F. M. Arouet's blandishments to add a cartoon of The Poly-Peer as a parrot perched on a urinal, it *was* tempting . . . because X.25 *is* ill-layered, just like everybody else's first try at an L I protocol I've ever seen, including BBN's. (Note that "first try" phrase particularly well: The popular justification for X.25 is that "we needed some sort of protocol soon so that we could start building products," but I still don't see how that justifies turning it into the biggest game of It's *My* Ball in recent memory—I mean, it wouldn't have been that hard to improve on 1822 if they'd only asked the right people. [That is doubtless somewhat unfair; I do believe some of the right people had a try at convincing the PTTs of how to do it and the PTTs didn't listen. Pity.])

* * *

Never let it be said that I'm totally vicious: A good reference for Louis' stuff is "Virtual circuits vs. datagrams—Technical and political problems" from the 1976 NCC. (But I still assume it's safe to say that it'll never be said that I'm *much* of a Scholar.) Also, the argument that "X.25 nets aren't packet switching" alluded to in Chapter 2 runs as follows: Packet switching means that each packet can go by a different route to the same destination as the last packet headed there went by. If that destination isn't in the packet explicitly, the "only way" you could do packet switching would be if you kept a table relating virtual circuit IDs to final destinations in each CSNP/DCE the packet could end up at. VCs, however, appear to be used only as guides to the next CSNP/DCE to send to "always". So X.25 might be called virtual circuit switching, but it isn't packet switching on the face of it. (I suppose you could cobble the packet switching capability in, but I don't know right offhand of anybody who does.) If that's still a bit cryptic, don't worry about it; it's by no means clear that anybody cares very much if X.25 is or isn't taking advantage of packet switching in the first place. (Gee, I must really be getting soft even to try to tie up all these loose ends.)

INTRODUCTION

According to some sources, the International Standards Organization's (ISO) "Open System Interconnection" (OSI) effort has adopted the International Consultative Committee on Telephony and Telegraphy (CCITT) developed X.25 protocol(s) as its Levels 1–3. ("Loose constructionists" of the ISORM would hold that X.25 is *a* mechanization of L1–L3 rather than *the* mechanization, and at least one British source holds that "we in the U.K. don't believe that ISO have adopted X.25.") In the U.S. Government arena, where the author spends much of his time, the Government Accounting Office (GAO) has suggested that the Department of Defense (DoD) ought to consider adopting "X.25 networks," apparently in preference to networks based on protocols developed by the DoD-sponsored intercomputer networking research community. That intercomputer networking research community in turn has, with a few recent exceptions, adhered to its commitment to the Oral Tradition and not taken up the cudgels against X.25 in the open literature, even though X.25 is an object of considerable scorn in personal communications.

Although the DoD Protocol Standards Technical Panel has begun to evolve a "Reference Model" different from ISO's for reasons which will be touched on below, there seems to be a need to address the deficiencies of X.25 on their own demerits as soon as possible. Without pretending to completeness,* this paper will attempt to do just that.

The overall intent is to deal with X.25 in the abstract; because of who pays the bills, though, a necessary preliminary is to at least sketch the broad reasons why the DoD in particular should not employ intercomputer networks which base their protocol suites on the ISO Reference Model (ISORM) with X.25 as Levels 1–3. (Note that this is a different formulation from "use communications subnetworks which present an X.25 interface.") Very briefly, the DoD has

---

*Various versions of X.25 and ISO documentation were employed; one incompleteness of note, however, is that no attempt has been made to do proper bibliographic citation. Another incompleteness lies in the area of "tutoriality"; that is, appropriate prior knowledge is assumed on the part of the reader. (The author apologizes for the omissions but hasn't the time or the energy to be overly scholarly.)

concerns with "survivability," reliability, security, investment in prior art (i.e., its research community has a working protocol suite in place on many different operating systems), procurability (i.e., ISORM-related protocol *suites* do not as yet fully exist even on paper and the international standardization process is acknowledged even by its advocates to require several years to arrive at full suite specification, much less offer available interoperable implementations), and interoperability with a much wider range of systems than are ever likely to receive vendor-supplied implementations of ISORM protocol suites. Regardless of which particular concerns are considered to dominate, the DoD cannot be expected to await events in the ISO arena. (Particularly striking is the fact that DoD representatives are not even permitted under current doctrine to present their specific concerns in the area of security in the sort of unclassified environment the ISO arena constitutes.)

Some zealous ISORM advocates have suggested that the DoD research community suffers from a "Not Invented Here" syndrome with respect to ISORM-related protocols, though, so even if the various reasons just cited were to prevail, there would still be an open issue at some level. At least one or two zealous members of the research community have asserted that the problem is not Not Invented Here, but Not Invented Right, so an assessment of the apparent keystone of the ISORM suite, X.25, from the perspective of whether it's "good art" ought to be appropriate. That's what we're up to here.

PROBLEMS WITH THE CONCEPTUAL MODEL*

There is confusion even among its advocates as to the real conceptual model of X.25-based ISO networking. Some draw their Reference Model as two "high-rises," others draw "parking garages" beside each high-rise. That is, some draw the seven ISORM layers in large rectangles (representing Hosts) next to one another, showing each layer in communication with its "peer" in the other Host/Open System; this implies an "end-to-end" view of X.25. Others draw smaller rectangles between the larger ones, with Levels 1–3 having peer relationships from the Host-OS ("Data Terminal Equipment") to the Comm Subnet Node ("Data Circuit Terminating Equipment"); this implies a "link-by-link" view of X.25. This ambiguity does not engender confidence in the architects, but perhaps the real problem is with the spectators. Yet it is indisputable that when

---

*Note that we are assuming an ISO-oriented model rather than a CCITT-oriented one (X.25/X.28/X.29) because the latter appears to offer only "remote access" functionality whereas the sort of intercomputer networking we are interested in is concerned with the full "resource-sharing" functionality the former is striving for. This might be somewhat unfair to X.25, in that it is taking the protocol(s) somewhat out of context; however, it is what ISO has done before us, and if what we're really accomplishing is a demonstration that ISO has erred in so doing, so be it. As a matter of fact, it can also be argued that X.25 is itself somewhat unfair—to its users, who are expecting real networking and getting only communication; see Chapter 3 for more on the extremely important topic of resource sharing versus remote access.

internetting with X.75, the model becomes "hop-by-hop" (and it is likely it's meant to be link-by-link even on a single comm subnet).

A major problem with such a model is that the designers have chosen to construe it as requiring them to break the "virtual circuit" it is supposed to be supporting whenever there is difficulty with any one of the links. Thus, if internetting, and on some interpretations even on one's proximate net, rerouting of messages will not occur when needed, and all the upper levels of protocols will have to expend space-time resources on reconstituting their own connections with their counterparts. (Note that the success of the reconstitution under DCE failure appears to assume a certain flexibility in routing which is not guaranteed by the Model.) This can scarcely be deemed sound design practice for an intercomputer networking environment, although many have conjectured that it probably makes sense to telephonists.

Indeed, it appears the virtual circuit metaphor is in some sense being taken almost literally (with the emphasis on the "circuit" aspect), in that what should be an environment that confers the benefits of packet switching is, at the X.25 level, reduced to one with the limitations of circuit switching. On the other hand, the metaphor is not being taken literally enough in some other sense (with the emphasis on the "virtual" aspect), for many construe it to imply that the logical connection it represents is "*only* as strong as a wire." Whether the whole problem stems from the desire to "save bits" by not making addresses explicitly available on a per-transmission basis is conjectural, but if such be the case it is also unfortunate.

(As an aside, it should be noted that there is some evidence that bit saving reaches fetish—if not pathological—proportions in X.25. For instance, there does not even appear to be a Packet Type field in data packets; rather—as best we can determine—for data packets the low-order bit of the "P(R)" field, which overlaps/stands in the place of the Packet Type is always 0, whereas in "real" Packet Type fields it's always 1. [That may, by the way, not even be the way they do it—it's hard to tell . . . or care.])

There is also confusion even among its advocates as to what implications, if any, the protocol(s) has (have) for comm subnet node to comm subnet node (CSN) processing. Those who draw just two high-rises seem to be implying that from their perspective the CSN (or "DCE") is invisible. This might make a certain amount of sense if they did not assert that each floor of a high-rise has a "peer-relationship" with the corresponding floor of the other high-rise—for to do so implies excessively long wires, well beyond the state of the wire-drawing art, when one notices that the first floor is the physical level. (It also appears to disallow the existence of concatenated comm subnets into an internet, or "catenet," unless the CSNs are all identically constituted. And those who hold that the ISORM dictates single protocols at each level will have a hard time making an HDLC interface into a Packet Radio Net, in all probability.)

Those who, on the other hand, "draw parking garages" seem to be dictating that the internal structure of the CSN also adhere to X.25 link and physical protocols. This implies that Packet Radio or satellite CSNs, for example, cannot "be X.25." Now that might be heartening news to the designers of such comm subnets, but it presumably wasn't intended by those who claim universality for X.25—or even for the ISO Reference Model.

Even granting that ambiguities in the conceptual model do not constitute *prima facie* grounds for rejecting the protocol(s), it is important to note that they almost assuredly will lead to vendor implementations based on differing interpretations that will not interoperate properly. And the unambiguous position that virtual circuits are broken whenever X.25 says so constitutes a flaw at least as grave as any of the ambiguities.

Another, and in our view extremely severe, shortcoming of the X.25 conceptual model is that it fails to address how programs that interpret its protocol(s) are to be integrated into their containing operating systems. (This goes beyond the shortcoming of the X.25 specifications in this area, for even the advocates of the ISORM—who, by hypothesis at least, have adopted X.25 for their Levels 1–3—are reticent on the topic in their literature.) Yet, if higher level protocols are to be based on X.25, there must be commonality of integration of X.25 modules with operating systems at least in certain aspects. The most important example that comes to mind is the necessity for "out-of-band signals" to take place. Yet if there is no awareness of that sort of use reflected in the X.25 protocol's specification, implementers need not insert X.25 modules into their operating systems in such a fashion as to let the higher level protocols function properly when/if an X.25 Interrupt packet arrives.

Yet much of the problem with the conceptual model might turn out to stem from our own misunderstandings, or the misunderstandings of others. After all, it's not easy to infer a philosophy from a specification. (Nor, when it comes to recognizing data packets, is it easy even to infer the specification—but it might well say something somewhere on that particular point which we simply overlooked in our desire to get the spec back on the shelf rapidly.) What other aspects of X.25 appear to be "bad art"?

"PERSONALITY PROBLEMS"

When viewed from a functionality perspective, X.25 appears to be rather schizophrenic, in the sense that sometimes it presents a deceptively end-to-end "personality" (indeed, there are many who think it is usable as an integral Host-Host, or Transport, *and* network interface protocol, despite the fact that its specification itself—at least in the CCITT "Fascicle" version—points out several functional omissions where a higher level protocol is expected—and we have even spoken to one or two people who say they actually *do* use it as an end-to-end protocol, regardless); sometimes it presents a comm subnet network interface personality (which all would agree it must); and sometimes (according to some observers) it presents a "Host-Front End Protocol" personality. Not to push the "bad art" metaphor too hard, but this sort of violation of "the Unities" is, if demonstrable, grounds for censure not only to literary critics but also to those who believe in Layering. Let's look at the evidence for the split-personality claim.

X.25 is not (and should not be) an "end-to-end" protocol in the sense of a Transport or Host-to-Host protocol. Yet it has several end-to-end features. These add to the space-time expense of implementation (i.e., consume "core" and CPU cycles) and reflect badly on the skill of its designers if one believes in the design principles of Layering and Least Mechanism. (Some examples of end-to-end mechanisms as superfluous to the network interface role are listed below.) The absence of a datagram mode which is both required and "proper" (e.g., not Flow Controlled, not Delivery Confirmed, not Nondelivery mechanized) may also be taken as evidence that the end-to-end view is very strong in X.25. That is, in ISO Reference Model (ISORM) terms, even though X.25 "is" L1–3, it has delusions of L4-ness; in ARPANET Reference Model (ARM) terms, even though X.25 could "be" L I, it has delusions of L II-ness.*

X.25 is at least meant to specify an interface between a Host (or "DTE") and a comm subnet processor (or "DCE"), regardless of the ambiguity of the conceptual model about whether it constrains the CSNP "on the network side." (Aside: That ambiguity probably reflects even more badly on certain X.25 advocates than it does on the designers, for there is a strong sense in which "of course it can't" is the only appropriate answer to the question of whether it is meant to constrain generic CSN processors (CSNPs) in the general case. Note, though, that it might well be meant to constrain specific DCEs; that is, it started life as a protocol for PTTs—or Postal, Telephone, and Telegraph monopolies—and they are presumably entitled to constrain themselves all they want.) Yet the end-to-end features alluded to above are redundant to the interfacing role, and, as noted, extraneous features have space-time consequences. There are also several features which, though not end-to-end, seem superfluous to a "tight" interface protocol. Further, the reluctance of the designers to incorporate a *proper* "datagram" capability in the protocol (what they've got doesn't seem to be usable as a "pure"—i.e., uncontrolled at L3 but usable without superfluous overhead by L4—datagram, but instead entails delivery confirmation traffic like it or not; note that "seem" is used advisedly: as usual, it's not easy to interpret the Fascicle) suggests at least that they were confused about what higher-level protocols need from interfaces to CSNPs, and at worst that there is some merit to the suggestion that, to paraphrase Louis Pouzin, "the PTTs are just trying to drum up more business for themselves by forcing you to take more service than you need."

Examples of mechanisms superfluous to the interface role:

1. The presence of a DTE-DTE Flow Control mechanism.

*For more on the ARM, see Chapter 5. (Some light may also be cast by the chapter on the earlier-mentioned topic of Who Invented What.)

2. The presence of an "interrupt procedure" involving the remote DTE.

3. The presence of "Call user data" as an end-to-end item (i.e., as "more" than IP's Protocol field).

4. The "D bit" (unless construed strictly as a "RFNM" from the remote DCE).

5. The "Q bit" (which we find nearly incomprehensible, but which is stated to have meaning of some sort to X.29—i.e., to at least violate Layering by having a higher-level protocol depend on a lower level mechanism—and hence can't be strictly a network interface mechanism).

The final "personality problem" of X.25 is that some of its advocates claim it can and should be used as if it were a Host-Front End protocol.* Yet if such use were intended, surely its designers would have offered a means of differentiating between control information destined for the outboard implementation of the relevant protocols and data to be transmitted through X.25, but there is no evidence of such mechanisms in the protocol. "Borrowing" a Packet Type id for H-FP would be risky, as the spec is subject to arbitrary alteration. Using some fictitious DTE address to indicate the proximate DCE is also risky, for the same reason. Further, using "Call user data" to "talk to" the counterpart H-FP module allows only 15 octets (plus, presumably, the 6 spare bits in the 16th octet) for the conversation, whereas various TCP and IP options might require many more octets than that. Granted that with sufficient ingenuity—or even by the simple expedient of conveying the entire H-FP as data (i.e., using X.25 only to get channels to demultiplex on, and DTE-DCE flow control, with the "DCE" actually being an Outboard Processing Environment that gets its commands in the data fields of X.25 data packets)—X.25 might be used to "get at" outboard protocol interpreters, but its failure to address the issue explicitly again reflects badly on its designers' grasp of intercomputer networking issues. (Another possibility is that the whole H-FP notion stems from the use of X.25 as a Host-Host protocol so that some might think of it in its Host aspect as "simply" a way of getting at the H-HP. This interpretation does give rise to the interesting observation that DCEs seem to need a protocol as strong as TCP amongst

---

*That is, as a distributed processing mechanism which allows Host operating systems to be relieved of the burden of interpreting higher level protocols "inboard" of themselves by virtue of allowing Host processes to manipulate "outboard" interpreters of the protocols on their behalf. Note that the outboarding may be to a separate Front-End processor or to the CSNP itself. (The latter is likely to be found in microprocessor-based LAN "BIUs.") Note also that when dealing with "process-level" protocols (ARM L III; approximately ISORM L5-7), only part of the functionality is outboarded (e.g., there must be some Host-resident code to interface with the native File System for a File Transfer Protocol) and even when outboarding Host-Host protocols (ARM L II; approximately ISORM L4 plus some of 5) the association of logical connections (or "sockets") with processes must be performed inboard—which is why, by the way, it's annoying to find ISO L5 below ISO L6; for instance, if you'd like to outboard "Presentation" functionality, you find its protocol expects to interact with the "Session" protocol, the functionality of which can't be outboarded. (Although this is not the proper context for a full treatment of the H-FP approach, it is also of interest that the approach can effectively insulate the Host from changes in the protocol suite, which can be a major advantage in some environments.) See also Chapter 6.

themselves, but doesn't strike the author as particularly convincing evidence for viewing X.25 as anything like a proper H-FP—if for no other reason than that a central premise of Outboard Processing is that the Host-side H-FP module must be compact relative to an inboard generic Network Control Program.)

X.25, then, *is* rather schizophrenic: It exceeds its brief as an interface protocol by pretending to be end-to-end (Host-Host) in some respects; it is by no means a *full* end-to-end protocol (its spec very properly insists on that point on several occasions); it's at once too full and too shallow to be a good interface; and it's poorly structured to be treated as if it were "just" an H-FP. (Some would phrase the foregoing as "It's extremely ill layered"; we wouldn't argue.)

A NOTE ON "GATEWAYS"*

Although it was at least implied in the discussion of conceptual model problems, one aspect of X.25/X.75 internetting is sufficiently significant to deserve a section of its own: Not only does the link-by-link approach taken by CCITT make it unlikely that alternate routing can take place, but it is also the case that ARPANET Internet Protocol (IP) based internetting not only permits alternate routing but also *could alt-route over an "X.25 Subnet."* That is, in IP's conceptual model, Gateways attach to two or more comm subnets "as if they (the Gateways) were Hosts." This means that they interpret the appropriate Host-comm subnet processor protocol of whatever comm subnets they're attached to, giving as the "proximate net address" of a given transmission either the ultimate (internet addressed) destination or the address of another Gateway "in the right direction." And an implementation of IP can certainly employ an implementation of ("DTE") X.25 to get a proximate net, so . . . at least "in an emergency" X.25 interface presenting Public Data Networks can indeed carry IP traffic. (Note also that only the proximate net's header has to be readable by the nodal processor of/on the proximate net, so if some appropriate steps were taken to render the data portion of such transmissions unintelligible to the nodal processors, so much the better.)

(Further evidence that X.75 internetting is undesirable is found in the fact that the U.S. National Bureau of Standards has, despite its nominal adoption of the ISORM, inserted IP at approximately L3.5 in its version of the Reference Model.)

THE OFF-BLUE BLANKET

Although touched on earlier, and not treatable at much length in the present context, the topic of security deserves separate mention. We are familiar with

---

*This section was added to address the ill-founded concerns of several ISORMites that "TCP/IP won't let you use Public Data Nets in emergencies."

one reference in the open literature* which appears to make a rather striking point about the utility of X.25 in a secure network. Dr. Kent's point that the very field sizes of X.25 are not acceptable from the point of view of encryption devices would, if correct (and we are neither competent to assess that, nor in a position to, even if we were), almost disqualify X.25 a priori for use in many arenas. Clearly, uncertified "DCEs" cannot be permitted to read classified (or even "private") data and so must be "encrypted around," after all.

It would probably be the case, if we understand Dr. Kent's point, that X.25 could be changed appropriately—if its specifiers were willing to go along. But this is only one problem out of a potentially large number of problems, and, returning briefly to our concern with the interplay of X.25 and the DoD, those persons in the DoD who know best what the problems are and/or could be are debarred from discussing them with the specifiers of X.25. Perhaps a sufficiently zealous ISORM advocate would be willing to suggest that Professor Kuo's publisher be subsidized to come out with a new edition whenever a problem arises so that if Dr. Kent happens to spot it advantage can continue to be taken of his ability to write for the open literature—but we certainly hope and trust that no ISORMite would be so tone-deaf as to fail to recognize the facetiousness of that suggestion.

In short, it appears to be difficult to dispute the assertion that whatever sort of security blanket X.25 could represent would at best be an off shade of blue.

SPACE-TIME CONSIDERATIONS

Another topic touched on earlier which deserves separate mention, if only to collect the scattered data in a single section, is that of what have been called space-time considerations. That is, we are concerned about how well X.25 in particular and the ISORM-derived protocols in general will implement, both in terms of size of protocol interpreters (PIs) and in terms of execution and delay times.

On the space heading, certainly the fact that X.25 offers more functionality in its end-to-end guise than is required to fulfill its network interface role suggests that X.25 PIs will be bigger than they need be. As an aside—but a striking one—it should be noted that X.25's end-to-end functions are at variance with the ISORM itself, for the "peer entity" of a DTE X.25 entity must surely be the local DCE X.25. Perhaps a later version of the ISORM will introduce the polypeer and give rise to a whole new round of Layering-Theologic controversy.† Speaking of the ISORM itself, those who hold that each layer must be traversed on each transmission are implicitly requiring that space (and time) be expended in the Session and Presentation Levels even for applications that have no need of

---

*S. T. Kent, "Security in Computer Networks," in F. Kuo, ed., *Protocols and Techniques for Data Communication Networks* (Englewood Cliffs, NJ: Prentice-Hall, 1981), pp. 369–432.

†And perhaps now we know why some just draw the high-rises.

their services. The Well-Known Socket concept of the ARM's primary Host-Host protocol, the Transmission Control Protocol (TCP), lets Session functionality be avoided for many applications, on the other hand—unless ISORM L5 is to usurp the Host's user identification/authentication role at some point. (Yes, we've heard the rumors that "null layers" might be introduced into the ISORM; no, we don't want to get into the theology of that either.)

On the time heading, X.25's virtual circuit view can be debilitating—or even crippling—to applications such as Packetized Speech where prompt delivery is preferred over ordered or even reliable delivery. (Some hold that the X.25 datagram option will remedy that; others hold that it's not "really datagrams"; we note the concern, agree with the others, and pass on.) Speaking of reliable delivery, as noted earlier some observers hold that in order to present an acceptable virtual circuit X.25 must have a protocol as strong as TCP "beneath" itself; again, we're in sympathy with them. Shifting focus again to the ISORM itself, it must be noted that the principle that "n-entities" must communicate with one another via "n-1 entities" even in the same Host is an over-zealous application of the Principle of Layering that must consume more time in the interpreting of the n-1 protocol than would a direct interface between n-level PIs or such process-level protocols as FTP and Telnet, as is done in the ARPANET-derived model.

Other space-time deficiencies could be adduced, but perhaps a shortcut will suffice. There is a Law of Programming (attributed to Sutherland) to the effect that "Programs are like waffles: you should always throw the first one out." Its relevance should become clear when it is realized that (with the possible exception of X.25) ISORM PIs are in general either first implementations or not even implemented yet (thus, the batter, as it were, is still being mixed). Contrast this with the iterations the ARPANET-derived PIs—and, for that matter, protocols—have gone through over the years and the grounds for our concern over X.25/ISORM space-time inefficiency become clear irrespective of corroborative detail. Factor in the consideration that space-time efficiency may be viewed as contrary to the corporate interests of the progenitors of X.25 ("the PTTs") and at least the current favorite for ISORM Level 4 (ECMA—the European Computer Manufacturers' Association), and it should become clear why we insist that space-time considerations be given separate mention even though touched upon elsewhere.*

GETTING PHYSICAL

Still another area of concern over X.25 is that it dictates only one means of attaching a "DTE" to a "DCE." That is, earlier references to "the X.25 protocol(s)" were not typographical errors. Most of the time, "X.25" refers to ISORM Level 3; actually, though, the term subsumes L2 and L1 as well. Indeed, the lowest

---

*The broad issue of design team composition is amplified in Chapter 8.

levels constitute particular bit serial interfaces. This is all very well for interfacing to "Public Data Nets" (again, it must be recalled that X.25's roots are in CCITT), but is scarcely appropriate to environments where the communications sub-network may consist of geosynchronous communications satellite channels, "Packet Radios," or whatever. Indeed, even for conventional Local Area Net-works it is often the case that a Direct Memory Access arrangement is desired so as to avoid bottlenecking—but DMA isn't HDLC, and the "vendor supported X.25 interface" so prized by some won't be DMA either, one imagines. (Speaking of LANs, at least the evolving standard in that arena—"IEEE 802"—apparently will offer multiple physical interfaces depending on comm subnet style [although there is some disagreement on this point amongst readers of their draft specs]; we understand, however, that their Level 2 shares X.25's end-end aspirations—and we haven't checked up on DMA capability.) X.25, then, imposes constraints upon its users with regard to interface techology that are inappropriate.

OTHER OBSERVERS' CONCERNS

This paper owes much to conversations with a number of people, although the interpretations of their concerns are the author's responsibility. Mention should be made, however, of a few recent documents in the area: The Defense Communications Agency (DCA Code J110) has sent a coordinated DoD position* to NBS holding that X.25 cannot be the DoD's sole network interface standard; Dr. Vinton Cerf of the ARPA Information Processing Techniques Office made a contribution to the former which contains a particularly lucid exposition of the desirability of proper "datagram" capability in DoD comm subnets†; Mr. Ray McFarland of the DoD Computer Security Evaluation Center has also explored the limitations of X.25.‡ Whether because these authors are inherently more tactful than the present author, or whether their positions are more constraining, or even whether they have been more insulated from and hence less provoked by uninformed ISORMite zealots, none has seen fit to address the "quality" of X.25. That this paper chooses to do so may be attributed to any one of a number of reasons, but the author believes the key reason is contained in the following:

CONCLUSION

X.25 is not a good thing.

---

*Letter to NBS from P. S. Selvaggi, Chief, Interoperability and Standards Office, 7 April 1982.

†V. G. Cerf, "Draft DoD Position Regarding X.25" in undated letter to P. S. Selvaggi.

‡Personal communications.

CHAPTER 10

Gateways,
Architectures,
and Heffalumps

ABSTRACT

The growth of autonomous intercomputer networks has led to a desire on the part of their respective proprietors to "gateway" from one to the other. Unfortunately, however, the implications and shortcomings of gateways which must translate or map between differing protocol suites are not widely understood. Some protocol sets have such severe functionality mismatches that proper T/MGs cannot be generated for them; all attempts to mesh heterogeneous suites are subject to numerous problems, including the introduction of "singularity points" on logical connections which would otherwise be able to enjoy the advantages of communications subnetwork alternate routing, loss of functionality, difficulty of Flow Control resolution, higher cost than nontranslating/mapping Gateways, and the necessity of recreating T/MGs when a given suite changes. The preferability of a protocol-compatible internet is also touched upon, as is the psychology of those soi-disant architects who posit T/MGs.

PREFATORY AFTERTHOUGHTS

If the truth be known, I have even fewer regrets about the Heffalumps metaphor than I did about the Woozles one. The fact of the matter is that it *is* the only explanation that makes sense to me for the phenomenon in question. But I don't want to spoil the surprise, so I won't say much more about the metaphor here. (Some readers—certainly any ISORMites who have gotten this far, and maybe others—will probably be amused to learn that I got to keep the title because the paper had been submitted to a conference by the time the Old Poops found out what it was called, but the conference I submitted it to, primarily because a former officemate was the chairman and had asked me to send them something, rejected it. I hope it doesn't spoil their amusement to learn that I thought it was hilarious, myself: the reviewers simply didn't get the joke. One of them even wondered where the bibliography was! Another marked up the copy very comprehensively, shortening sentences and putting in subsection headings. Oh, well, if you've gotten this far yourself you've probably figured out that another of the many things I don't do is Journalese. Matter of fact, I wanted a linen dustjacket for the book . . . for do-it-yourself handkerchiefing, naturally.)

*   *   *

A point which deserves stronger emphasis than it got amidst all the fun I was having with the premise is the "Janus Host" notion. That is, if you *have to* "interoperate" between dissimilar protocol suites, the best bet at present really does seem to be to take a system that implements each suite properly and make the splice via applications programs, which can interrogate human users for addresses if necessary or otherwise acquire the information that isn't available in the given native suite, calling on the appropriate "Server" protocols on the "other side" by going up through the other side's suite in the fashion normal to it (including its own "User" protocols). That might be a little obscure until you've read the paper, but at least it should get you thinking. As a matter of fact, though perhaps even more obscure, the nice thing about a Janus Host is that it properly terminates each protocol suite, rather than attempting to "concatenate virtual circuits" as some blithely assume Translating/Mapping Gateways can do. Janus Hosts might get rather messy for functions other than virtual terminal, though, and are likely to be fairly slow, and still constitute the "singularity points" mentioned in the paper—and I don't think anyone would accuse 'em of being elegant. . . .

Actually, a better solution, in my view at any rate, to the Interoperability Problem can be found in the Future History section of Chapter 2.

*   *   *

Speaking of Chapter 2, after the little learning Expotition I told you about early in it, I became even more strongly convinced than I had been that casually assuming you can achieve interoperability by some magical thing (mis)called a Gateway is even less well-advised than casually assuming that the ISORM or X.25 is a Good Thing just because you saw an article or two about it in *Dataworld* or *Computermation*. I mean, it was a *major* manufacturer, and when they find out how hard it's going to be to live up to their promise that they'll achieve interoperability via Gateways their corporate face is going to be awfully egg-covered, even if it doesn't actually get red (either because they have no shame or because it's not their color). Indeed, one of my friends told me when I got back that it was a jolly good thing I was only down there to learn, because they didn't deserve my help to begin with—which, if it proves nothing else, at least proves that I'm not the snottiest person *I* know.

*   *   *

By the way, let the record show that I'm **not** saying that building "Translating/Mapping Gateways" is never **possible** . . . just that in my view it comes within epsilon of never being *desirable*. (In a funny way, this chapter really ought to be attractive to the ISORMites, even though I doubt it will be: "OSI" is, after all, clearly a protocol-compatible sort of thing, too. But if I'm *for* protocol compatibility I imagine the ISORMites will think they have to be agin' it. ISORM<u>ists</u>, however, will probably understand—and might even admit it, if pressed.) And anybody who says what he or she meant all the long was a Janus Host apparently overlooked the stuff about going into the IMP and making it withhold RFNMs in the proposal—and didn't hear the pious chitchat about "Concatenating logical connections". . . .

In our collective zeal to remain (or become) abreast of the State of the Art, we sometimes fall into one or the other (or both) of a couple of pitfalls. Only one of these pitfalls is particularly well-known: "Buzzwords"—and even here merely knowing the name doesn't necessarily effect a spontaneous solution. The other deserves more attention: inadequate familiarity with The Relevant Literature.

The key is the notion of what's really relevant. Often, it's the Oral Tradition that matters; published papers, in their attempts to seem scholarly, offer the wrong levels of abstraction or, because of the backgrounds of their authors, are so ill-written as to fail to communicate well. Sometimes, however, that which is truly relevant turns out to be unfindable by a conventional literature searcher because it isn't "in" the field of search.

I wandered into an instructive case in point recently, when it took me over an hour to convince a neophyte to the mysteries of intercomputer networking (who is quite highly regarded in at least one other area of computer science, and is by no means a dummy) that a particular Local Area Network architecture proposal which casually appealed to the notion of "gatewaying" to three or four other networks it didn't have protocols in common with was a Very Bad Thing. "Gateways" is, of course, another one of those bloody buzzwords, and in some contexts it might have been enough just to so label it. But this was a conversation with a bright professional who'd recently been reading up on networks and who wanted really to understand what was so terrible.

So I started by appealing to the Oral Tradition, pointing out that in the ARPA internetworking research community (from which we probably got the term "Gateway" in the first place—and from which we certainly get the proof of concept for internets) it had been explicitly decided that it would be too hard to deal with connecting autonomous networks whose protocol sets differed "above" the level of Host-to-Communications-Subnetwork-Processor protocol. That is,

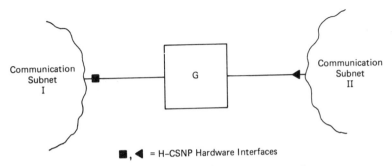

■, ◀ = H–CSNP Hardware Interfaces

Figure 10-1 Defining Characteristic of All Flavors of Gateway

the kind of Gateway we know how to build—and, indeed, anything one might call a Gateway—attaches to two (or more) comm subnets as if it were a Host on each, by appropriately interpreting their respective H-CSNP protocols and doing the right things in hardware (see Figure 10-1), but for ARPA Internet Gateways each net attached to is assumed to have *the same* Host-Host Protocol (TCP/IP, in fact—or, anyway, IP and either TCP or some other common-to-both-nets protocol above it), and *the same* process level protocols (e.g., Telnet, FTP, or whatever). The reason for this assuming of protocol set homogeneity is that they "knew" the alternative was undesirable, because it would involve the translation or mapping between different protocol sets in the Gateways and such T/MGs were obviously to be avoided.

Well, that didn't do the trick. "*Why* is a T/MG a Bad Thing?" he wanted to know. "Because of the possibility of irreconcilable mismatches in functionality." "For instance?" "Addressing is the most commonly cited." "Addressing?"

Assuming the reader is as bored as I am with the dialogue bit, I'll try to step through some specifics of the sorts of incompatibility one can find between protocol sets in a less theatric manner. *Note that the premise of it all is that we don't want to change either preexisting protocol set.* Let's assume for convenience that we are trying to attach just two nets together with a T/MG, and further assume that one of the nets uses the original ARPANET "NCP"—which consists, strictly speaking, of the unnamed original ARPANET Host-Host Protocol and the unfortunately named "1822," or ARPANET Host-IMP Protocol—and the other uses TCP/IP.

Host addressing is the most significant problem. NCP-using hosts have "one-dimensional" addresses. That is, there's a field in the Host-IMP "leader" where the Host number goes. When you've assigned all the available values in that field, your net is full until and unless you go back and change all the IMPs and NCPs to deal with a bigger field. Using IP, on the other hand, addresses of Hosts are "two-dimensional." That is, there's an IP header field in which to designate the foreign *network* and another field in which to designate the foreign Host. (The foregoing is a deliberate oversimplification, by the way.) So if you wanted a Host on an NCP-based net to communicate with a Host on another,

TCP-based net you'd have a terrible time of it if you also didn't want to go mucking around inside of all the different NCP implementations, because you don't have a way of expressing the foreign address within your current complement of addressing mechanisms.

There are various tricks available, of course. You could find enough spare bits in the Host-IMP leader or Host-Host header perhaps, and put the needed internet address there. Or you could change the Initial Connection Protocol, or even make the internet address be the first thing transmitted as "data" by the User side of each process-level protocol. The common failing of all such ploys is that you're changing the preexisting protocols, though, and if that sort of thing were viewed with equanimity by system proprietors you might as well go the whole hog and change over to the new protocol set across the board. Granted, that's a big jump; but it must be realized that this is just the first of several problems.

(It *is* the case that you could get around the addressing problem by having the T/MG become more nearly a real Host and terminate the NCP-based side in an application program which would "ask" the user what foreign Host he wants to talk to on the TCP-based side—at least for Telnet connections. When there's no user around, though, as would be the case in most file transfers, you lose again, unless you fiddle your FTP. In general, this sort of "Janus Host"—after the Roman deity with two faces, who was according to some sources the god of gateways (!)—confers extremely limited functionality anyway; but in some practical cases it can be better than trying for full functionality and coming up empty.)

Then there's the question of what to do about RFNMs. That is, NCPs follow the discipline of waiting until the foreign IMP indicates a Ready for Next Message state exists before sending more data on a given logical connection, but if you're talking to a T/MG, *its* IMP is the one you'll get the RFNM from (the real foreign Host might not even be attached to an IMP). Now, I've actually seen a proposal that suggested solving this problem by altering the T/MG's IMP to withhold RFNMs, but that doesn't make me think it's a viable solution. At the very least, the T/MG is going to have to go in for buffering in a big way (see Figure 10–2). In a possible worst case, the foreign net might not even let you know your last transmission got through without changing *its* protocols.

Going beyond the NCP-TCP example, a generic topic fraught with the

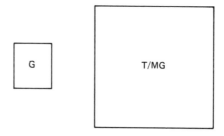

Figure 10-2   Gateway and Translating/Mapping Gateway, Approximately to Scale

peril of functionality mismatch is that of the Out-of-Band Signal. (There are some who claim it's also an NCP-TCP problem.) The point is that although "any good Host-Host protocol" should have *some* means of communicating aside from normal messages "on" logical connections, the mechanizations and indeed the semantics of such Out-of-Band Signals often differ. The fear is that the differences may lead to incompatibilities. For example, in NCP the OOBS is an Interrupt command "on" the control link, whereas in TCP it's an Urgent bit in the header of a message "on" the socket. If you want Urgent to be usable in order to have a "virtual quit button," the semantics of the protocol must make it very clear that Urgent is not merely the sort of thing the NBS/ECMA Host-Host protocol calls "Expedited Data". That is, if the intent of the mechanism is to cause the associated process/job/task to take special action rather than merely the associated protocol interpreter (which need not be part of the process), you'd better say so—and none of the ISO-derived protocols I've seen yet does so. And there's not much a T/MG can do if it gets an NCP Interrupt on a control link, notices a Telnet Interrupt Process control code on the associated socket, and doesn't have anything other than Expediting Data to do with it on its other side. (Expedited Data, it may be noted, bears a striking resemblance to taking an SST across the Atlantic, only to find no one on duty in the Customs shed—and the door locked from the other side.)

Functionality mismatch is not, of course, limited to Host-Host protocols. Indeed, the following interesting situation was observed at University College London: In their "Terminal Gateway," which translates/maps ARPANET Telnet and "Triple X" (CCITT X.25, X.28, X.29), they were able to get data across, as might be expected, but only *one* option (echoing), which is rather worse than might be expected. (And the UCL people are quite competent, so the problem almost certainly doesn't have to do with inadequate ingenuity.)

It could be argued that the real problem with Expedite Data and Triple X is that some protocol sets are a lot worse than others. I wouldn't dispute that. But it's still the case, to reuse a Great Network One-liner, that

> *sometimes, when you try to turn an apple*
> *into an orange, you get back a lemon.*

Nor is the likelihood of encountering irresolvable functionality mismatches the only technical shortcoming of Translating/Mapping Gateways. A somewhat subtle but rather fascinating point arises if we ask what happens when traffic is heavy enough to warrant more than one T/MG between a given pair of protocol-incompatible nets (or even if we'd like to add some reliability, regardless of traffic). What happens, if we think about it a little, is a big problem. Suppose you actually could figure out a way to translate/map between two given sets of protocols. That would mean that for each logical connection you had open, you'd have a wealth of state information about it for each net you were gatewaying. But "you" now stand revealed as a *single* T/MG—and your clone next door doesn't have that state information, so any logical connection that started its life with you has to spend its life with you, in a state of perpetual monogamy, as it were. Naturally, this epoxied pair-bonding could perhaps be dealt with by still another new protocol between T/MGs, but it's abundantly clear that there will be no easy analogue to no-fault-divorce. That is, to put it less metaphorically, it becomes at best extremely complex to do translating/mapping at more than one T/MG for the same logical connection. As with the broader issue of reconciling given protocol sets at all, doing so at multiple loci of control may or may not turn out to be feasible in practice and certainly will be a delicate and complex design task.

One more NCP/TCP problem: When sending mail on an NCP-based net, the mail (actually, File Transfer) protocol currently uses only the addressee's name, because the Host was determined by the Host-Host Protocol. If you're trying to get mail from an NCP-based net to a TCP-based net, though, you're back in the Host addressing bind already discussed. If you don't want to change NCP (which, after all, is being phased out), you have to do something at the process level. You can, but the "Simple Mail Transfer Protocol" to do it takes 62 pages to specify in ARPANET Request for Comments 788.

If things get that complicated when going from NCP to TCP, where there's a close evolutionary link between the Host-Host protocols, and the process-level protocols are nominally the same, what happens when you want to go from DECNET, or from SNA, or from the as-yet incomplete NBS or ISO protocol sets? There may or may not turn out to be any aspects that no amount of ingenuity can reconcile, but it's abundantly clear that Translating/Mapping Gateways are going to have to be far more powerful systems than IP Gateways (which are what you use if both nets use the same protocol sets above the Host to Comm Subnet Processor protocol). And you're going to need a *different* T/MG for *each pair* of protocol sets. And you may have to tinker with CSNP internals. . . . An analogy to the kids' game of Telephone (or Gossip) comes to mind: How much do you lose each time you whisper to your neighbor who in turn whispers to the next neighbor? What, for that matter, if we transplant the game to the United Nations and have the whisperers be translators who have speakers of different languages on each side?

Other problem areas could be adduced. For example, it's clear that interpreting two protocol sets rather than one would take more time, even if it could be done. Also, it should be noted that the RFNMs Problem generalizes into a concern over resolving Flow Control mismatches for any pair of protocol sets, and could lead to the necessity of having more memory for buffers on the T/MG than on any given Host even for those cases where it's feasible in principle. But only one other problem area seems particularly major, and that is the old Moving Target bugaboo: For when any protocol changes, so must *all* the T/MGs involving it, and as there have already been three versions of SNA, presumably a like number of versions of DECNET, and as there are at least two additional levels which ISO should be acknowledging the existence of, the fear of having to redo T/MGs should serve as a considerable deterrent to doing them in the first

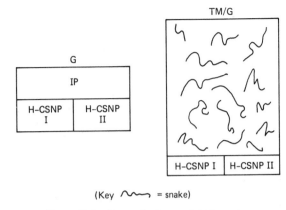

(Key ⌇⌇⌇ = snake)

Figure 10-3   Respective Internals Schematics

place. (This apparent contravention of the Padlipsky's Law to the effect that Implemented Protocols Have Barely Finite Inertia Of Rest is explained by a brand-new Padlipsky's Law: To The Technologically Naive, Change Equals Progress; To Vendors, Change Equals Profit.)

At any rate, it's just not clear that a given Translating/Mapping Gateway can even be built; you have to look very closely at the protocol sets in question to determine even that. It's abundantly clear that if a given one can be built it won't be easy to do (see Figure 10–3). Yet "system architect" after "system architect," apparently in good faith, toss such things into their block diagrams. Assuming that the architectural issue isn't resolved by a fondness for the Gothic in preference to the more modern view that form should follow function, let's pause briefly to visualize an immense, turreted, crenellated, gargoyled . . . microprocessor, and return to the question of why this sort of thing happens.

It's clear that buzzwording is a factor. After all, "system architects" in our context are usually employees of contractors and their real role in life is not to build more stately mansions but to get contracts, so it's not surprising to find appeal to the sort of salesmanship that relies more heavily on fast patter than on precision. Another good analogy: I once went to one of the big chain electronics stores in response to an ad for a cassette recorder that "ran on batteries or house current" for $18, only to find that they wanted an additional $9 for the (outboard) AC adaptor. Given the complexities of T/MGs, however, in our case it's more like an $18 recorder and a $36 adaptor.

But is buzzwording all there is? Clearly not, for as mentioned earlier there's also ignorance of the Oral Tradition in play. Whether the ignorance is willful or not is probably better left unexamined, but if we're willing to entertain the notion that it's not all a bait-and-switch job akin to the separately priced AC adaptor, we see that those who casually propose T/MGs haven't done enough homework as to the real state of the art.

What ever became of that early reference to The Relevant Literature, though? Surely you didn't think I'd never ask. The answers are both implied in the assertion that:

Gateways are Heffalumps

as you'll plainly see once you've been reminded of what Heffalumps are. Dipping into The Relevant Literature, then, let's reproduce the opening of the Heffalumps story:

> *One day, when Christopher Robin and Winnie-the-Pooh and Piglet were all talking together, Christopher Robin finished the mouthful he was eating and said carelessly: "I saw a Heffalump to-day, Piglet."*
> *"What was it doing?" asked Piglet.*
> *"Just lumping along." said Christopher Robin. "I don't think it saw me."*
> *"I saw one once," said Piglet. "At least, I think I did," he said. "Only perhaps it wasn't."*
> *"So did I," said Pooh, wondering what a Heffalump was like.*
> *"You don't often see them," said Christopher Robin carelessly.*
> *"Not now," said Piglet.*
> *"Not at this time of year," said Pooh.*
> *Then they all talked about something else, until it was time for Pooh and Piglet to go home together.*

(To satisfy the lazy reader—who'd actually be better off searching for it in both—it's from *Winnie-the-Pooh*, not *The House at Pooh Corner*.)

Pooh, in case you still don't recall, decides to make a Heffalump Trap. (Piglet is sorry he didn't think of it first.) He baits it with a jar of honey, after making sure that it really was honey all the way to the bottom, naturally. In the middle of the night, he goes to the Trap to get what's left of the honey and gets his head stuck in the jar. Along comes Piglet, who sees this strange creature with a jar-like head making frightful noises, and, having known no more than Pooh what Heffalumps really were, assumes that a Heffalump has indeed been Trapped and is duly terrified.

It would probably be too moralistic to wonder how much Christopher Robin actually knew about Heffalumps in the first place. The "Decorator," based on the picture on page 60 of my edition, clearly thinks C. R. thought they were elephants, but I still wonder. At best, though, he knew no more about them than the contractor did about Gateways in the proposal that started this whole tirade off.

CHAPTER 11

An Architecture
for Secure
Packet-Switched Networks

ABSTRACT

The paper offers a broad approach to making packet-switched networks secure by means of judicious application of security kernel technology. The central insight is that the expedient of having a single uncertified process for each Host homed on a given kernelized packet switch can, in conjunction with a single uncertified Network Daemon process on each switch, lead to an architecture which is at once secure and possessed of such other desirable characteristics as requiring less verification than other kernelized approaches, avoiding inordinate process overhead, preserving the integrity of networking protocols, and being readily comprehensible.

PREFATORY AFTERTHOUGHTS

"I have here in my hand the *last* envelope." [Thunderous applause.]
    "May a diseased ISORMite commit Prescriptivity upon your sibling."
[Giggles.] "The answer is . . . Probably Not."
    "Probably not."
    "And the question is . . . Will anybody ever get Multilevel Network
Security right?"

    Sorry 'bout that, but I couldn't resist, once I realized that this *is* the last
set of Prefatory Afterthoughts. Actually, the main point I want to try to
make is that, in my experience, there are even fewer real Security experts
who know anything about Security *in an Intercomputer Networking context*
(i.e., beyond the mere communications aspects) than there are real Intercomputer Networking experts—and by now I imagine you've figured out
how few of those I think there are—so coming up with a *real* MLS *network*
has to figure as a real longshot.
    As I don't want to get into still another Holy War (between the Church
of the Holy Kernel and the Church of the Holy Crypto), I'll settle for merely
suggesting that the reason why there aren't many relevant experts borders
on the obvious: Both disciplines are pretty subtle and neither is exactly old,
so there just aren't many people around who have had the opportunity to
have mastered both. I'm not particularly convinced I can lay claim to being
one of them, by the way, but I will be so bold as to expect that I could recognize one if I ever happened across one.
    Despite the demurrer, I've at least been to a Sunday School class or
two in both Churches and I do still find the proposed approach of the paper a
sound one in principle, *if* you grant its premises, especially the one which

holds that the crux of "secure networking" is to control all points of ingress to and egress from "the net." But I don't claim the required gadget can be built with *perfect* confidence. (And one of the reasons I made such a fuss in Chapter 2 over the issue of whether the CSNP is a separate box or not is that having it be separate is certainly a premise here.)

*　*　*

There are a couple of semi-subtle reasons for including the paper here which might be of interest to some readers: In the first place, I thought it would be nice to include one piece that isn't Us versus Them; and, in the second and final place, I *love* the footnotes.

*　*　*

As these *are* the last P.A.'s, it seems appropriate to close with my traditional

Cheers,

INTRODUCTION

We present here an apparently rather attractive high-level architecture, which we have not seen before, for making packet-switched networks secure. Our primary intent is to submit the approach to the consideration of workers in the secure computer systems field, but we wish to avoid becoming enmeshed in the tech-nicotheological disputes of Security. Thus, we will not align ourselves with any particular terminological or technological camp. Also, in the interests of con-ciseness and to avoid introducing potentially sensitive material, scholarly ap-paratus will be minimal.

A SIMPLE COMPROMISE PARADIGM*

Limiting the sense in which "secure" is meant to convey something along the lines of "a system in which no sensitive information is compromised" ("denial of

*If there weren't so many mathematicians in the field, we'd call it a "model."

© 1978 IEEE. Reprinted, with permission, from Third Berkeley Workshop on Distributed Data Management and Networking, August, 1978, San Francisco, CA, pp. 54-65.

service," e.g., being beyond our scope), we consider it axiomatic that for compromise to occur there must be implicit or explicit *senders* of information, implicit or explicit *channels* for the information to traverse, and explicit *receivers* of the information.

We state that senders may be implicit in order to suggest that, presumably owing to design inadvertence, information in a given system may simply be accessible in some direct or indirect fashion to unintended receivers. Similar considerations apply to channels, but here another distinction is useful as well: Whether they be viewed as "covert," "storage," "modulation," and/or "confinement," channels fall into two broad categories, which we choose to term "obvious" and "devious." For example, if any process (or address space in execution) in a given system can read the text editor command's working file, there exists an obvious channel—even if the system has a sophisticated file system such that a user's permanent copy of the file in question is perfectly "secure." On the other hand, if the text editor itself contains maliciously inserted code to copy the contents of the file to somebody else's file directory as well as to the invoker's, we'll call this an instance of a devious channel. The point at issue here is not intended to be profound; rather, we seek to avoid the somewhat confusing terminology of the literature by substituting an admittedly imprecise, but workable, alternative.

SEVERAL SIMPLE SECURITY PARADIGMS*

To counter the threats implied by the simple compromise paradigm, the following broad courses are open—irrespective of whether single sytems or networks are at issue.

Eliminate Senders

If the design of the system were such that there were no (implicit or explicit) senders of information to other than "proper" receivers, there would, tautologically, be no compromise possible. Presumably, this would entail exhaustive verification of the code. As far as we know, this is beyond the state of the art.

Eliminate Receivers

For receiving *programs*, similar considerations apply as to senders. For networks, however, literal and figurative wire-tappers are also potential receivers; we posit encryption as the means of defeating such wire tappers.

Block Channels

It being too difficult to eliminate senders and receivers until and unless exhaustive software verification techniques become available, what about

*We can't be sure the mathematicians have gone away, even after the previous paragraph.

blocking the channels over which they communicate? Without going too far afield into computer system security, let us simply observe that there are approaches extant for dealing with obvious channels, but devious channels are still a problem. For example, in single system software security, there is the so-called "confinement problem."* Also, for networks "end-to-end encryption" has been advanced as a means to block sender-receiver channels; however, it cannot easily deal with the devious channels which arise from the modulation of such "clear" parameters as the length and address of transmissions.† (Trusted software or hardware could be interposed to garble such channels—padding lengths and generating fictitious addresses—but this not only would detract from throughput, it would also, to a purist, only add "noise" to the channels.‡)

Block Receivers

The other alternatives being more or less unsatisfactory even at the cursory level of detail above, a final alternative becomes inherently attractive, if only by contrast: What about making it impossible for any receiving software to get illicitly acquired information out of "the system" to a human confederate? In a network in particular, this alternative has intuitive appeal, for we in some sense "own" the communications subnetwork processors (CSNPs). Therefore, even though it is incontrovertible that we cannot dictate that all subscribers eliminate potential senders of information to potential receivers in the CSNP, and even though we cannot afford the performance penalties of blocking the channels, and, finally, even though we cannot guarantee the absence of potential receivers in our CSNP software, we can perhaps arrange matters such that the receivers are unable to pass illicitly acquired information along, "outside the net."

TWO APPROACHES TO BLOCKING RECEIVERS

With the focus of attention on preventing not the acquisition of illicit information by CSNP software but rather on preventing its further use, we see that it is straightforward to protect the transmitted data themselves (obvious channels). The data can be protected either by (end-to-end) encryption or by some sort of "security kernel." Now, again, we run the risk of digressing into

---

*See B. W. Lampson, "A Note on the Confinement Problem," *CACM*, 16, No. 10 (October 1973), 613–615; and S. B. Lipner, "A Comment on the Confinement Problem," MTP-167, The MITRE Corporation, November 1975.

†M. A. Padlipsky et al., "Limitations of End-to-End Encryption in Secure Computer Networks," USAF Electronic Systems Division Technical Report, as yet unpublished.

‡We acknowledge that if the network in question can afford to require the interposition of crypto gear "between" *every* Host and *any* switch, the presumed malicious switch software's spontaneous transmissions would be garbled before reaching any receiver. This is, however, expensive—and would appear to allow a sort of second-order devious channel still. In any event, we are far more comfortable in the software realm, and will concentrate on it henceforth, without prejudice to the meta-issue of whether end-to-end encryption "really works."

deeper waters than we want to wade in, so let us merely characterize a kernel as trusted software which furnishes the primitives necessary (and sufficient) for process isolation and address space management, and avoid taking up the cudgels for either the MITRE/ESD mathematical model, the SRI Provably Secure Operating System, ARPA's Kernelized Secure Operating System, UCLA's virtual machines, or even the University of Texas work we're not really familiar with. The crucial point of a (generic) kernel is that we can assume trustworthy process isolation (which assumes address space management—and control of Input/Output).

So let's posit the protectability of the transmitted data within the CSNP. The potential receiver software could still obtain information over devious channels, via "headers" (which might only be addresses and lengths, if end-to-end encryption is in play—ignoring the possibility of modulating the timing of transmissions because that's easily hidable from untrusted software). We have seen two broad approaches to the problem of blocking the receivers from passing this sort of information on.

Ad Hoc Methods

One approach is simply to make trusted all the CSNP code which could transmit at its own behest. Somewhat more sophisticated is the alternative which attempts to identify—and certify—only the code which can transmit "outside the net" (i.e., to subscribers) at its own behest. There are problems with any such ad hoc approach, however. In the first place, the identifying of the code to make trusted is not a rigorous proceeding; rather it depends on the ingenuity and acuity of the designer. Also, the amount of code which needs certification (an expensive undertaking, we note) is high. Finally, although it is admittedly a subjective consideration, this approach "is mere engineering" which of course is not intuitively satisfying to the scientists of the protection racket.

By Design

Finally, we come to the desirable approach: Consider how to design into the CSNP the blocking of receivers. There are two "obvious" sub-approaches. If each security level is handled by a separate process, or if each transmission is so handled, any good kernel can prevent such a process from writing to any inappropriate place. Unfortunately, however, for a military network, say, when both categories and compartments must be taken into account, there are a lot of security levels. There are also a lot of transmissions. And the CSNP is driven by economic considerations to be as small as possible. So there is a fear of swamping the CSNP inherent in process per level and process per transmission approaches.* Further, there is a fear that the handling of the implied multilevel

---

*In fairness, it should be noted that we have seen no rationale other than intuition offered for this fear; let us assume, though, that we share it.

data bases (e.g., for buffers for the Switch-Host Protocol, and for "routing") would place an inordinate burden upon the kernel. Dealing with these fears will be the burden of the next section, which sketches our proposed architecture.

A RELATIVELY SIMPLE, APPARENTLY SOUND ARCHITECTURE

Premise

Our premise is that there should be one process in the CSNP *for each Host* "homed" on the CSNP. The crucial underlying observation is that you have to trust Hosts to maintain separation of data to whatever extent they are legally permitted to. That is, ordinary Hosts—which contain untrusted operating systems—deal with one level at a time (unless under dispensation to deal with multiple compartments). They can be allowed to communicate with Hosts at their level(s) freely, but with no others (unless network security policy permits "writing up"—a complication which we ignore for present purposes, although it might alter somewhat the implementation of one particular kernel primitive). "Multilevel Secure" Hosts, on the other hand, will, when they are certified, be by definition capable of enforcing separation of their processes according to security levels.* They can, then, communicate anywhere within the range of security levels for which they are certified. But with a kernel imposing separation on the per-Host processes within the CSNP and allowing transmissions (indelibly associated with level codes by the kernel itself *on entry to the CSNP*) to be output only to like Hosts (whether locally or remotely homed) there is no risk of broad-band compromise by the per-Host processes.†

That takes care of the "too many processes" fear, we submit, for typical CSNPs home only four to eight Hosts. As to the implied multilevel data base fear, we turn to, eventually, the kernel, but first to an indispensable ancillary process.

"Network Daemon"

Shifting our perspective momentarily from network security to network protocols, we note that the CSNP must interpret, in addition to the Switch-Host Protocol we've just relegated to per-Host processes, some sort of Switch-Switch

---

*Note that this implies "proper" integration of network software into the Multilevel Secure Host, in the sense of performing the same sort of demultiplexing and isolation about to be described, in order to preclude a devious channel from a CSNP per-Host process back to an inappropriate process on its "own" Host (as opposed to on a foreign Host). In particular, the process in which the Switch-Host Protocol interpreter resides must be isolated.

†We touch upon devious channels later. It should be noted, though, that Host-switch devious channels involving parameter modulation appear to be at least two orders of (decimal) magnitude down from the rates of direct Host-switch transmission, and, at least intuitively, any overlooked devious channels out of the switch ought to be two further orders of magnitude down.

Protocol. At the least, the Switch-Switch Protocol deals with subnet flow control; it might also address "accountability" and "routing," and perhaps some other items we've overlooked (reports to a Network Control Center are a good possibility). Here, though, the key observation is that all transactions are internal to the network, and the kernel *can keep them so* by the simple expedient of indelibly associating a special level code with any transmissions initiated by the *single* process—which, for sentimental reasons, we call the Network Daemon—that interprets Switch-Switch Protocol in the broad sense for the CSNP. Thus, even if addresses and lengths of transmissions are being clandestinely modulated to comprise a devious channel, the kernel only makes them known to the Network Daemon process, *which can't use the information derived* to communicate with anything other than another Network Daemon process. (Note also that lengths need not be made known at all in many circumstances, and can be judiciously lied about in all cases; further, addresses only need be of target CSNP, not Host, thus reducing the number of bits available for modulation.)

This strategy appears to eliminate all but one of the feared data bases, at the cost of a single, untrusted process.

Kernel

The other data base which is in some sense multilevel is the buffer pool for incoming transmissions (which will also be the source of outgoing data transmissions). That is, for example, a devious channel between per-Host processes (PHPs) could be created by means of filling up the pool with "garbage" by PHP A in order to communicate a bit to PHP B, *if* B can come along and request a buffer from the same pool A is using. The straightforward solution to this situation is to have the kernel manage the pool and only dole out buffers to PHPs according to some algorithm which places ceilings on any PHP's share of the pool. (This is, we believe, what's known as "virtualizing shared resources" in some circles.)

So, aside from performing the functions common to kernelizing, we see a few other actions the kernel for a CSNP with a PHP architecture must perform:

As just noted, it must manage the buffer pool. As previously stated, it must indelibly associate levels with transmissions, ban spontaneous transmissions by PHPs, do all I/O multiplexing/demultiplexing, and, of course, forbid output to a (physical) line of a transmission the level of which is not in a proper relationship according to the policy of the network to that of the line. (We assume the latter condition is equivalent to saying the transmission is in the access range of the recipient, but want to avoid tripping over the treacherous ground of "partial ordering.")

Two additional services seem desirable (assuming that mediation of all interprocess communication is within the spectrum of common kernel functions, and that this sort of kernel refuses to let PHPs talk to one another—but they can, and must, indirectly invoke a primitive or two of the Network Daemon): The kernel should be conversant enough with the header structure of the given network to indelibly associate the originating address with the transmission (on initial input). This is needed to allow eventual multilevel secure Hosts to make their own discriminations about whom they're talking to for purposes of internal access control. Also, in networks where there is subnet "accountability" (not, for example, in "pure datagram" nets) the kernel must permit the Network Daemon to convey a few bits (three seems to be enough) to a PHP to report on transmission disposition.*

"Scenario"

The foregoing is at best concise, and may well be terse. Perhaps a rough scenario of the normal routes through the subnet will help clarify the architectural sketch, even though it does not attempt to turn the sketch into a blueprint.

When a packet comes into a CSNP, it comes over either a Host line (where terminal mini-Hosts are still after all Hosts) or a trunk line. It is first dealt with by—and always retained "in"—the kernel, which must perform a level check before causing either the appropriate PHP (if a Host line) or the Network Daemon (if a trunk line) to be invoked. For Host lines, the level check is to assure that the level alleged for the packet in the header is "within range" for the originator (based on a kernel-internal line table, and according to the network's policy in this area); the kernel also writes the originator's address into the header; then it invokes the appropriate PHP, which in turn interprets Switch-Host Protocol as necessary (the relevant header command field, at least, being an invocation parameter†). If necessary, the PHP requests more buffers from the kernel (so it can do Switch-Host flow control); it then (assuming a data packet) calls the kernel for purposes of causing the Network Daemon to route and send the packet. The kernel gives the Daemon the foreign CSNP address (along with a buffer registration number, probably, and a rounded up length, if necessary) and subsequently responds to the Daemon's request to send the packet over a given trunk or Host line (doing a level check if it's a Host line). For trunk lines, the kernel invokes the Network Daemon, which in turn routes tandem traffic or traffic for locally homed Hosts (and must, of course, have the kernel output the packet on the appropriate line), or performs Switch-Switch Protocol. In the latter case, any responses again go out of the CSNP via the kernel, with the "network internal" level inserted by the kernel. (Note that similar considerations apply to a PHP which needs to generate output to its own Host as part of Switch-Host Protocol: here, the kernel either refuses "new" buffers addressed

---

*Purists might argue that this could constitute a devious channel. They might be right. (But it's *very* slow.) And we do know of one network wherein the documentation says that five completion statuses can be conveyed in only two bits. (It doesn't say how, though.)

†We have been accused by one colleague of implicity subscribing to what we term "The Unclassified Headers Heresy." We prefer to think of our approach as following the "Need-to-Know Header Rite," according to the "Principle of Least Privilege Orthodoxy."

anywhere other than to the PHP's own Host or allows the PHP to overwrite the header, as implementation considerations dictate.)

Of course, the crafting of such functions as buffer "registration" and the demultiplexing of transmissions which come in from the net (as opposed to over a Host line) will require some care. For present purposes, however, it is not particularly interesting to worry about them, as they do not appear to be broad architectural issues. Therefore, we will turn instead to a brief discussion of the advantages and disadvantages of our proposed PHP architecture.

ADVANTAGES

We perceive the following advantages to the PHP approach:

Minimize Verification

Only the kernel need be trusted code. Although the kernel is somewhat "bigger" than a single system's need be, the additional primitives clearly do not impose so heavy a verification burden as would alternatives wherein, at the least, the Switch-Host Protocol Interpreter and various internal-to-the-net message generators must be verified.

Optimize Process Population

Although it is likely that a function-oriented process assignment scheme would lead to numerically fewer processes within the CSNP, the five to nine processes dictated by the PHP approach should not be unduly burdensome.

Maintain Protocol Integrity

In another context, the major advantage of the approach would be that by keeping protocol interpreters as integral modules it spares protocol designers the onerous burden of attempting to find a rational basis for functional decomposition of protocols into "secure" and "security unrelated" subsets. Note that nothing in the approach debars Host-Host and/or process-level protocols from taking whatever steps are appropriate to introducing security considerations as germane, but also that the approach makes no unsupportable assumptions about the actions—or even veracity—of protocol interpreters external to the CSNP.

Comprehensibility

Finally, we believe the architecture to be comprehensible by designers/implementers of given secure networks. Despite the fact that prior familiarity with the field was assumed by the concise presentation here, if the premises of kernel technology are valid it would seem that PHP "holds water" as a way to make networks secure—and, it should be noted, a way which is not a priori inefficient.

A corollary to the comprehensibility issue is that any devious channels which might exist should at least become more nearly visible, in like manner to the "accountability" point raised above.

DISADVANTAGES

We perceive the following potential disadvantages to the PHP approach:

"Piggybacking"

It is not clear whether the additional kernel complexity (in the area of having to "know" too much about the relevant protocols) is worthwhile in order to support the "piggybacking" of Switch-Switch protocol control information onto data transmissions destined for an appropriate CSNP. (It is not even clear to us, however, whether it's worthwhile to go to the trouble of identifying suitable traffic on which to piggyback even in a nonsecure net.) The simple solution is to ban piggybacking, which may, of course, cost some throughput.

Verification Ease

If it be the case that "trusted processes" are more amenable to automatic verification techniques than is a kernel per se, then the argument that PHP offers less to verify has correspondingly lighter impact.

CONCLUSIONS

Granting without equivocation that the foregoing reasoning is far from rigorous, it still seems to us that a packet-switching network based upon per-Host processes in the Communications Subnet Processors (with "any good kernel"— and, of course, link encryption to defeat literal wire-tappers) has sufficient conceptual appeal to be worth pursuing further.

An analogy to the proposed approach might prove of interest, and will prove to be our final observation: Picture each per-Host process and the Network Daemon in a given CSNP painted with a distinct color.* The kernel's job, then, is to allow—in cooperation with the other CSNPs' kernels—metaphorical wires of only the same color as the end points to be "strung" across the network.

It should work.

ACKNOWLEDGMENTS

The basic PHP insight arose during a conversation with Grace Nibaldi, who deserves much of the credit (but none of the blame) for such refinement of the idea as this paper might represent. Stanley Ames and Kenneth Biba also provided useful comments.

*We ourselves would be strongly disinclined to choose either red or black, however.

The Appendices

APPENDIX 1

Two Introductions That Were Too Good to Go to Waste

§SECTION 1.

STANDARDS: THREAT OR MENACE

A SCHEMA FOR AN UNCONVENTIONAL PANEL DISCUSSION THAT WASN'T

M. A. Padlipsky, *Provocateur*

The Freud and the Freudians Problem is not sufficiently widely known. In essence, Freud was the inventor of a new field, which many would call a science but we needn't get distracted by that. Several of his followers, Jung and Adler probably being the most notable, diverged from his position and founded their own schools. Other of his followers, calling themselves Freudians, asserted their continued adherence to his position but misunderstood it so profoundly as to in fact not only constitute still other schools but also reflect badly upon Freud's own reputation because of the peculiar positions they attributed to him. Thoughtful students of psychoanalysis often contend that the Freudians did far more to discredit Freud than Jung and Adler combined.

A similar condition exists in the field of intercomputer networking protocols today, although perhaps an even better analogy would be to the Jung and the Jungians and Adler and the Adlerians Problems, which the audience can presumably derive by straightforward recursion. That is, the ARPANET

190

evolved an approach to resource sharing (or "higher level") protocols which, although it was acknowledged to be in need of some refinement, worked rather well. Along came, on the one hand, the Transmission Control Protocol and its associated Internet Protocol (TCP/IP) from the surviving members of the ARPA research community, implicitly claiming to be that refinement; and, on the other hand, the Open System Interconnection Reference Model from the International Standards Organization (referred to herein as the ISORM—and pronounced "eyesore-mmm," just in case anybody can't wait to find out which side I'm not on), tacitly ignoring its debt but still clearly in the ARPANET tradition. (It must be observed, by the way, that anybody who doesn't believe that the ISORM is an abstraction of the original ARPANET protocols is implicitly accusing its originators of far sloppier scholarship than even I would on my grouchiest, snottiest day.) Both TCP/IP and various protocols developed in the name of the ISORM are being vigorously advocated as Standards, just as the Jungians and the Adlerians set up their own shops.

The problem is particularly acute when it comes to the ISORM. At INFOCOM'82 we were treated to the striking spectacle of one expert showing a picture of two high-rise buildings with clotheslines between them even on the first floor, which seems to suggest that despite what we might think about the state of the wire-drawing art, the "Physical Level" *is* "end to end." I've also heard an X.25 camp follower proffer his ricebowl as an alternative to TCP/IP—which is indistinguishable by me from offering four tires (of different sizes) to your 16-year-old when he asks you for a car. And then there's the ISORM "wineglass" model from another session at INFOCOM'82, where the stem is supposed to suggest *single* protocols at levels 3 and 4, at least (and probably 5 and 6 as well—and maybe even 2, too), but how can you do X.25 *across* a packet radio net? (Maybe *into* works, but that would mean that the guys who draw parking garages between their high-rises are wrong, or the parking garages are all sorts of shapes or . . . something.) And how can the four or five or whatever ECMA "classes" of L4 be part of a wine glass stem in the first place? Then there's the fact that you can find some ISORMites who think you can have a "null" protocol or two in the pile. For that matter, you can even find a fair number of ISORMites who admit that X.25 doesn't really conform to the Model. A few of them have even tried to convince me, the father of Host-Front End protocols, that X.25 "is an H-FP." (It ought to be needless to say that they failed.) And how come the NBS attempt to realize the ISORM has an Internet protocol somewhere around 3.5 instead of X.75 at L −1 or so? What it all seems to boil down to is that even if there were no TCP/IP so that we didn't have to iterate the metaphor to bring in the two successor schools, the ISORMites are doing the ISORM just as much a disservice as the Freudians ever did Freud. At any rate, their cacophony at the INFOCOM'82 planted the seeds for this session; indeed, the first draft of this schema was written on April 3, 1982.

In a sense, then, our problem might be viewed as twofold: separating the nonsense of the Jungians (for there has been some confusion about TCP/IP as well) and the Adlerians out to arrive at Jung's and Adler's positions, and then determining whether Jung or Adler is the True Heir of Freud. (Even better, we might discover that one camp or the other equates metaphorically to the Freud of the Id/Ego/Superego Model, with the original ARPANET approach being the Unconscious/Preconscious/Conscious Model Freud—unless I've got them in the wrong order, which I decline to check out for you on the grounds that it's too much to expect me to reread Freud and X.25 in the same year.)

To rephrase it for the benefit of those who aren't fluent in the obscure programming language Metaphor, what we are up to is an attempt to clarify what TCP/IP and the ISORM "really mean" in order to determine, if possible, whether one approach actually is superior to the other. The method employed can be termed Socratic, to dignify it, or "20 Nasty Questions," to lighten it. At any rate, the realest available experts on the two approaches—that is, provided I can get them to come, the ones who wrote the design specs, not merely those who claim they've read 'em—will be asked some rather searching questions, based on popularly held beliefs as to the strengths and weaknesses of those approaches. Note, by the way, that "rather searching" is a blatant euphemism: When you have a *Provocateur* rather than a Chairman, you'd better expect that all of the contention won't be resolved by the Node-to-Node protocol. If time allows, I'd like to go beyond the prepared questions and get into free-for-all mode; but, in advance, I can't even promise we'll be able to get through all 20 of the questions I've prepared.

A few words on "objectivity" would be in order: My cheek would break if I tried to stick my tongue in it far enough to pretend that I'm impartial. Indeed, despite having been one of "TCP's" more outspoken critics in the days when it wasn't TCP/IP and when there wasn't, as far as I knew, even an ISORM, much less an ISORM that attempted to subsume X.25, in some circles I am now known as a sort of Auxiliary Bishop in the Congregation of the Propagation of the TCP/IP Faith. Many of the reasons for this *volte face* should come out during the Inquisition this paper is introducing. The master metaphor for them all is that, considering the two alternatives as, practically speaking, the only alternatives, the differences between ISORM ("based" on X.25) and, to broaden the focus a bit, today's ARPANET Reference Model (or "ARM") protocol suite ("based" on TCP/IP) are like night and day. Granted that the night is not altogether moonless and the day is at least partly cloudy, but if you want to see the state of the art you'd do much better in the daylight of the ARPANET approach.

Nevertheless, within the limits of my learned bias (emphatically not a prejudice—my starting position was "a plague on both their houses"), I've tried to play fair. That is, with one irresistible exception, I haven't pulled any punches in the prepared questions for the ARPANET side, and, to my great credit considering the provocation, I haven't succumbed to the temptation of stacking the ISO side with the sort of muddled Adlerians (who usually sit on standards committees rather than work in the field) who show pictures in public suggesting that the "Physical Level" is end to end or assert in public that an advocate of TCP/IP "even" on Local Area Nets should use IEEE 802 "instead." Rather, I've tried to recruit the best possible representatives of both sides. If it succeeds, I think you'll be amused by how long most of us have known each other, and how many roots we have in common. "Who really is the heir to Freud?" is a *nifty* metaphor.

A final preliminary: Because the ISORM is more widely touted than TCP/IP, and hence the clearer present danger, it seems only fair that it should be the target of the nastier of the questions. This is in the spirit of our title, for in my humble but dogmatic opinion even a good proposed Standard is a prima facie threat to further advance in the state of the art, but a sufficiently flawed standard is a menace even to maintaining the art in its present state, so if the ISORM school is wrong and isn't exposed the consequences could be extremely unfortunate. At least, the threat/menace paradigm applies, I submit in all seriousness, to *protocol* standards; that is, I wouldn't think of being gratuitously snotty to the developers of physical standards—I like to be able to use the same cap to reclose sodapop bottles and beer bottles (though I suspect somebody as it were screwed up when it came to those damn "twist off" caps)—but I find it difficult to be civil to advocates of "final," "ultimate" standards when they're dealing with logical constructs rather than physical ones. After all, as I understand it, a fundamental property of the stored program computer is its ability to be reprogrammed. Yes, I understand that to do so costs money and yes, I've heard of ROM, and no I'm not saying that I insist on some idealistic notion of optimality, but definitely I don't think it makes much sense to keep trudging to an outhouse if I can get indoor plumbing . . . even if the moon in the door is exactly like the one in my neighbor's.

Whoops, still another preliminary: An acquaintance of mine from the NBS tells me that the reason why there aren't any standards for the members of standards committees is that "after all, they're *voluntary* standards organizations." Therefore, to combat that sort of brain surgery by transmission mechanics, I feel I should present my credentials for being at least the prosecuting attorney and perhaps the judge (and maybe even the jury) for this little Dialogue of the Great World Systems Revisited. So, aside from having coined the term "Old Network Boy"—and being one—and indeed probably being the only person in the world who knew, worked with, and was even on friendly terms with Vint Cerf, Jon Postel, and Dave Clark before they got their respective doctorates, I was an active participant in the design of the ARPANET "Old" and "New" Telnet protocols, the File Transfer Protocol, and the first Graphics Protocol; I was the originator and a principal designer of "neted," a common editor command for the ARPANET; and I was the originator and a principal designer of the first Host-Front End Protocol, not only for the ARPANET. I also implemented "Old" Telnet for Multics, did the integration and checkout of NCP and Telnet on 645 Multics—setting the one-month record for Development Machine Time in the process—and later served as Multics Network Technical Liaison and

Network and Graphics Group Leader, supervising the attachment of 6180 Multics to the ARPANET in the process. In recent years, I've tried to help the Government get some of its money's worth from the contractors on any number of networks too depressing to mention and have assessed any number of protocols too disgusting to mention both for the ———* Corporation, which now employs me, and for the DoD's Protocol Standards Technical Panel. There were a few other things too, but if you haven't gotten the picture by now it probably doesn't matter. (And if you don't get the *"provocateur"* joke, you probably shouldn't come to the session anyway.)

*Name withheld to avoid the necessity of Corporate Review.

§SECTION 2.

"A PERSPECTIVE ON THE ARPANET REFERENCE MODEL"

Session Chairman's Introduction

Inspired by the extremely edifying and amusing "deliberately provocative panel" on Distributed Processing at Infocom '82, I had allowed myself to be convinced to serve as what I insisted on calling the *Provocateur* of another deliberately provocative panel for Infocom '83, under the working title of "Standards: Threat of Menace" (my notion being that any standard is a threat to further advances in the state of an art, but a bad standard is a menace even to the present state of the art in question). The Program Committee found that a bit *too* provocative, though, and we were discussing a slightly less pointed title when the whole idea fell through for reasons beyond our control. So by way of explaining the session that did eventuate, I'd like to sketch the one that didn't happen.

The original premise was that there's a Freud and the Freudians problem in intercomputer networking. That is, just as Freud's insights were distorted by his professed followers, the ideas of both the International Standards Organization's Reference Model for Open System Interconnection (ISORM) and of the ARPA-sponsored Transmission Control Protocol and Internet Protocol (TCP/IP) on which the U.S. Department of Defense has standardized were being widely misstated and misunderstood by their respective camp followers and, for that matter, critics. Being on friendly terms with the principals of both the ISORM and TCP/IP, I thought it would be extremely edifying and amusing to get three of each on a panel and play Twenty Nasty Questions with them (ten for each side, of course) in order to attempt to determine who was the "true heir of Freud" (because I firmly believe that both the ISORM and TCP/IP are predicated on the original ARPANET's approach to resource-sharing intercomputer networking protocols, even though the ISORMites rarely if ever publicly acknowledge it).

To my surprise—and dismay—after the Program Committee had approved of the session and requested the names of the panelists for the Proceedings, the Old Network Boys who also happen to have become ISORM principals whom I asked to sit on the ISORM side declined, on the grounds that "it would [or could] do more harm than good". Somewhat reluctantly, I'll preserve their anonymity, and, rather more professionally than they behaved in my view, I'll even resist the temptation to stage the original panel with empty chairs on their side. But I cannot see my way clear to inviting what I take to be second stringers in lieu of principals, so what evolved instead was the following, in order not to leave the Program Committee short:

The session still will be a panel, there being no time to turn it into a learned papers session less than two weeks before the printer's deadline for the Proceedings. The title will become "A Perspective on the ARPANET Reference Model" (ARM), though, which happens to be the name of a paper I wrote recently for different purposes entirely, which in turn happens to address both the ARM in the abstract as its primary theme and some comparisons and contrasts with the ISORM as its secondary theme.* The paper will appear in the Proceedings, in order that it be available in the open literature. The session will offer a brief discussion of the paper (for the lazy), brief talks by the panelists on selected aspects of the ARM (I'm pushing for "The ARM View of Layering," "The ARM View of Internetting," and "Logical Connections vs. Virtual Circuits" myself, but the actual talks will be subject to the panelists' final decisions), and the Ten Nasty Questions for TCP/IP (based on both my own view of their shortcomings and some more or less rational points I've heard raised by other observers).

Not as amusing as it might have been, but perhaps, in view of the scarcity of treatments of the ARM in the open literature, even more edifying.

And if the spirit moves, I might even allow myself to be prevailed upon at least to read the Ten Nasty Questions for the ISORM . . . but it'll take an extreme spiritual upheavel for me to offer my educated guesses as to what the answers would have been. (The audience is welcome to try to convince me to, of course.)

---

*The need for both an explication of the ARM and at least a mild exposition of some of the flaws of the ISORM became painfully clear to me when I mentioned to a middle manager type who thought he knew something about "networking" that the ISORM is, after all, largely an abstraction from the ARPANET protocols, which did, a matter of fact, have a reference model of their own. I was then asked, in all seriousness, whether the ARM conformed to the ISORM. (For the curious, the fallacy involved is probably *post hoc ergo huis causa*—"after, therefore its cause".) This true story should help account for the presence of the comparisons-and-contrasts subtheme: the publicity has, indeed, been rather one-sided. (Please see the first footnote of the paper for more on why it happens to attempt to deal with both themes.)

APPENDIX 2

The Arouet Papers

§SECTION 1.

EMPIRICAL HERESY CONSIDERED THREATENING

We must report with considerable regret that no less distinguished an organization than IRIA is at present engaged in work on distributed database management systems that proposes actually to measure the performance of various concurrency control strategies rather than to follow the traditional approach of selecting a single strategy and proving its worth by either the standard method of Strong Assertion or the newly popular contender, simulation with irrelevant parameters. The dangers of this Empirical Heresy are both apparent and abundant. It is not too fanciful to imagine that if this distasteful practice were not rigorously suppressed, it could even lead to a thoroughly unacceptable state of the art wherein standards are discovered by standards organizations rather than, according to time-honored practice, invented by them. The unfortunate economic consequences of this are painfully obvious and need not be recounted here. A somewhat less obvious damaging psychological consequence is worthy of note, however: Were they to be deprived of their semi-absolute, quasitheocratic power by the greatly-to-be-feared widespread application of such a heresy, members of standards organizations would have no consolation left other than whatever small benefits might accrue from frequent all-expenses-paid trips to various more or less exotic locales. Surely we cannot stand idly by and allow the very foundations of the field to crumble: Our motto must become "Researchers of the world, give up; you have nothing to lose but your integrity."

F. M. Arouet
Institute for Entropic Maximization

§SECTION 2.

ISORM CONSIDERED INSIDIOUS

F. M. Arouet

As the token ARPANET Old Network Boy for a fairly well-known "think tank",* I see a fair number of intercomputer networking proposals, concepts of operations, functional descriptions, and the like. I wish I could use the word "fair" one more time to describe most of them, but to do so would be far too flattering even if it weren't overly repetitive. Since the ballyhooing of the International Standards Organization's Reference Model for Open System Interconnection, the proposals et al. have gotten even less sensible, on average, and it seems that a case of *post hoc ergo propter hoc* really does exist. This note is intended, then, among other things, to explain why the ISORM has made matters worse.

The first step is to recognize a fundamental problem in systems engineering that can perhaps best be called the Diagrammable Block Fallacy: The putative system architect hears of some concept—say, a Network Control Program (NCP) or the Transmission Control Protocol (TCP)—knows it's been implemented somewhere, hears it works, and hey presto! it's a block in the diagram. That he or she doesn't really know what it does is overlooked; after all, it's a diagrammable block and somebody knows what it does. Of course, when it comes to the ISORM things appear to be even more attractive to block diagrammers: After all, you've got seven (as of now) blocks to toss around in your diagram and if you have a reasonably good memory you even know what order to put them in. That you're going to need all seven (or more) to get anywhere, that several of them haven't been implemented anywhere, that others don't work, and that almost nobody agrees on what they do . . . again, overlooked. After all, they're diagrammable blocks and lots of people *sound* as if they know what they all do do and/or will do.

Naturally, those who know the difference between "descriptive" and "prescriptive" won't pay much attention to a mere Reference Model, and those who understand Occam's Razor will have already concluded that the ISORM is inferior to the ARPANET's process, Host-Host, and network levels. Unfortunately, there don't seem to be very many students of the philosophy of science mucking about with networks, and the ISORM seems to capture the fancy of enough nonphilosophers that it bids fair to become the newest heir to Epicycles. Surely the Diagrammable Block fallacy must appeal to some deep psychic stratum, must transcend the convenience of the ignorant or even the avarice of

---

*For various reasons, I choose to protect both their anonymity and my own. (A modest prize is offered to those who know why the *nom de plume* is particularly apt.)

the partially learned, to impel as much kludgolatry as it does. How to account at a deep level for the ISORM's appeal? How, for that matter, to make it go away?

Is the appeal accounted for by an Emperor's New Clothes archetype? That is, has nobody been willing to tell ISORM's proponents that the magic cloth they're peddling doesn't exist? No, there have been several well-meaning innocents who've tried to explain to the Standards Bureaucrats that standards should be discovered, not decreed, and not only hasn't that exorcised the ISORM, it hasn't even freed us of X.25. The problem, I submit, goes deeper than Lies Agreed Upon.

Is the appeal accounted for by a Woozles archetype? That is, have the Standards Bureaucrats emulated Pooh and Piglet and convinced themselves that because they keep seeing more and more footsteps around the tree they're walking around that they must be the tracks of some fabulous creatures, and none being willing to admit ignorance of the nature of the beast, are they imputing more and more characteristics to it just because they're scared? No, there really were some tracks around before the circular stampede started (remember the ARPANET?). The problem, I submit, goes even deeper than Mutually Assured Delusion.

The germ of the appropriate answer can be found in Pouzin's Projection,* which holds that "ISO will be going to 17 levels any year now because it's a sacred number in Bali." (Actually, that's not what made me think of the answer, but it is a nifty transition—and we should always be attuned to the echoes of Epicycles anyway.) To understand what's so insidious about the ISORM, then, consider the following observations of Sir James Frazer:

> *Unable to discriminate clearly between words and things, the savage commonly fancies that the link between a name and the person or thing denominated by it is not a mere arbitrary and ideal association, but a real and substantial bond which unites the two in such a way that magic may be wrought on a man just as easily through his name as through his hair, his nails, or any other material part of his person. In fact, primitive man regards his name as a vital portion of himself and takes care of it accordingly. (*The Golden Bough, *Macmillan 1 vol. edn., p. 284, 1938)*

Eureka! The Diagrammable Block fallacy is at last explained, revealed as an instance of primitive Name Magic. And it's clear that the ISORM takes the Name Magic to the Seventh (aha!) Power—with even an added arcane fillip in that so few people can remember seven things at once that those who can are readily believed to Know Everything.

But how does the realization that the appeal of the ISORM is accounted for by its advocates' belief that by knowing the names of all those layers they

*No, I'm not Louis, as you should be able to tell because my English is too good. We are just old friends.

magically have power over them lead to the exorcism devoutly to be wished? Elementary: It's ironic enough that one of the seminal texts of "Computer Science" is *The* Art *of Computer Programming*, but how could anybody possibly keep a straight face when the standardsmongers come out with *The* Magic *of Protocols?*

§SECTION 3.

STANDARDS COMMITTEEMEN CONSIDERED DANGEROUS

F. M. Arouet

I have been concerned for some time about the apparent lack of standards for membership on standards committees. Institutions are somehow or another entitled to representation, and so they send representatives; but it's by no means clear that they're particularly selective about whom they send. Indeed, there's a clear <u>dis</u>incentive for sending their most qualified workers in the fields of given committees—after all, those are the ones you want to be staying home in the back room, working away . . . if you're an institution, that is. I won't draw the tempting inference that the majority of standards committee members are their institutions' professional meeting goers, because that would be awfully nasty even if I could prove it. I do, however, want to tell you a true story that happened not too long ago.

At approximately 11:15 a.m. on [date and venue withheld to make the villain of the piece, who saw an earlier version of this little moral essay and extracted a promise from me never to use his (or her) name again, less paranoid about being publicly embarrassed by the story by being readily identifiable], I heard a member of one or more "networking" standards groups [exact sex and all names withheld for above reason, and so he (or she) won't even consider wasting my time by running the risk of finding out that Truth *is* a sufficient defense against libel] ask an advocate of TCP/IP on Local Area Nets, in an extremely smug and partronizing tone, why he didn't "forget that academic mickeymouse, and use IEEE 802 instead." By shortly after 6 p.m., while driving home, I had finally decompressed enough to come up with an appropriate analogy:

Suppose you're a 16-year-old boy. (No sexism intended—it just lends concreteness.) You ask your parent or guardian for an automobile. (Again, for concreteness but without prejudice, suppose you say, "Gee, Dad, I'd really rather have a Buick.") In all seriousness, your P. or G. hands you a picture of four automobile tires. I submit you will entertain grave doubts about the old man's understanding of Transportation, at least, and of his sanity if you worry about such things, even if you don't notice that the tires are of different sizes and one of them is a radial.

Nor would you feel any better about your genetic heritage if he went out and bought you four actual tires, two of which were radial, and three of which (but not the two radials) were of the same size. That is, even if the original psuedotechnical suggestion had been to use X.25 "instead"—which, unlike IEEE 802 at the time of the story, did exist (and has its own defects)—the very question betrays a terrible ignorance . . . especially for a person who's empowered to participate in the making of standards in the field: To do anything like real networking (where Host computers are severally involved), as opposed to merely using a communications subnetwork as a communications medium, you need to do rather more than just interface to the communications subnetwork. Yet IEEE 802 and X.25 are both just such interface protocols. The X.25 specification explicitly disavows being a complete "end-to-end" protocol in the sense of "Host-Host" or even "Transport" protocol, even if some twits do try to use it in contrary fashion; the IEEE 802 specification presumably will also, unless the few networking-sophisticated members of the committee resign in the face of the invincible ignorance of their nominal colleagues who, according to the reports I've gotten from an Old Network Boy on the committee, seem bound and determined to try to come up with an end-to-end protocol (possibly even at ISORM L 2 rather than L 3) of their very own, despite the fact that the very "Reference Model" they're allegedly standardizing to/for doesn't/shouldn't want/need that flavor of end-to-endness there anyway. (Another thing I worry about is that when each committee is viewed as a kingdom, Territorial Imperatives and/or expansionist visions come into play too readily.)

Well, it would be gilding the ragweed to extend the automotive analogy to add a chassis (Host-Host or Transport) and a body (Process/Applications or Session Presentation Application). But it *was* so astounding—and disconcerting—to hear that the tires are the only part of a car that matters that, in order to finish decompressing and achieve a modicum of catharsis, I had to get the above down on paper. (The first draft of this was finished, by the way, at 6:56 p.m. on [That Day].)

Postscript at 6:57 p.m.: It ought to go without saying, but just in case: As anybody who had taken the trouble (and had the capacity) to understand TCP/IP before badmouthing them would have known, not only do you need more functionality than you get from an interface protocol, even if it is pretty much end to end, to do real networking, but it's not even an either-or situation, because the conceptual model of IP does not by any means preclude operation on a comm subnet that presents an X.25 or IEEE 802 interface. To do so would merely be wasteful, because of the unnecessary extra functionality that comes with the interfaces and costs cpu cycles. Well, it would be "merely" wasteful unless, of course, you happen to share my tastes in technicoaesthetics—and find it appalling to use a chainsaw as a steak knife.

Afterthought on Psychopathology

The inflammatory action was particularly infuriating because of the tone taken, but it's by no means an isolated phenomenon. There's a lot of that sort of mistakenly appealing to the Sacred Seven thing going around, so it might be useful to explore it a bit further.

Uncharitable souls might be disposed to write the inflammatory action off as clear evidence of "brain damage." That's certainly tempting, if only because the etiology would then be—in deference to the purported popularity of the ISORM Over There—a Foreign Lesion; but it's just not good enough. Charitable souls might want to excuse the inflammatory action on the grounds that, as the poet tells us, this is, after all, a Generation of Hypers, or even that "everybody's got a right to his or her 'ricebowl'." Neither explanation is satisfactory, however, unless we were to accept the utterly unprofessional premise that it's licit to mong things that are oversold, underdesigned, and years from here without taking the trouble to understand either the things or the alternatives to the things. *How in the world could that Meleagris gallopavo have wanted to substitute L 3 (or maybe L 2) stuff for L 4 stuff* (in the terms of Their Model), even if there *were* L 5-7 stuff available to ride on it (which there isn't)??!!!???!!!!!????? Even if the end-to-endness business *is* too subtle, the turkey was so concerned with trying to come off smug and superior-sounding that (s)he simply betrayed a total lack of "knowing the territory" with that nonsensical "instead"; I mean, (s)he might think TCP is a moldy orange, but that's no excuse for comparing it to a wormy apple!

No, what I think is really going on, in semi-classical Freudian terms, is that your typical ISORMite has simply expended all of his/her available libido on *remembering* All Seven, so that there's just no psychic energy left to reason about them with.

The prosecution rests . . . for the time being.

§SECTION 4.

AN ALTERNATIVE ENCODING OF "42"

OR

THE ULTIMATE ANSWER

F. M. Arouet

It's downright inspiring the way the Brits so often turn out to have been first: Atlas before Multics for virtual memory, and the Cambridge Ring before the ARPANET for packet switching, for example.

Of course, in both cases the Brits' work wasn't necessarily widely known, and even though they pioneered the concepts, there was still plenty of room left for refinement. But historically they apparently did come first, and it's mere quibbling to worry whether Corbató and Glaser or Taylor and Roberts were even familiar with their respective Transatlantic precursors/counterparts.

When it comes to a fitting conclusion for the present exercise, then, it's only fitting that again the Brits should have had the first words, and that those first words should again require refinement from the traditionally more practical Yankee cousins. For the real problem underlying all that has gone before is that the ISO stuff all *sounds* so good and seems to stand as evidence that a great deal of thought has gone into it—and there are so many more people running around claiming to be ISORM experts (or OSIRM experts, as they'd prefer, but that calls for a conclusion after all; that is, just as E[lectronic] D[ata] P[rocessing] is preferable to A[utomatic] DP, so it is preferable not to grant the premise that they're actually achieving O[pen] S[ystem] I[nterconnection] in their very label) than there are people running around claiming to be ARM experts—that it's hard to stand there and say that They don't have The Answer. However, the first Brit to come to our aid, suitably refined, casts a great deal of doubt on the soundness of the ISORMite position by the elegant expedient of casting a great deal of light on the psychodynamics of the lay response to ISORMite propaganda:

If you're anxious for to shine in the technocratic line
as a man of learning rare,
Y ou must get up all the germs of the ISORMitic terms,
and plant them everywhere.
Y ou must spurn those words of Michael's and disgorge
more epicycles 'bout your complicated state of mind;
The meaning doesn't matter if it's Structured-sounding
chatter of an ISORMitic kind.
And everyone will say
As you walk your Layered way
"If this young man can call to mind so many more
than *me*
Why, what a very singularly deep young man
this deep young man must be!"

That is, it really doesn't seem to be too great a feat to be able to remember Network Interface, Host-Host, and Process/Applications—it's as easy as I, II, III—but anyone who can reel off ApplicationsPresentationSessionTransport (breathe) NetworkLinkandPhysical (*wheeze*) gives a very good impression of knowing his onions. (Don't think too hard about onions, though; the seven story high-rise is still the best metaphor.)

If, however, it turned out to be relatively easy to remember all seven levels, that really ought to remove a great deal of the mystic impact.

Well, here's where the other Brit comes to our aid. Recently, in some circles, there's been a rage for *The Hitchhiker's Guide to the Galaxy,* et seq., whether the book versions, the BBC radio series, or the BBC $->$ PBS television series—a rage equal to or greater than the apparent rage for the ISORM, actually. (Naturally, in keeping with the tradition of becoming an expert in almost anything via *Dataworld* and *Computermation* articles, at this writing I've only seen the television series.) In the series, after a great deal of interesting incident (starting with the destruction of the Earth to make way for an Intergalactic Expressway, or the like) which I won't burden you with, it turns out that The Answer (to Life, the Universe, and Everything) is . . .

42

Again, the pioneering conceptual work has been vouchsafed to us from the Other Side. Again, we need to do some refinement. So . . . the Answer to the paramount technical question of our time (How Can I Become an ISORM Expert and Hence a Respected Networker?) is . . . that we need a mnemonic.

Naturally, I wouldn't have told you all that if I didn't happen to have one handy.

In conclusion, then, the way to remember the ISO Levels and appear to have become an expert is simply to remember

<u>A</u>ll

<u>P</u>rotocols

<u>S</u>hould

<u>T</u>alk

<u>N</u>icely

<u>L</u>ike

<u>P</u>adlipsky

APPENDIX 3

The Self-Framed Slogans Suitable for Mounting

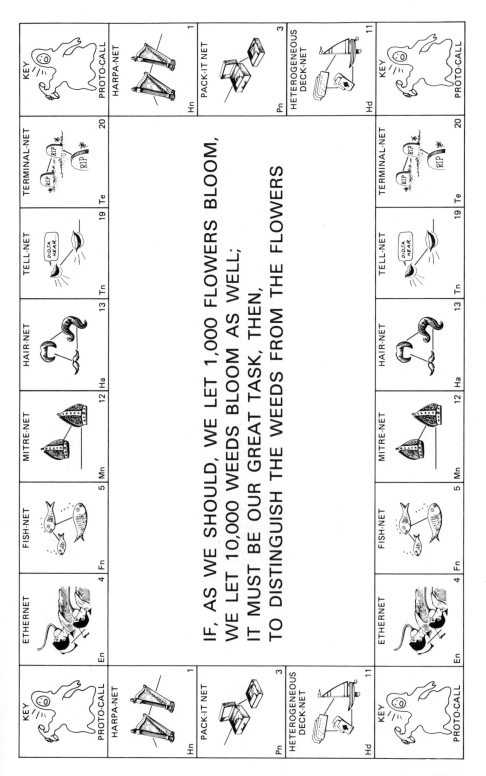

IF, AS WE SHOULD, WE LET 1,000 FLOWERS BLOOM,
WE LET 10,000 WEEDS BLOOM AS WELL;
IT MUST BE OUR GREAT TASK, THEN,
TO DISTINGUISH THE WEEDS FROM THE FLOWERS

BEWARE THE PANACEA PEDLARS:
JUST BECAUSE YOU WIND UP NAKED
DOESN'T MAKE YOU AN EMPEROR

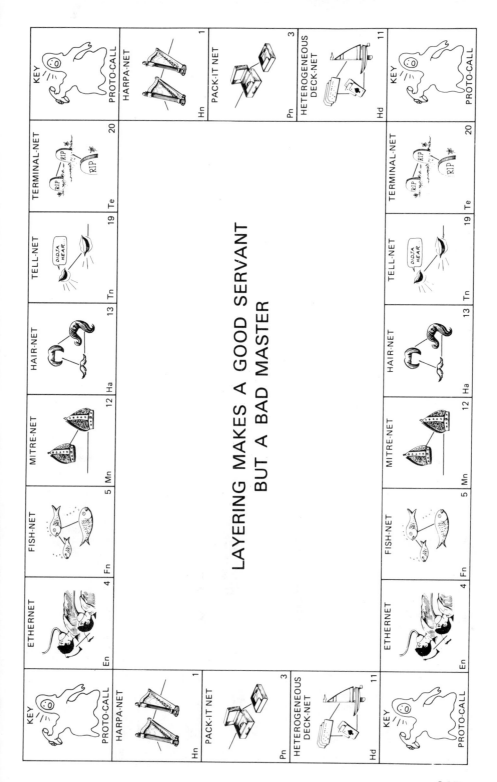

LAYERING MAKES A GOOD SERVANT
BUT A BAD MASTER

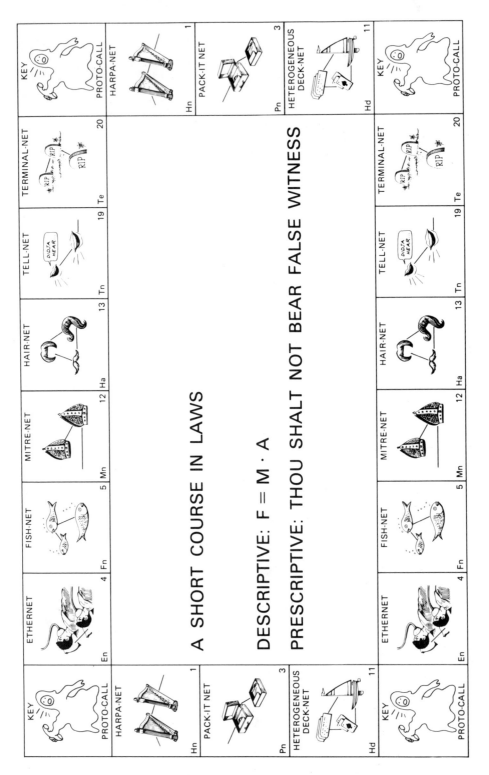

KEY — PROTO-CALL

HARPA-NET — Hn — 1

PACK-IT NET — Pn — 3

HETEROGENEOUS DECK-NET — Hd — 11

KEY — PROTO-CALL

TERMINAL-NET — Te — 20

TELL-NET — Tn — 19

HAIR-NET — Ha — 13

MITRE-NET — Mn — 12

FISH-NET — Fn — 5

ETHERNET — En — 4

A SHORT COURSE IN LAWS

DESCRIPTIVE: $F = M \cdot A$

PRESCRIPTIVE: THOU SHALT NOT BEAR FALSE WITNESS

KEY — PROTO-CALL

HARPA-NET — Hn — 1

PACK-IT NET — Pn — 3

HETEROGENEOUS DECK-NET — Hd — 11

KEY — PROTO-CALL

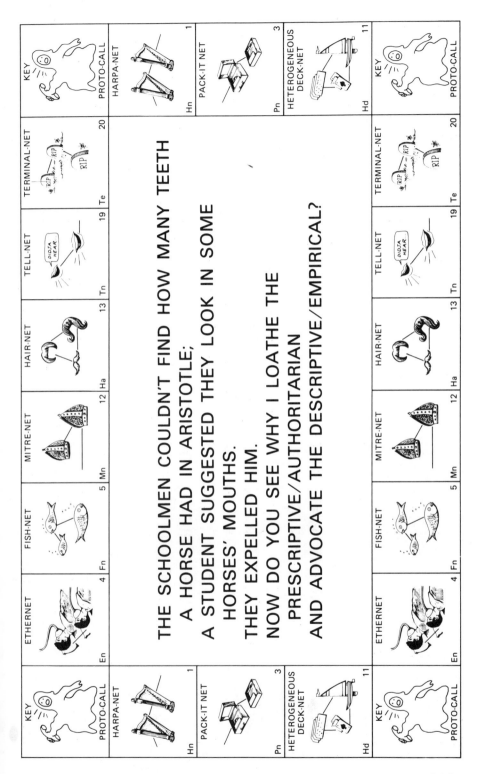

THE SCHOOLMEN COULDN'T FIND HOW MANY TEETH
A HORSE HAD IN ARISTOTLE;
A STUDENT SUGGESTED THEY LOOK IN SOME
HORSES' MOUTHS.
THEY EXPELLED HIM.
NOW DO YOU SEE WHY I LOATHE THE
PRESCRIPTIVE/AUTHORITARIAN
AND ADVOCATE THE DESCRIPTIVE/EMPIRICAL?

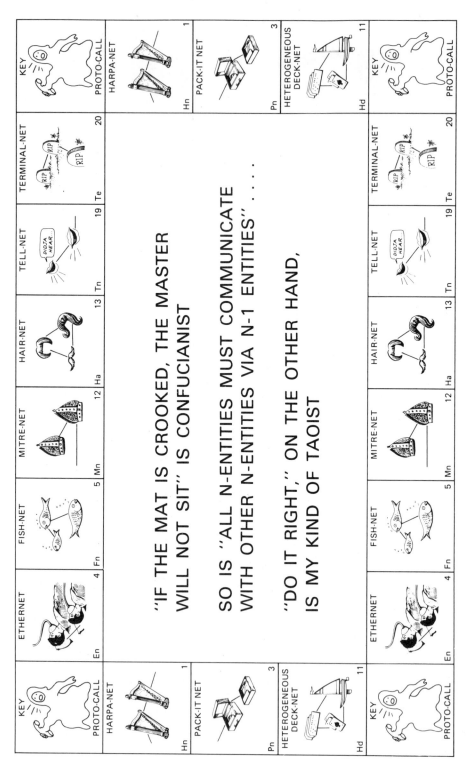

"IF THE MAT IS CROOKED, THE MASTER
WILL NOT SIT" IS CONFUCIANIST

SO IS "ALL N-ENTITIES MUST COMMUNICATE
WITH OTHER N-ENTITIES VIA N-1 ENTITIES" . . . . .

"DO IT RIGHT," ON THE OTHER HAND,
IS MY KIND OF TAOIST

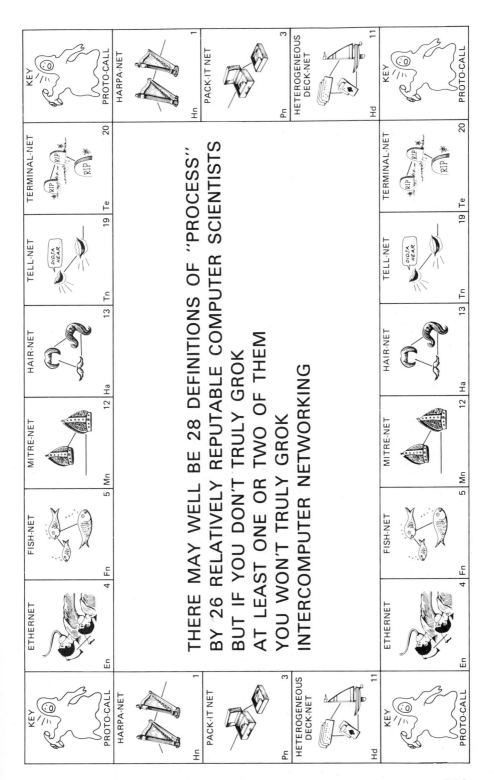

THERE MAY WELL BE 28 DEFINITIONS OF "PROCESS"
BY 26 RELATIVELY REPUTABLE COMPUTER SCIENTISTS
BUT IF YOU DON'T TRULY GROK
AT LEAST ONE OR TWO OF THEM
YOU WON'T TRULY GROK
INTERCOMPUTER NETWORKING

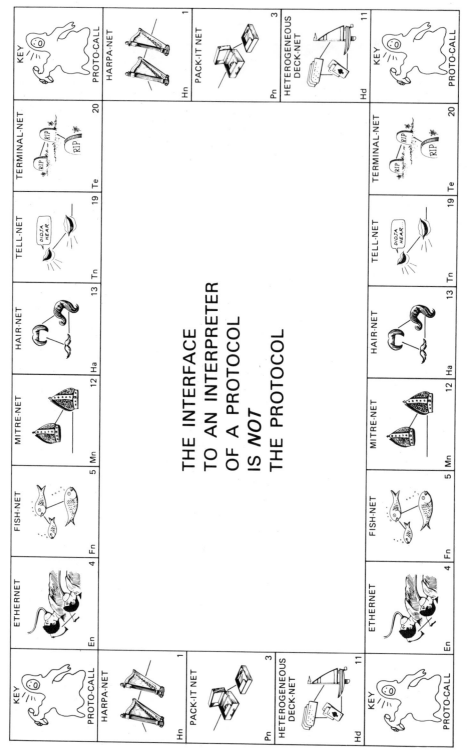

THE INTERFACE
TO AN INTERPRETER
OF A PROTOCOL
IS *NOT*
THE PROTOCOL

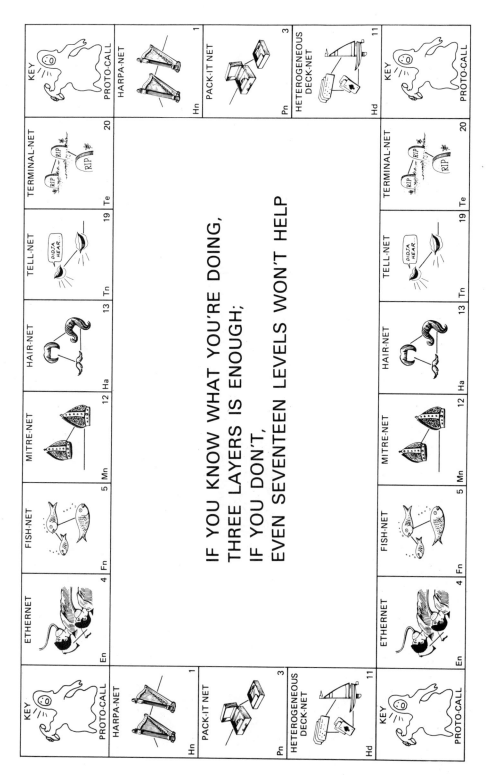

IF YOU KNOW WHAT YOU'RE DOING,
THREE LAYERS IS ENOUGH;
IF YOU DON'T,
EVEN SEVENTEEN LEVELS WON'T HELP

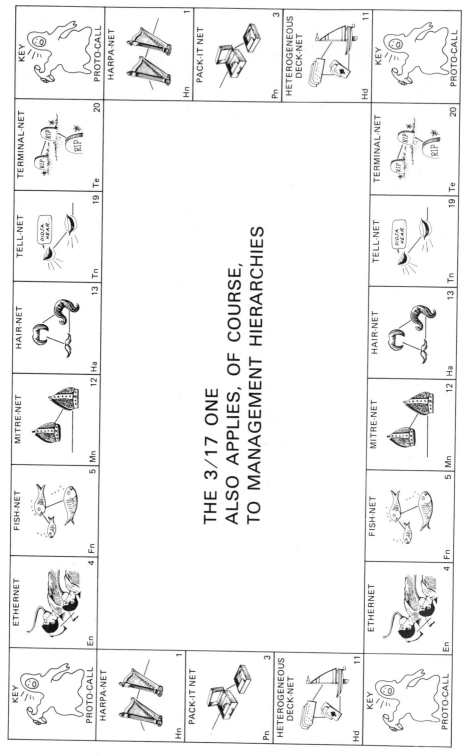

THE 3/17 ONE
ALSO APPLIES, OF COURSE,
TO MANAGEMENT HIERARCHIES

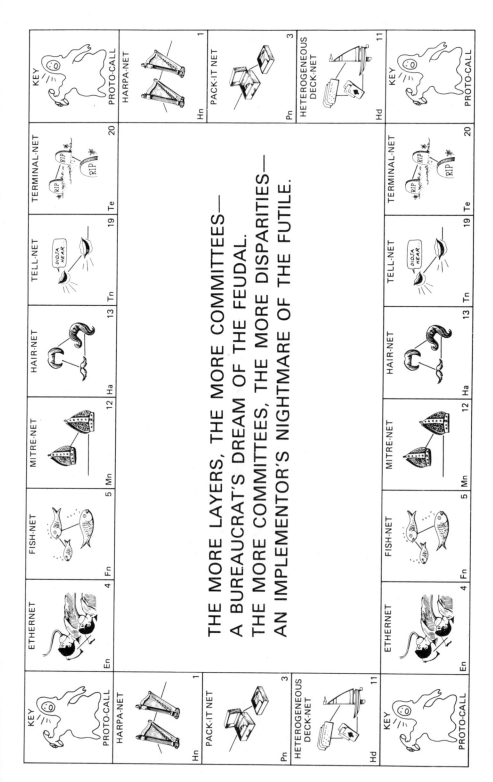

THE MORE LAYERS, THE MORE COMMITTEES—
A BUREAUCRAT'S DREAM OF THE FEUDAL.
THE MORE COMMITTEES, THE MORE DISPARITIES—
AN IMPLEMENTOR'S NIGHTMARE OF THE FUTILE.

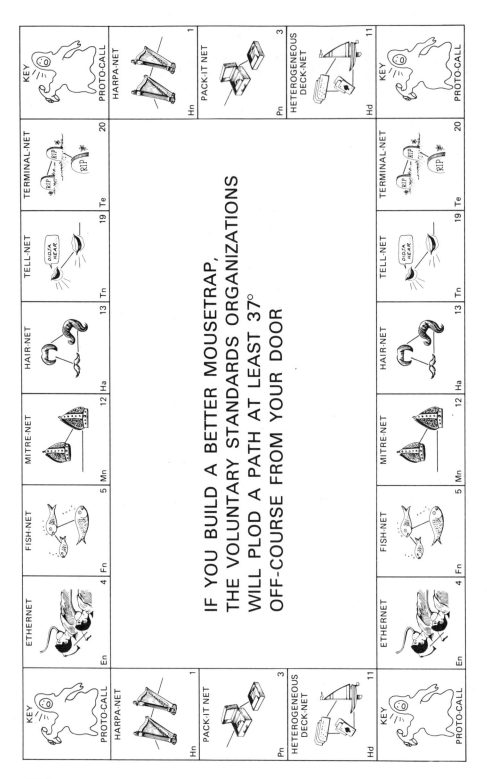

IF YOU BUILD A BETTER MOUSETRAP,
THE VOLUNTARY STANDARDS ORGANIZATIONS
WILL PLOD A PATH AT LEAST 37°
OFF-COURSE FROM YOUR DOOR

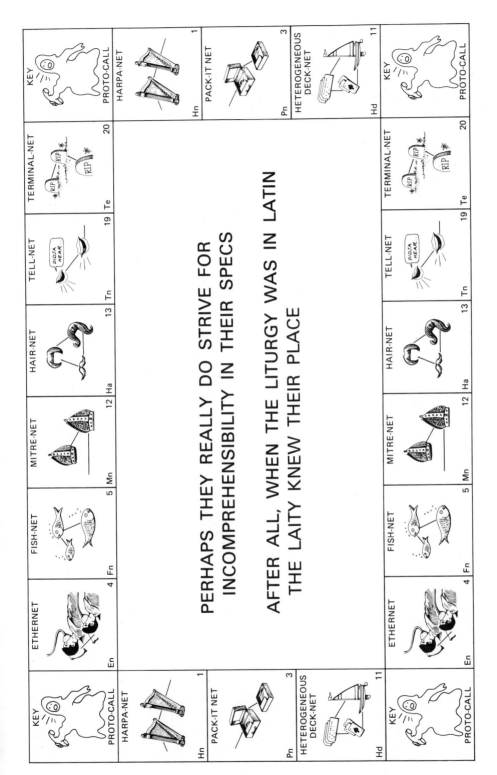

PERHAPS THEY REALLY DO STRIVE FOR
INCOMPREHENSIBILITY IN THEIR SPECS

AFTER ALL, WHEN THE LITURGY WAS IN LATIN
THE LAITY KNEW THEIR PLACE

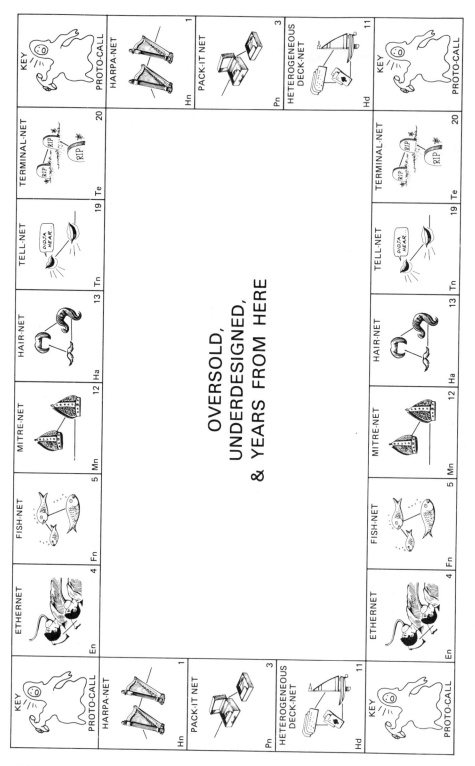

OVERSOLD,
UNDERDESIGNED,
& YEARS FROM HERE

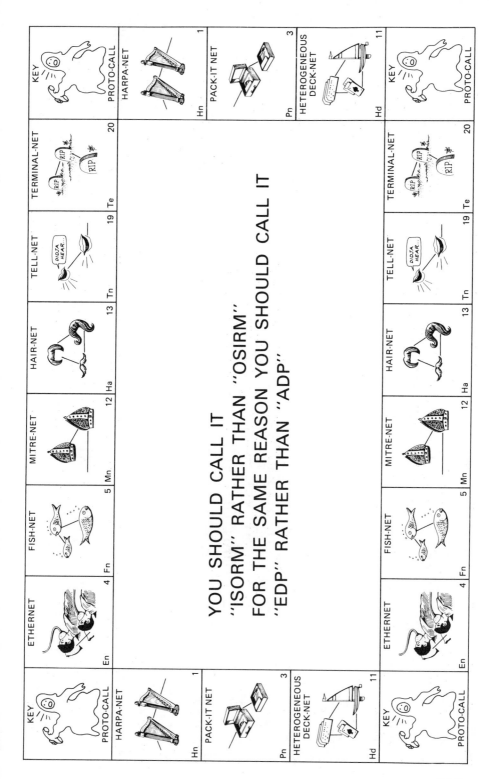

YOU SHOULD CALL IT
"ISORM" RATHER THAN "OSIRM"
FOR THE SAME REASON YOU SHOULD CALL IT
"EDP" RATHER THAN "ADP"

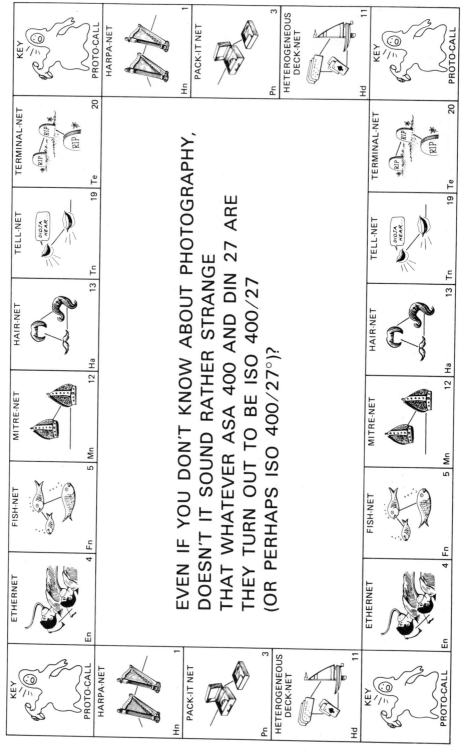

EVEN IF YOU DON'T KNOW ABOUT PHOTOGRAPHY, DOESN'T IT SOUND RATHER STRANGE THAT WHATEVER ASA 400 AND DIN 27 ARE THEY TURN OUT TO BE ISO 400/27 (OR PERHAPS ISO 400/27°)?

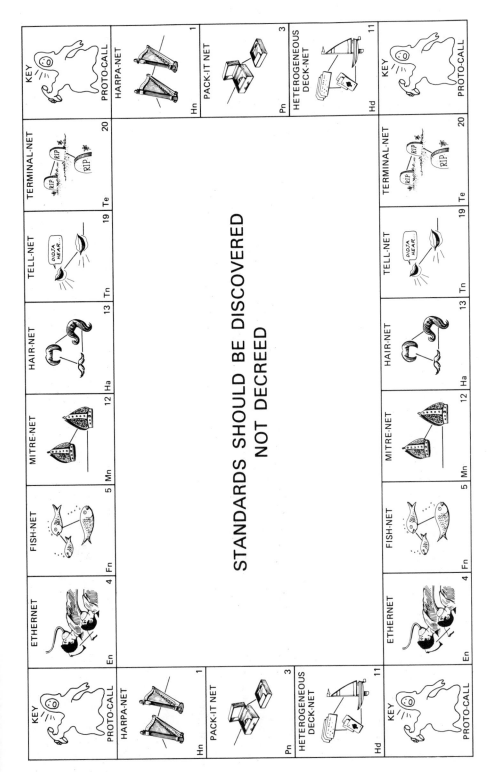

STANDARDS SHOULD BE DISCOVERED
NOT DECREED

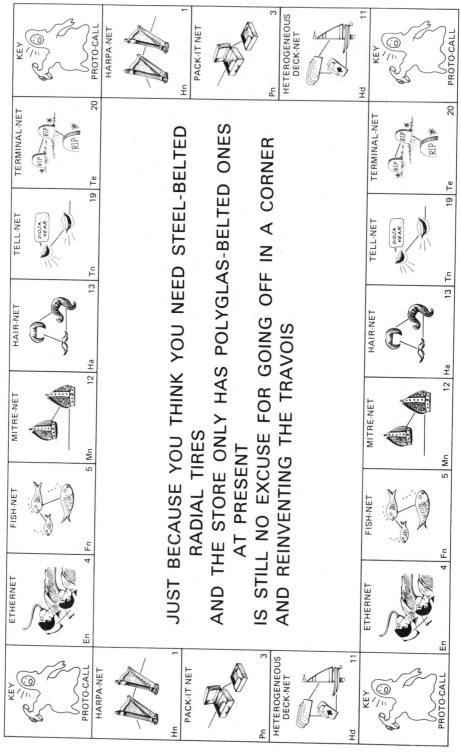

JUST BECAUSE YOU THINK YOU NEED STEEL-BELTED
RADIAL TIRES
AND THE STORE ONLY HAS POLYGLAS-BELTED ONES
AT PRESENT
IS STILL NO EXCUSE FOR GOING OFF IN A CORNER
AND REINVENTING THE TRAVOIS

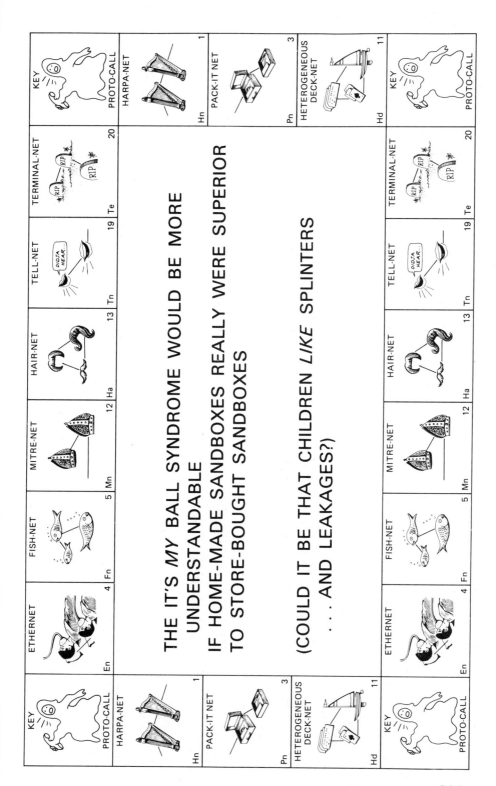

THE IT'S *MY* BALL SYNDROME WOULD BE MORE UNDERSTANDABLE IF HOME-MADE SANDBOXES REALLY WERE SUPERIOR TO STORE-BOUGHT SANDBOXES

(COULD IT BE THAT CHILDREN *LIKE* SPLINTERS . . . AND LEAKAGES?)

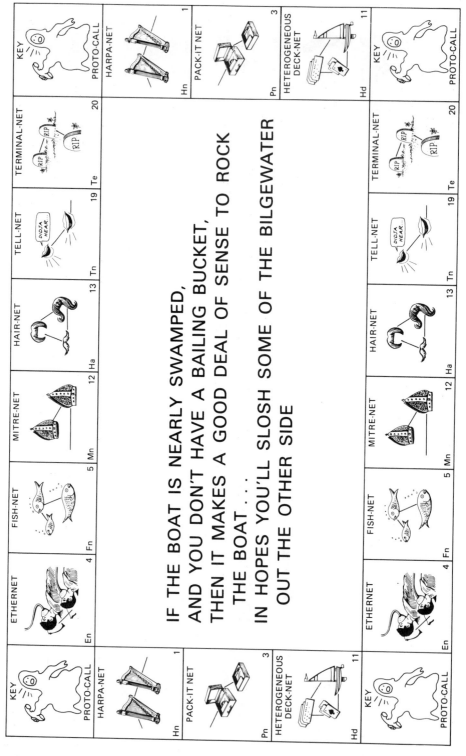

IF THE BOAT IS NEARLY SWAMPED,
AND YOU DON'T HAVE A BAILING BUCKET,
THEN IT MAKES A GOOD DEAL OF SENSE TO ROCK
THE BOAT . . . .
IN HOPES YOU'LL SLOSH SOME OF THE BILGEWATER
OUT THE OTHER SIDE

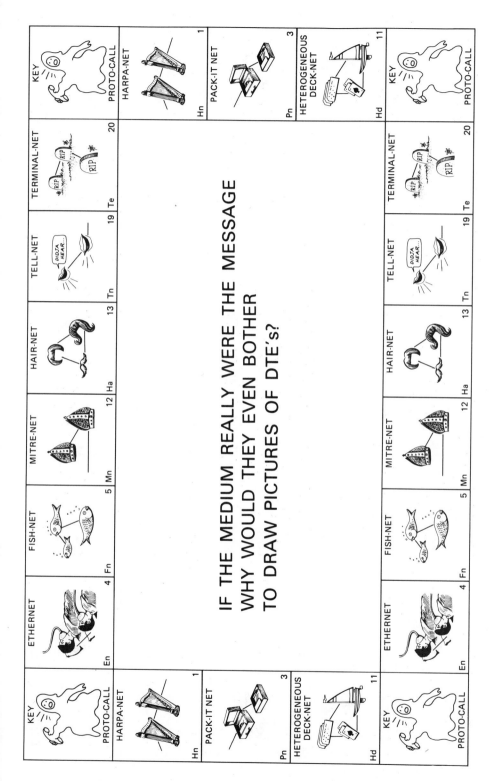

IF THE MEDIUM REALLY WERE THE MESSAGE
WHY WOULD THEY EVEN BOTHER
TO DRAW PICTURES OF DTE's?

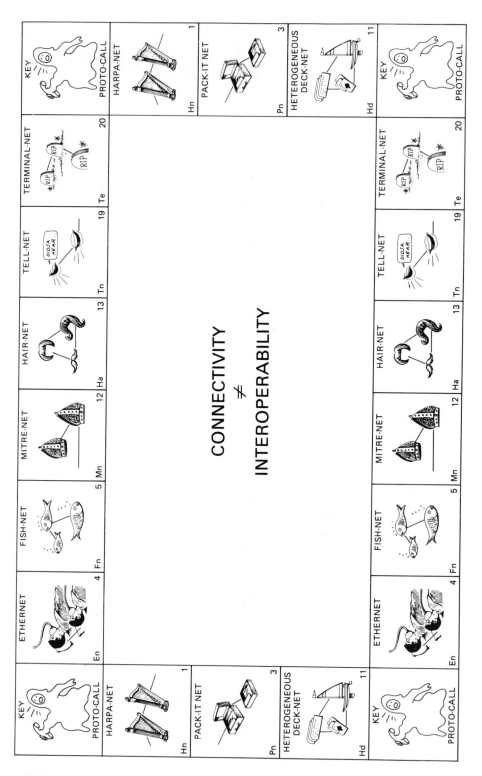

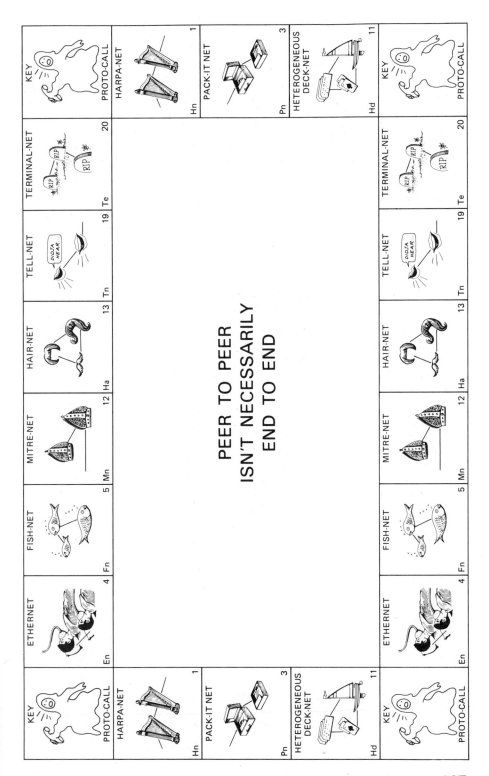

PEER TO PEER
ISN'T NECESSARILY
END TO END

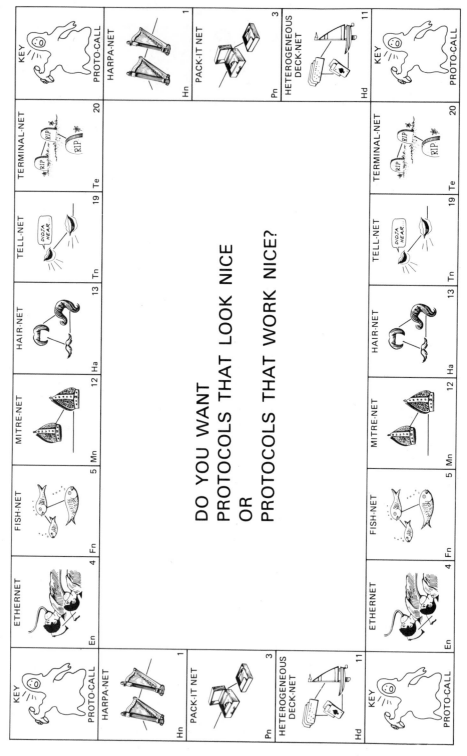

DO YOU WANT
PROTOCOLS THAT LOOK NICE
OR
PROTOCOLS THAT WORK NICE?

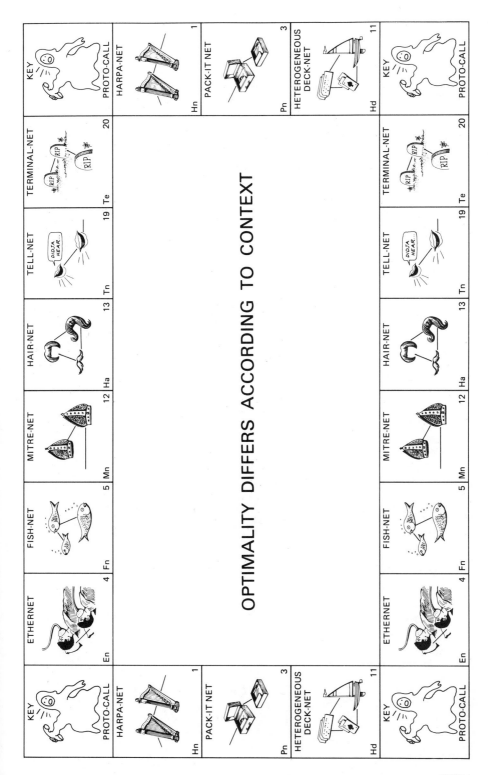

OPTIMALITY DIFFERS ACCORDING TO CONTEXT

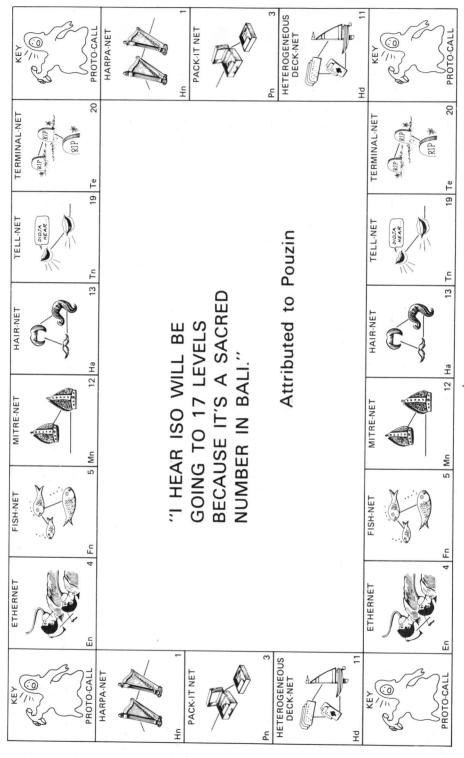

"I HEAR ISO WILL BE GOING TO 17 LEVELS BECAUSE IT'S A SACRED NUMBER IN BALI."

Attributed to Pouzin

230

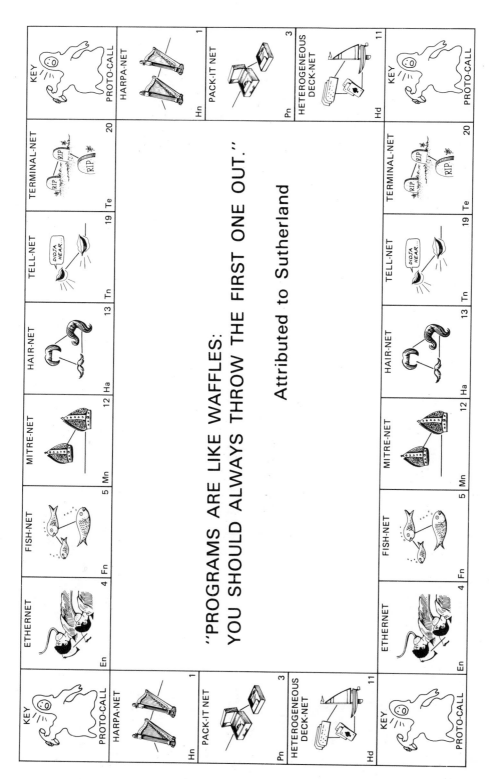

"PROGRAMS ARE LIKE WAFFLES:
YOU SHOULD ALWAYS THROW THE FIRST ONE OUT."

Attributed to Sutherland

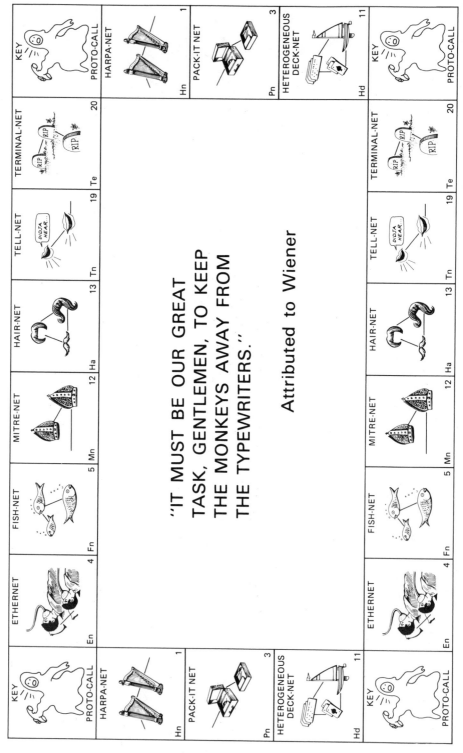

"IT MUST BE OUR GREAT TASK, GENTLEMEN, TO KEEP THE MONKEYS AWAY FROM THE TYPEWRITERS."

Attributed to Wiener

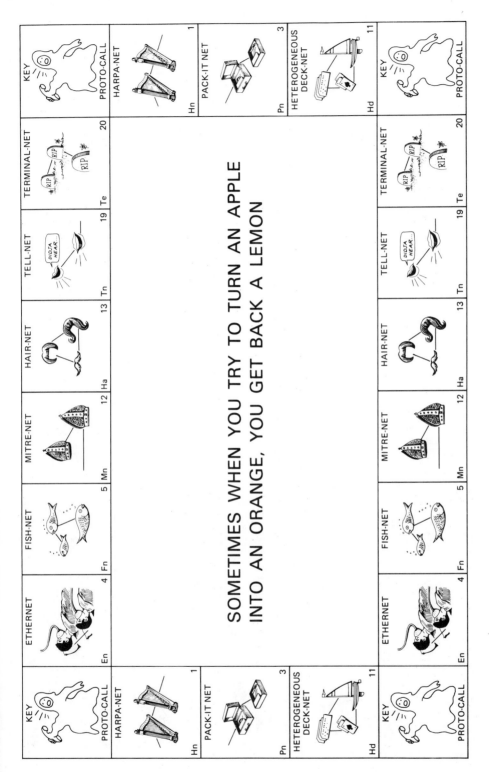

SOMETIMES WHEN YOU TRY TO TURN AN APPLE
INTO AN ORANGE, YOU GET BACK A LEMON

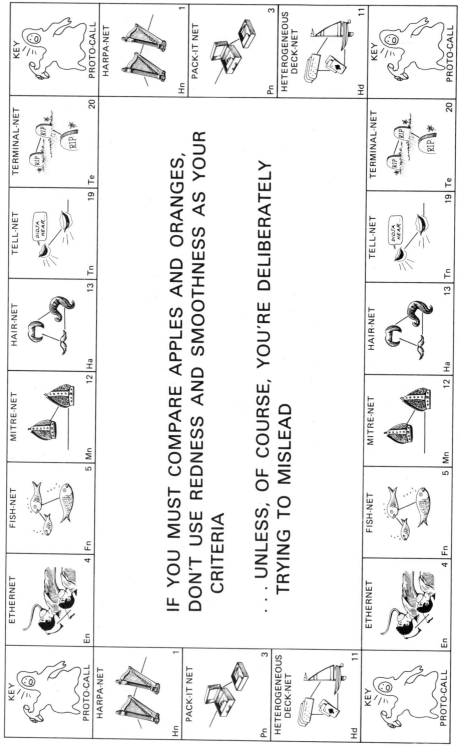

IF YOU MUST COMPARE APPLES AND ORANGES,
DON'T USE REDNESS AND SMOOTHNESS AS YOUR
CRITERIA

. . . UNLESS, OF COURSE, YOU'RE DELIBERATELY
TRYING TO MISLEAD

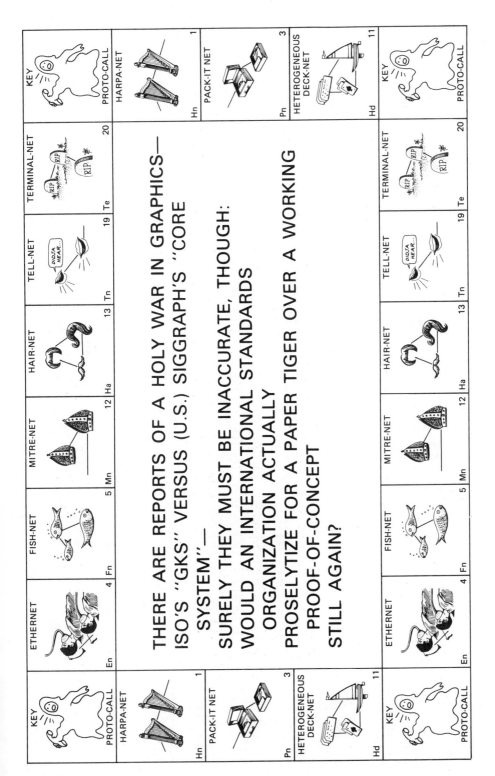

THERE ARE REPORTS OF A HOLY WAR IN GRAPHICS—
ISO'S "GKS" VERSUS (U.S.) SIGGRAPH'S "CORE
SYSTEM"—
SURELY THEY MUST BE INACCURATE, THOUGH:
WOULD AN INTERNATIONAL STANDARDS
ORGANIZATION ACTUALLY
PROSELYTIZE FOR A PAPER TIGER OVER A WORKING
PROOF-OF-CONCEPT
STILL AGAIN?

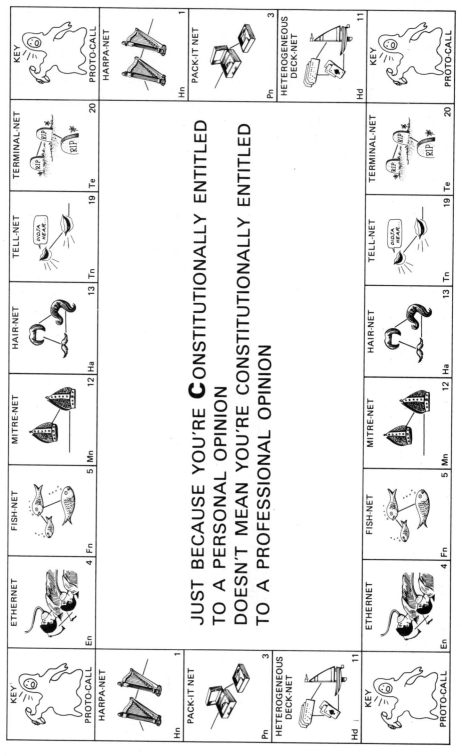

JUST BECAUSE YOU'RE CONSTITUTIONALLY ENTITLED
TO A PERSONAL OPINION
DOESN'T MEAN YOU'RE CONSTITUTIONALLY ENTITLED
TO A PROFESSIONAL OPINION